OVERTAKEN
on the Information Superhighway

How the U.S. Lost Internet Leadership
and What to Do About It

Thomas Bleha

Published in the United States by BookSurge Publishing,
Charleston, South Carolina, 2009

ISBN: 1-4392-2385-8
ISBN-13: 9781439223857
Library of Congress Control Number 2009902258

Visit www.amazon.com to order additional copies.

Dedicated to the memory of my parents:

Esther FitzGerald Bleha

and

Charles J. Bleha

"Second only to a weapon of mass destruction detonating in an American city, we can think of nothing more dangerous than a failure to manage properly science, technology, and education for the common good over the next quarter century."

– U.S. Commission on National
Security/21st Century (2001)

"Technology shapes possibility in the long run, but politics determines results in the short run."

– Former FCC chairman
Reed Hundt

CONTENTS

Chapter 1.
A look ahead – to 2015

Consider these two scenarios set in 2015.

Hiroshi Saito, an old friend and engineering professor at Keio University in Japan, had agreed to bring me up to date on Japan's Internet progress in the decade since 2005. So we met to talk at the elegant, mahogany-paneled coffee shop *Inoshishi*, in Yokohama, just west of Tokyo, on October 25, 2015.

Saito-*san* began by saying Japan had advanced greatly during the past decade. Now nearly all Japanese could access "ubiquitous networks," completely integrated, ultra-fast, fiber broadband and wireless networks that are 70 to *700* times faster than American broadband was in 2005. Three-quarters of the Japanese were now using these networks. And to access them, most had become heavily dependent on fourth-generation mobile phones introduced in 2012. Now called Personal Communications Devices (PCDs), these handsets were used for just about everything: cash, subway and train tickets, identification, keys, scheduling, controlling home appliances, listening to music, watching movies, reading books, navigating streets, and in many other ways. Best of all, we Japanese now simply speak to our PCDs and computers to control them. "But rather than just talk about all that," Saito-*san* said, "let me tell you some of the things my family did yesterday....

"Early in the morning, my PCD warned me of an accident on the road I usually take to the university. The PCD also gave me train schedules, but I decided to drive a short distance along my usual route and then detour around the accident – using my PCD as my car's global positioning system. That worked, and I arrived in plenty of time to teach my class.

"I do some consulting as well, and yesterday afternoon, a client called from Sapporo, a city about 500 miles away. I was out running errands at the time, so I held a videoconference with my client using my portable 20 x 25 centimeter (8" x 10") tablet-screen that connects wirelessly to my PCD. I was not only able to see my client, I could also observe his body language and facial expressions – and I resolved his problem. Ten years ago, I would have had to take a bullet train to Sapporo – over three hours each way.

"Last night I sat down with a beer to watch some *Sumo* [Japanese wrestling] matches from the 1980s that I told my PCD to download that afternoon. We can now watch thousands of sports events, movies, and TV programs, or photos, calligraphy, and movies we create ourselves wherever we want to."

Assured that I wanted to hear more, Saito-*san* continued: "Yesterday morning, my wife, Kazue, who was at home in Yokohama, had a four-way video consultation with her mother, who has heart trouble, and her mother's doctor, who were about 100 miles away in Kanazawa on the Japan Sea, as well as a heart specialist in Tokyo. All of mother's medical records, including MRIs, are online, so the doctors could easily review them. After some discussion, they decided the best course would be to monitor mother's vital signs around the clock with sensors that connect to her doctor's information center. If her vital signs reach dangerous levels, her doctor's PCD will alert him. If her condition becomes worse, we can have all of her activities monitored at home with an array of sensors. That kind of medical attention is a great comfort to us because mother is now 88, and we live so far away.

"Except for one day a month when she must go to her Tokyo workplace, Kazue now telecommutes. She calls or videos her supervisor or colleagues on their PCDs whenever she needs to, and she participates in virtual office meetings with video-conferencing from home or with her PCD tablet-screen elsewhere. Nearly half of Japan's workers telecommute these days, and many of us will move to the country as soon as our children finish high school.

"At home, we can control heating, air conditioning, and almost any appliance with our PCDs from wherever we are. We can also track our food. When Kazue passes her PCD over a bar code next to fish at the supermarket, she receives instant information on her PCD screen about when and where the fish were caught and when they reached the store. She can also learn whether pesticides were used on fruits and vegetables and how fresh they are. When she's made her choices, she pays with her PCD linked to a credit card. We seldom use cash any more.

"Our daughter, Hiroko, who's in high school, is obsessed with Korean pop singers. She's so involved that she's now taking a Korean-language course three times a week by video link with a language school in Seoul. She's also taking an online weekly video class in popular-song writing and music-video production from a young Japanese woman who studied at a music school in Boston. Now Hiroko is creating her own music videos and putting them on her website.

"As you can see," Saito-*san* concluded, "the way we live has changed dramatically over the past decade. And all of this innovation has meant a big boost for our economy and many new jobs."

Two weeks after talking with Saito-*san*, I asked Joan Nelson, a computer-science professor at George Washington University in Washington, D.C., to chat with me about the Internet's role in American life in 2015. She agreed, and we met at a Starbucks coffee shop on Pennsylvania Avenue.

Joan began by saying, "The U.S. government never did develop a plan to promote high-speed broadband or the wireless infrastructure. But, as you know, gradually increasing competition between the cable and telephone companies led to substantial progress. Fiber-optic cable now reaches half of American families, and one-third subscribe to fiber service that is 15 to 30 times faster than the average Internet connection was in 2005. High-speed, fourth-generation mobile phones were introduced last year, and 250,000 Americans in about twenty cities are now using them. And nearly 20% of the people with mobile phones subscribe to wireless Internet access for news, streaming video, and entertainment.

Unfortunately, the wireless infrastructure is still far from complete, so some calls still won't go through or are dropped. And, unfortunately, most Americans are still tied to their laptops – and their keyboards – for most things.

How far have we really come?, I asked. Joan replied, "Although we live in northern Virginia, not far from the self-proclaimed Internet capital of the world, we can only get cable Internet – about 20 times faster than our 2005 broadband Internet connection. That's because most of the houses in our area are on large lots, and it's expensive to bring in fiber. So for most of my work, I have to go to my office in Washington – ten miles away – to use the university's fast, fiber Internet connections. For example, I'm now participating in an online MIT project, and I have to use my university computer to work with the three-dimensional displays.

"My consulting practice is easier than it used to be. I can videoconference with some of my larger clients, and that has cut my travel in half. But my smaller clients usually don't have fast Internet connections. So they have to use an expensive commercial videoconferencing studio if one exists nearby, or I have to travel to them. Usually I travel.

"As the computer scientist in the family, I'm in charge of our home's heating, air conditioning, and security systems. These systems work reasonably well after they are programmed. But we can't control our appliances with our mobile phones, because the United States has still not completely transitioned to the new Internet address system that would give all of our appliances their own Internet addresses. And, unlike in Japan. which I visited last year, when I go to the supermarket, there's no online information about perishable items.

"The family's main worry now is my husband Phil's elderly father, who lives in a small town in northern Wisconsin. He's approaching 95 and has lung problems. His local doctor orders X-rays and MRIs, but these have to be sent by mail to a specialist in Madison for review, because the rural Internet connections are too slow to transmit them. So when Phil talks with the specialist in Madison, it is always a few days after the X-rays and MRIs were taken, and something might have happened in the meantime. Also, my father-in-law's vital signs can't be monitored without going into the hospital. It's a worrisome situation.

"Phil now telecommutes three days a week, but his boss insists that he and his colleagues come to the office on the other two days for meetings. The boss isn't being unreasonable: some of Phil's colleagues still can't get Internet connections fast enough for real-time videoconferencing."

There have been, Joan hastened to add, some good developments. "Phil is in charge of our family finances, and the Internet makes them much easier to manage. We can pay the bill with our mobile phone in some stores. And because most Americans now have faster Internet connections than they did ten years ago, a wide variety of TV programs, movies, music, games, and instructional programs for children are now available. Many people can quickly download these programs with their fiber broadband connections.

"Our daughter, Anne, is now in college studying anthropology. Last summer, she went to northern Arizona on an anthropology field trip. She was able to use her mobile phone to take pictures and short movies and to dictate brief notes there. She could also use her laptop to write up longer descriptions of what she saw and heard. But she couldn't use her mobile phone to make calls or her laptop to reach the Internet. There simply wasn't any wireless service in that area. She had to use an old-fashioned pay telephone to call us. So we still have some problem areas."

Joan took a couple of sips of coffee and summed up: "All in all, there has been progress, particularly the expansion of fiber Internet access, and substantial innovation. This has helped the economy. But America is still well behind the Internet front runners in Asia and Europe. Moreover, limited competition in the United States has meant that the cost of Internet access has remained higher than it should be. And rural parts of the country and the inner cities still don't have fiber broadband service, because those areas are unprofitable for the communications companies. Mobile-phone technology remains years behind Asia's; the wireless infrastructure is far from complete; and mobile use of the Internet lags well behind Asia and even Europe. Most troubling of all, most Americans don't realize how far behind we are."

This book is about Internet leadership: what it is, why it matters, and the essential role of government in achieving it. The book centers on a leadership race between the United States and Japan that began with an announcement in 2000. That fall, Japan's then-prime minister, Yoshiro Mori, asserted that his country would be the world's Internet leader by 2005. He wasn't taken seriously in Japan or overseas:

The United States was the globally acknowledged Internet champion, and Japan trailed behind substantially. But in early 2001, Japan's new Koizumi government began implementing a bold plan to achieve Internet leadership, and the incoming Bush administration turned its back on information technology. By the end of 2005, Japan led the United States and most of the world in the availability and usage of ultra-fast broadband and mobile-phone Internet use, the two most important dimensions of Internet leadership. And the United States was drifting *further* behind.

Japan also narrowed the gap with the United States in other dimensions of Internet leadership. With less than half of the U.S. population, Japan continued to produce more native-born Internet engineers than the United States did – and Japan attracted tens of thousands of foreign information-technology (IT) specialists. It made IT a main focus of government research and development funding and invested nearly as much in information technology R&D as the United States did from 2001 to 2005. It encouraged commercially oriented university IT research, and the number of Japanese patents, second only to the United States, increased. Moreover, Japan smoothed the path for bringing university research ideas to market, and promoted venture-capital funding.

The United States is still among the world's leaders in electronic government and remains well ahead of Japan in that respect. And the United States may have better integrated the Internet into the K-12 curriculum, although the schools in both countries are well connected. But Japan now leads in computer-based e-commerce, and it has surged well ahead in mobile-phone-based m(obile)-commerce. Further, the Japanese government is succeeding in providing universal fiber broadband service, which may be more than a decade away in the United States. And the Japanese accomplished all of this in just eight years of concerted effort.

Does it make a difference which country has the Internet lead? It makes a *huge* difference. As the Bill Clinton-Al Gore era demonstrated, technological advance is a major driver of sustainable economic growth. From 1996 to 2000, information technology accounted for fully one-third of U.S. economic growth. Moreover, one 2001 study indicates that the U.S. economy might have grown by $500 billion yearly if all Americans had enjoyed even the very slow broadband Internet access of that day – and that such access, if universal, might have created as many as 1.2 million new jobs.[1] Universal broadband would also have helped solve other pressing problems, such as energy independence, healthcare, education, and homeland security.

Technological advances also bring with them opportunities for innovation. Five large, new, Internet-related markets now exist or are in the offing: high-speed (advanced DSL and cable) broadband; ultra-fast (fiber) broadband; third-generation mobile-phone; fourth-generation mobile-phone; and ubiquitous (combined ultra-fast broadband and wireless) networks. Once 10 million people or so begin using each of those new technologies, a new market emerges that strongly encourages innovation: new applications, products, services, and "content." With nearly nationwide fiber and advanced wireless infrastructure already in place, three of those five markets already exist in Japan (high-speed and ultra-high-speed broadband; third-generation mobile phone). This means that Japan (and her Asian neighbors) have first crack at innovating for those markets.

Japan plans to launch ultra-fast mobile phones and ubiquitous networks in 2010. When ten million subscribers begin using *those* new services, the Japanese will have additional opportunities for innovation. America's Microsofts and IBMs are unlikely to be left behind; they are deeply involved in what is happening overseas, particularly in Asia. But America's smaller firms, where the bulk of our innovation takes place, will suffer.

Furthermore, Internet leadership brings special, quality-of-life advances suggested in the 2015 scenarios. So securing it, or at least keeping pace with the leaders, looms as a crucial factor in America's current – and future – economic and social wellbeing

Why did Japan rise so quickly and the United States fall behind? This book tells the story of the decisions and events in both countries that determined their present positions in each dimension of Internet leadership. In a nutshell, the Japanese government in 2001 took the Clinton-Gore-era economic success – and the 21st Century's likely economic trends – more seriously than the American government did. The Japanese government understood the critical importance of information technology to the nation's future welfare, and it recognized the essential role that government must play in achieving Internet leadership.

But it's time to get on with our story.

Chapter 2.
America takes the lead

Jack Ruina had a problem. Appointed director of the Pentagon's blue-sky Advanced Research Projects Agency (ARPA) in 1961, early in the Kennedy administration, he reluctantly agreed to take over a huge Q-32 mainframe computer in Santa Monica and the staff that ran it, because the Air Force could no longer afford to pay the staff. At about the same time, Ruina's Pentagon superiors saddled him with an improbable research project: one of the Army brass thought that social-science techniques could be used to squeeze usable intelligence from cocktail-party conversations. Ruina now had to find someone who knew something about computers and social science.

Ruina quickly learned there were only two qualified people in the entire country. One was Harvard professor Fred Frick; the other, MIT professor J.C.R. Licklider. Both were then working at MIT's Lincoln Lab, and neither wanted to leave. Ruina was, however, able to persuade them to come to Washington to listen to his pitch. Ruina failed to convince either man, but another Pentagon official got them to agree the job was so important that one should take it. After neither could convince the other to take the job, they decided to flip a coin. Licklider lost the toss. As the first head of ARPA's information processing office, he would soon spread his enthusiasm for interactive computing across the country. In the process, he became the Internet's visionary.

Thus began an extraordinary, four-decade-long process that produced the Internet itself – and America's global Internet leadership. For the first two of those decades, the U.S. government led the way, because it had to: No other entity would fund an unproven technology without obvious commercial value. Several universities did critical research, and the private sector provided hardware and transmission lines. But with few exceptions, all of this was done with government contracts. By the mid-1980s, the third decade, government leadership (and funding) had demonstrated the technology's feasibility, proven its usefulness, and extended the network across the country – and the private sector's role grew. In the 1990s, the fourth decade, the U.S. government laid out a vision that inspired the world.

Licklider (LICK-lye-der) was an original. Tall and blue-eyed with an Ozark twang, "Lick" – as he insisted on being called – was a St. Louis native. While studying for his doctorate at Washington University, he developed an interest in psychoacoustics and eventually became an expert on the auditory nervous system. After a stint at Harvard and MIT's acoustics lab, he agreed to set up a human-engineering group at the institute's newly constructed Lincoln Lab. At Lincoln, Lick had his first exposure to computers. The lab's enormous SAGE (Semi-Automated Ground Environment) computer was designed to collect data from tracking radars along the northern approaches to the United States and, if unidentified aircraft were detected, aim anti-aircraft guns at the intruders. SAGE's ability to do that led Lick to see computers as more than huge calculating machines; they were potential human partners in solving complex problems.

When Licklider agreed to take the ARPA information-processing job, he insisted on – and got – complete freedom to take the program wherever he chose. At the time, he had three strong convictions: that time-sharing – giving several experienced researchers, using separate keyboards, direct access to a single computer– was the next critical step in computer technology; that he should enlist the smartest computer scientists and let them do what they pleased; and that the best way to proceed was to systematically award ARPA research contracts to the nation's fledgling computer-science centers with the aim of creating three or four major new centers, like MIT, and several minor ones.

Lick backed his convictions with government money. Using his ARPA budget, he permitted research-project directors to purchase mammoth mainframe computers on the understanding that the machines would be shared by several researchers. By pursuing this strategy, he funded the first twelve time-shared computers ever developed, and by the end of his two-year stay at ARPA, he had underwritten 70% of all computer research in the United States.

Lick referred to the very best computer scientists of the day – at MIT, Stanford, UCLA, Berkeley, and a handful of companies – as the "Intergalactic Computer Network." In April 1963, he addressed a memo to this group describing the possibility of a "network of computers." Even if they interacted only rarely, he wrote, it was important to develop the possibility of an integrated network that might even extend overseas.[1] When Licklider left ARPA in 1964, he had turned the attention of the nation's best computer scientists to interactive computing and had given them a vision of what they might achieve.

One man's frustration

Two years after Lick returned to Cambridge, Robert Taylor, improbably another psychoacoustics specialist, took over ARPA's information-processing office. He soon became frustrated with three computer terminals, located just outside his office, that connected to the separate, off-site mainframe computers that Taylor oversaw. These computers required different keyboards, used different operating systems that required different passwords, and received commands in different programming languages. As he moved from terminal to terminal communicating with the computers, Taylor often made mistakes; he was frustrated.

Taylor decided to do something about that. He went to see his boss, Charlie Herzfeld, who directed ARPA, and came straight to the point. Everyone proposing a new research project for funding, Taylor said, now wanted their own mainframe computer. As a result, research computers were multiplying, and so was unused computing capacity. And because by law the Defense Department could not favor particular computer makers, computer incompatibility was increasing as well.

Taylor then proposed a solution: a "networking experiment." If the growing number of computers were connected in a network, he explained, fewer would be needed, and researchers would still have access to all the computer power they needed. Moreover, if these machines were connected, they could communicate with one another despite their different operating systems.

Would it be difficult to build such a network?, Herzfeld asked. "Oh no," Taylor lied, "we already know how to do it." Praising Taylor's "great idea," Herzfeld told him he would get another $1 million in his budget to pursue it, and he should get started immediately. The entire conversation – and the beginning of the Internet – had taken less than twenty minutes.[2]

Taylor now had to find someone to design and direct his networking experiment. The choice was critical because, for the first time, the ARPA information office itself would manage the project. In fact, Taylor already had someone in mind: Larry Roberts, a young electrical engineer and computer specialist at the Lincoln Lab.

The son of two chemists, Roberts had become bored with his undergraduate studies at MIT and drifted into computing. After logging over 760 hours on an X-2 computer, and writing most of the operating code that controlled it, he ranked as the world's leading expert on the machine. So Roberts, though still a graduate student, was put in charge of the computer when the two professors who built it left after a bitter argument over whether a cat belonging to one of them should be permitted in the lab.

Anxious to get started with his networking experiment, Taylor tried unsuccessfully to recruit Roberts over several months. Refusing to consider anyone else, Taylor turned again to his boss, Charlie Herzfeld. He asked Herzfeld to call Lincoln's director, remind him that ARPA provided more than half of his lab's funding, and tell him it would be in his best interest if one of the lab's computer graphics researchers, Larry Roberts, took the network project manager's job at ARPA. Two weeks later, Roberts accepted.[3] He was 29 years old.

Designing a network

Now, at the Pentagon, Roberts chose the simplest design for the new network of diverse computers: computer A would connect to B, which would connect to C, which would connect back to A. Telephone lines would link all four. Roberts presented this preliminary idea to a conference of information-office project managers held in Ann Arbor, Michigan, in early 1967. But the managers didn't like it. They quickly understood that *they* would have to figure out how to connect the computers and then use *their* computers' limited capacity to transmit the network's messages – with no obvious benefit to them.

But one of the conference participants, computer-scientist Wesley Clark from Washington University, had a solution. He told Roberts he should use a subnetwork of same-model computers. Such a subnetwork wouldn't drain host computer capacity. And it would make fewer demands on technicians, employ machines that all spoke the same language and, best of all, be under Roberts' exclusive control.

Roberts adopted Clark's subnetwork suggestion, labeling the subnetwork computers, inelegantly, "interface message processors," or IMPs (pronounced "imps"). As news of the subnetwork idea spread among the ARPA information-processing community, opposition to the proposed network subsided. The managers now realized their own computers wouldn't be affected – and they would have another machine to play with. Moving quickly, Roberts pitched a new "ARPAnet" built on a subnetwork of IMPs at a conference in Gatlinburg, Tennessee, later that year. But he said little about how the network would work or how data would be transmitted. How could he? He didn't know how.

By pure chance, the answers came in a paper presented at that same conference by an Englishman, Roger Scantlebury. Scantlebury introduced the idea of a digital, "packet-switching" network. That concept had been developed by Donald Davies and his team at the British government's National Physical Laboratory in London, and Scantlebury, a member of the team, was chosen to present the research. When Roberts expressed keen interest in this new approach, Scantlebury revealed, to Roberts' amazement, that the packet-switching concept was based on even earlier work by an American named Paul Baran.

While working at RAND, the U.S. Air Force's think tank in Santa Monica, Baran, an electrical engineer, became interested in making the fragile U.S. military communications system reliable in the event of nuclear attack. With an analog telephone system, a message can travel on only one path, making it highly vulnerable to attack. To overcome this, Baran designed a digital, "packet-switching" network that resembled a fishnet. If one network connection point (a knot in the fishnet) were destroyed, the message would simply take another route around it, redirected by constant computer updating of the network map. To complete his network concept, Baran conceived short message-blocks that could take alternate routes and be reassembled at their destination, much like furniture in separate moving vans is reassembled at a family's new home.

Baran completed his design of a more reliable, digital network for the entire United States in 1962 – five years before Scantlebury's presentation. But it took Baran three more years to persuade his RAND colleagues and Air Force superiors to implement his idea. By that time, Defense Secretary Robert McNamara had created the Defense Communications Agency to handle all military communications. The new agency was heavily influenced by AT&T representatives who believed (incorrectly) that digital networks were incompatible with analog networks – and unnecessary as well. Faced with this certain opposition, the Air Force and Baran decided to move on to other things.

As Baran was moving on in 1965, the British lab's Donald Davies developed an interest in computer time-sharing after seeing some experiments at MIT. In an effort to make computer time-sharing more efficient, Davies began working out his own system for transmitting digital message segments that he called "message packets." After he gave a lecture in London on his "packet switching" (message-packet transmission) concept some months later, a man who said he was from the Defense Ministry asked Davies whether he knew of very similar work done by an American, Paul Baran.

Davies didn't, but he soon found it. After reviewing Baran's work, Davies wrote a 25-page proposal for a five-year, experimental "digital communications network" that he estimated would cost □50,000 per host computer. He submitted the proposal to the U.K. Ministry of Posts, which turned him down, saying such a network was too costly and of uncertain value. (Had the ministry approved, the Internet might well have begun in Britain.) It was the concept under-lying Davies' unsuccessful proposal that Scantlebury pre-sented to the Gatlinburg conference sixteen months later.

The birth of ARPAnet

Almost miraculously, all of the elements of the "net-working experiment" had come together. Roberts studied Davies' proposal carefully and nearly wore out the Baran reports he found gathering dust in a nearby office closet. In early 1968, Roberts met Baran and invited him to become an informal adviser to a group Roberts had assembled to design the new network. Baran agreed, and provided very useful advice. When the design group finished its work, Roberts prepared a formal request for bids to build a subnetwork of IMPs that would form the core of "ARPAnet." The request went to 140 interested companies in August of that year.

Two of the most promising potential bidders, IBM and Control Data Corporation, the leading maker of medium-sized computers, declined to bid. They were convinced there were no computers small enough to make the subnet-work cost-effective. But eventually more than a dozen bids came in. Most of the interested firms planned to use a just-introduced, medium-sized computer, the Honeywell DDP-516, which cost $80,000 each. Raytheon, the well-known defense contractor, was the bidding frontrunner. So it came as a surprise when, a few days before Christmas, the contract was awarded to Bolt Beranek and Newman (BBN), a small, MIT-connected, Cambridge, Mass. consulting firm. In fact, it may not have been so surprising: According to one account, Roberts had alerted Frank Heart at BBN of the pending request, and the company spent $100,000 getting ahead of the competition.[4]

Heart was smart and energetic, and he got things done. That was essential, because there was very little time to complete the project. Under the terms of the contract, BBN had to deliver four IMPs and bring the network online in a single year – by the end of 1969 – for just over $1 million.

The biggest challenge turned out to be reconfiguring and debugging the Honeywell computers to serve as IMPs. But Heart and BBN delivered IMP #1 to UCLA on August 30, 1969, two days ahead of schedule. And IMPs #2, #3, and #4 were delivered at monthly intervals to SRI (formerly the Stanford Research Institute) in Palo Alto, the University of California at Santa Barbara, and the University of Utah. Thanks to Heart's determination and a lot of hand-wiring, a four-terminal ARPAnet was in place at the end of 1969, as scheduled.

In the following months, the software that permitted the "network" to actually exchange data was created by a small group of extraordinary graduate students led by UCLA's Steve Crocker, Vinton Cerf, and Jon Postel. Developing the new connection procedures and message-packet handling rules was anything but easy. As Crocker later put it, the task was like trying to invent two-by-fours with the buildings and village already in mind. But they succeeded in creating transmission software (the File Transfer Protocol), and by the summer of 1970, ARPAnet was able to function as envisioned.[5]

From start to finish, the entire process had been conceived, designed, directed, and funded by the government's ARPA information processing office. The cost: something over $1 million. Thanks to ARPA's work, the United States had taken the Internet lead.

The existence of the new network, although still primitive, spurred innovation. In 1971, Roy Tomlinson, then working at BBN, sent the first e-mail message between two computers in his own office. Unlike the well-known first messages sent by telegraph ("What hath God wrought?") and telephone ("Mr. Watson, come here; I need you"), Tomlinson later couldn't remember the text of his message. But he did recall cautioning a colleague not to tell anyone else what he had done: they were supposed to be working! After the necessary software was developed two years later, e-mail became ARPAnet's most popular application, or "killer app"; a year after that, in 1974, e-mail accounted for fully three-quarters of ARPAnet traffic.

Pushed by Roberts, ARPAnet continued its steady advance, and by 1973, it connected more than 40 host computers. Roberts then tried to *give* the network to the private sector. The ARPAnet technology had been proven, and the growing network was costing his office about $1 million a year that might be better spent on other projects. But both AT&T and IBM rejected Roberts' free offer. Neither company understood the technology involved nor had confidence in it, and their business offices couldn't figure out how to make any money with the network. So, with no private-sector takers, ARPAnet was transferred to the Defense Communications Agency in 1975, and the Pentagon continued to manage and fund it for two more decades.

From ARPAnet to inter-networks

Vietnam-War-related Congressional pressure in the late 1960s and early '70s caused the Defense Department to change ARPA's name to the *Defense* Advanced Research Projects Agency (DARPA) and required the renamed agency to focus almost exclusively on militarily relevant research. So, as the first IMPs were being delivered, Robert Taylor funded a digital packet-switching *radio* network experiment in the Hawaiian islands. Called ALOHAnet, the network proved workable but was vulnerable to air attack. To overcome that, Taylor's office established a satellite network, SATnet, the first packet-switching *satellite* network. Due to the great distances involved, the satellite network was slower than landline networks. But the existence of the radio and satellite networks, along with ARPAnet, raised the question of how they might be connected.

That question first occurred to Robert Kahn, an early member of Frank Heart's ARPAnet team at Bolt Beranek and Newman. Kahn joined DARPA's information processing office in 1972. By then, Donald Davies had finally received funding for his own small, experimental, packet-switching network in Britain, and Louis Pouzin had built a French version of ARPAnet, named "Cyclades" after the cluster of Greek islands. Soon an international working group was formed to build a "network of networks," with

Vinton Cerf, the one-time UCLA graduate student, as chairman. This set the stage for an extraordinary collaboration between Cerf and Kahn that led to the next critical stage in the Internet's development.

The two men were remarkably different. Kahn, an electrical engineer with graduate degrees in mathematics from Princeton, was a quiet, cerebral man whom Frank Heart described as a "consummate theoretician." Cerf, a dapper, outgoing Californian, had studied mathematics at Stanford before shifting to computer science at UCLA. He loved programming where "[y]ou created your own universe, and you were the master of it."[6] Kahn had already worked with Cerf and turned to him for help in connecting the networks.

They began intense discussions about various approaches. The ARPAnet subnetwork idea was a nonstarter for several reasons, including cost. Several kinds of gateways between the networks were possibilities, but none was quite right: different networks used different message-packet sizes and different transmission speeds. Pondering the problem in a San Francisco hotel lobby one spring day in 1973, Cerf came up with the crucial concept: the gateways should act as *network* go-betweens, rather than *computer* intermediaries (like ARPAnet).

In Cerf's plan, a gateway computer would translate the operating rules of one network – message-packet sizes, transmission speeds, and all other aspects of its communications – into those of the other; no more, no less. With gateway computers acting in this fashion, a series of completely dissimilar networks could be connected. That idea formed the conceptual basis of the "network of networks."

Working in tandem, the two men hammered out the outlines of the new inter-network. After discussing their ideas with Cerf's international working group and doing more intensive work, they published their new concept, titled "A Protocol for Packet Network Intercommunication," in May 1974. Like Frick and Licklider 13 years earlier, they flipped a coin – this time to determine whose name would go first on the paper's title page. Cerf won the toss, so it was Cerf and Kahn. They developed the TCP/IP (Transmission Control Protocol/Internet Protocol) protocols that are used to this day by gateway "routers" standing between the world's unlike networks.

Beginning in the mid-1970s, three private-sector inventions fueled the Internet's advance. The Altair "home computer," first advertised in *Popular Mechanics* magazine in 1975, attracted the attention of hobbyists around the country. Among those who took note were Paul Allen and Bill Gates who, working from an Arizona motel, developed the *Altair*'s operating system. The *Altair* led to the Apple personal computer, and in 1982, to the IBM PC that set the global standard for these new machines.

At about the same time, Xerox was developing its own PC. Xerox assigned a young researcher, Bob Metcalfe, to create a network that would connect PCs within a limited area, such as an office, an office suite, or a building. Metcalfe invented a digital, local-area network (LAN), computers linked to each other by thin cables and software, which he called an "Ethernet." A LAN with perhaps hundreds of computers could then be connected to a digital network, rather than connecting each computer to the network separately.

And finally, moving in the opposite direction, Sun Micro-systems developed an extremely powerful PC called a "work station" that could exchange large files and perform other heavy-duty tasks; but it connected directly to the Internet.

In the early 1980s, the Defense Communications Agency, then controlling ARPAnet, made two decisions that also contributed to the Internet's advance. The agency decided that ARPAnet would shift to the TCP/IP inter-networking protocols, and it provided funding for U.S. computer makers to build the protocols into their machines. That went a long way toward making TCP/IP the global standard. And be-cause unauthorized people were accessing ARPAnet, along with a growing number of hackers, the agency decided to split ARPAnet in two: into an experimental ARPAnet and an operational MILnet. Although no one knew at the time, this was an essential precondition to making the Internet public some ten years later.

Those were the last major Internet decisions made at the Pentagon. But by this time DARPA, and more broadly the Defense Department and the U.S. government, had brought to life a breathtaking new technology – inter-networking – that would form the heart of the coming information revolu-tion. The Internet leadership baton now passed to another U.S. government agency, the National Science Foundation.

Creating a nationwide "Internet"

The National Science Foundation (NSF), established in 1950 to promote scientific research, had a reputation for cau-tion: it made modest, peer-reviewed grants to universities around the country. But by the late 1970s, some academic departments – math, physics, electrical engineering, and nascent computer science faculties – were facing a crisis. Many of their ablest young researchers were leaving universities for the private sector. Although some left for money, most simply wanted access to ARPAnet and the leading-edge research it permitted. Of some 120 academic computing centers, only fifteen had ARPAnet access. The problem could not be easily fixed. An ARPAnet connection came in only one size – extra large, costing $100,000 a year – and to qualify for a connection, a university had to be engaged in defense research. That created two groups of academic computer scientists: the "haves" with an ARPAnet connection and the "have-nots" without one.

A group of the have-nots, led by networking pioneer Lawrence Landweber, met at the University of Wisconsin in late 1979 to discuss what to do about the situation. Landweber and his colleagues David Farber and Rick Adrion then developed a proposal to the NSF for a new network that would be open to all computer scientists – at universities or in government or the private sector. The cost of running this network would be much cheaper than ARPAnet, because it would use a commercial service provider, run at slower transmission speeds, and use the TCP/IP protocol, eliminating the need for a subnetwork of IMPs.

The NSF was skeptical, mainly because it had never managed a network. But in 1980, it approved the proposed three-tier network with access charges ranging from a few thousand dollars to $21,000 per year. The NSF also agreed to manage the new network for two years and underwrite it for five more at a cost of $5 million. The result was the

Computer Science Network, CSnet, which, for the first time, connected the entire computer science community and gave it access to ARPAnet. Soon thereafter, those involved began referring to the new network as the "Internet."

After the success of CSnet, non-governmental networks began to appear. One of these, BITnet (for "Because It's Time"), linked many IBM mainframe computers. Another network based on the Unix-to-Unix Copy Protocol emerged after AT&T distributed hundreds of free copies of the UNIX operating system. A third network, which began with a (UUCP) connection between Duke University and the University of North Carolina, eventually became USEnet, which distributed news. And around this time, the mid-1980s, many research institutes created their own networks using the TCP/IP protocol. A few years later new academic research networks also appeared in Canada, Europe, and Asia.[7]

But it was the government, again in the form of the NSF, that would take the next major step in the Internet's advance. Once the computer-science departments in America's universities were connected, another group of have-nots moved to center stage: physicists who wanted access to the nation's small number of supercomputers (CRAY-1's at the time). Some physicists working on Department of Energy projects, mostly related to nuclear weapons, had access to the department's supercomputers. Others begged for time on them at the national labs. A few others received NSF travel money permitting them to use supercomputers in Europe and Japan. But most of America's physicists couldn't gain access to a supercomputer.

A panel of experts proposed that the government purchase more supercomputers; but physicists *with* access feared that would mean cuts in their research budgets, and the proposal died. Unexpectedly, Japan came to the rescue when its powerful Ministry of International Trade and Industry (MITI) announced its fifth-generation computer project, aimed at combining supercomputing with artificial intelligence. This caused the Defense Department, the Energy Department, and NASA to join the NSF in proposing a new study group. Its chairman, the distinguished mathematician Peter Lax, would soon describe the Japanese challenge as a "new *Sputnik*" that required immediate, concerted action. The Lax group recommended a $100-million proposal: five linked supercomputer centers stretching across the country. During the House Science Committee hearings on the proposal, the committee members (including Al Gore) learned of ARPAnet and the importance of supercomputers for the first time.

The legislators understandably worried about coordination of the several governmental units involved in the proposal. To meet these Congressional concerns, the President's science office created a coordinating council that would be responsible for monitoring the purchase of the new supercomputers and access to them. Eventually, Congress agreed to invest $40 million in the project, and approved the construction of five new supercomputer centers that were spread across the country and linked by high-speed telephone lines.

But the legislation left open the question of whether researchers would have to go to the supercomputer sites or might access the machines from elsewhere. Stephen Wolff, who would later become the second head of the NSF's networking programs, recalled that "as soon as anyone thought about it, the idea of using the [supercomputer-center] network *only* to connect the supercomputing centers lasted about fifteen nanoseconds. It was instantly apparent that the network could be a tool for general scientific communication."[8]

There was disagreement over the nature of the new network, however, and it became obvious that the NSF itself would have to create it – or there wouldn't be one. Again, some NSF officials had serious misgivings. Yet because of their success with CSnet, they decided to proceed. To design the new network, the NSF chose an outsider, Dennis Jennings, an Irish networking expert who had built a higher-education network in Ireland.

Quickly getting down to work, Jennings, with the help of an advisory committee, made three controversial decisions that determined the nature of the new network. It would be, he decided, a general purpose network, open to all researchers not only physicists. It would also be hierarchical and pyramid-shaped: at the top would be the network "backbone," the high-speed telephone lines connecting the supercomputer centers, managed and funded by the NSF; in the middle, connected to the backbone, would be regional networks run by large research universities; and at the bottom, would be a host of university and college-campus local-area networks that would connect to the regional ones. The entire system, Jennings decreed, would use the TCP/IP protocols.

Those decisions led to a rapidly expanding national network called the NSFnet. Soon the major governmental networks (including ARPAnet) and the academic ones (including CSnet) were connected to the NSF backbone. Jennings then spurred the development of regional, research-university groups that would create the new network's middle level. He did that by offering five-year grants of $20,000-$50,000 so the regional groups could buy the equipment needed to establish the regional networks and connect them to the backbone. The northeastern region's universities (NYSERnet) were the first to accept Jennings' offer, followed closely by their southeastern counterparts (SURAnet). Next, Jennings made short-term grants to permit colleges and universities to connect to the regional networks. By 1987, all of the regions had networks linked to the NSF backbone. The hierarchical, general-purpose, nationwide network Jennings had envisioned was in place.[9]

Now researchers in all of the nation's colleges and universities could gain access to the supercomputers and the major government networks, including ARPAnet. Many elements of the private-sector gained access to NSFnet as well. That happened because NSF made clear from the outset that its grants would not be extended beyond five years. Worried about paying for their network connections after that, many colleges and universities offered network access to nearby private companies willing to help them foot the bill. At about that time, several overseas networks (including Japan's WIDE) began connecting to NSFnet as well. The NSF laid down only one rule: no commercial use of the NSFnet backbone that linked all of the regional networks.

Creation of the NSFnet was inspired public policy, the work of thoughtful and imaginative individuals in government and the universities. Above all, it was a tribute to the superb leadership of Dennis Jennings, who, during his 15 months at the NSF, made the difficult decisions and created the incentives needed to produce the nationwide network. As the use of personal computers quickly spread, and new applications, such as word processing and spreadsheets, became available, the NSFnet's growth was exponential. For months on end, the number of network users grew ten percent a month. To cope with such rapid growth, the NSF twice sharply increased the speed of its backbone service. With NSFnet in place, there was little need for the relatively slow ARPAnet, which was quietly decommissioned in 1989.

Although the private sector linked the computers to connection points and provided the (leased) telephone lines that connected the networks, it played no role in directing or funding this major network advance. One reason was that the entire sector was undergoing a painful restructuring as a result of the AT&T breakup in the early 1980s. There were other reasons as well. The telephone companies lacked networking experience, and they did not believe the research community was a viable market. Their main concern, then as now, was to make sure the new network did not compete with them. So it was not until 1988, when the NSF contracted with Merit (a private Michigan firm), IBM, and MCI to manage the NSF backbone, that private-sector involvement became significant. By that time, an informal group of federal technology bureaucrats had set up a personal network of their own, committed to advancing the Internet, along with other IT objectives.

Chapter 3.
Gore galvanizes the government

As a junior Congressman in the early 1980s, Al Gore was deeply interested in information technology and spent a great deal of time learning more about computers and networking. By the end of the decade, Gore had become one of a handful of politicians who was interested in technology and really understood it.[1] As a strong proponent of the nation's five National Science Foundation supercomputer centers, he became intrigued with the possibility of connecting the centers with ultra-fast, fiber-optic cable. That would permit far more data traffic than the vastly slower leased telephone lines that were planned to connect the supercomputer centers.

So Gore in 1986, as part of the NSF reauthorization bill, proposed a study by the President's Office of Science and Technology Policy that would answer three questions: What computing and IT resources did the nation's research community need? What benefits would an improved computer network offer? And what networking options – including a fiber-optic backbone – were available? A supercomputer and networking committee, headed by Paul Huray, a senior policy analyst in the President's science office, took on Gore's questions.

A new member of the group, Gordon Bell, inventor of the popular VAX computer and then head of NSF computing and networking, quickly persuaded his colleagues to seize on the Gore request as a means of getting additional funding for a number of expensive items on their respective agendas. Named chairman of a Huray-committee subgroup examining computer networking, Bell quickly commissioned essays on high-speed networking from experts in government, the research universities, and industry. In February 1987, he convened a San Diego workshop that was attended by nearly 100 network researchers to consider the essays and make recommendations.

To cover all bases, Bell asked the National Research Council to form yet another study group to suggest the kind of research network that would best serve the country. That group concluded that government and university researchers should decide the nature of the network, government should fund research and development of the network, and industry should consider the network's commercial potential once it matured. Most important, the study group said, industry should be included in planning from the outset – to avoid a parallel private-sector network.

With all this information in hand – more than 700 pages – the Bell group urged the government to fund research on how to develop, within five years, a high-speed "national research network" aiming at one gigabit-per-second (one billion bits transmitted per second) capability. Another Huray committee subgroup considering U.S. computing research needs called for a high-performance computer with "teraflop" (one trillion operations per second) capacity, also within five years.

In setting those goals and the ways to reach them, the Huray committee laid out an overall, federal-government IT strategy that would bring about huge leaps in U.S. networking and computing capacity. The committee had brought the research universities and industry into the planning process, insuring the best possible thinking and getting everyone to agree on the goals. Moreover, the process had produced a near consensus on the respective roles of government, academia, and the private sector. It was a rare example of a critical national strategy being decided in a thoughtful, comprehensive, and decisive way.

A federal coordinating group takes the lead

Al Gore was astonished when the committee's thick study arrived in his office in November 1987. Instead of the expected short account of the best way to connect the supercomputers, he received a comprehensive, five-year plan for advancing computing and networking research. Gore had little time to consider the impressive new strategy: He was running for President. Ten months later, however, after giving up his Presidential bid, he held hearings on the five-year plan before his Senate science, technology, and space subcommittee.

Kicking off the hearings, Gore noted that his study request two years earlier had marked the 30th anniversary of the interstate highway system that his father was instrumental in creating. Now Congress had the ability to create an "information superhighway" for the 1990s.[2] "[W]e must," he declared, "develop a national plan to take advantage of our computing technology...."[3] He pronounced the cost – $1.7 billion over five years for supercomputing, networking, and other items – well worth the money.

The experts invited to the hearings agreed. Paul Huray, the committee chairman, stressed the importance of the proposed network in encouraging U.S. innovation. Leonard Kleinrock, who chaired the National Research Council's network study, reminded the Senators of the Japanese challenge: "They believe that in the future, computing will be done with silicon and communications with fiber."[4] Robert Kahn, co-inventor of the TCP/IP Internet transmission protocol, stated flatly that government *must* take the lead in creating the advanced research networks: "They will simply not happen any other way." But industry must also be included, Kahn said, otherwise it would oppose the entire project.[5]

Having received a wonderful tutorial, Gore sponsored legislation authorizing government funding of research on both high-performance computers and the high-speed "national research and education network." But for three years, top Presidential aides in the George H.W. Bush White House, working with Senate Republicans, blocked the Gore bill. They believed government had no business supporting this kind of research – and they certainly didn't want to make Gore, a potential Presidential opponent, look good.

White House resistance was overcome when ten top high-tech CEOs, including IBM's Lew Gerstner and John A. Rollwagen of Cray Research, stepped in. With the support of a newly created lobbying coalition, they convinced George H.W. Bush himself that the high-performance computer research was both needed and urgent. With that, Congress quickly passed that portion of the Gore bill, and Bush signed it in November 1991. (The networking portion of the original Gore bill would be passed in early 1993 and signed by Clinton.) The federal agencies involved now had approval to proceed – but no additional funds. The Bush administration had not requested money, and Congress had not appropriated any.

Little time was lost, however. In the four years following the completion of the networking strategy, a small group of NSF, the renamed DARPA, Energy Department, and space-agency bureaucrats simply moved ahead following their own clear road map. By fall 1989, they had developed a detailed implementation plan while extending their gigabit network deadline several years, to 1999. Then they got to work with the money they had. As one member of the small group, Charles Brownstein, then-deputy director of the NSF's computer and networking office, put it: "We just found it more useful to cooperate than fight. ...[I]f they [the group of officials] came up with a good idea, they would go out and find the money in someone's budget to do it."[6]

These men and a handful of women, particularly those at the NSF and DARPA, cooperating closely, carried the baton of Internet leadership until Gore took office as vice president in 1993. And they succeeded: in 1999, as rescheduled, the NSF's 2.4 gigabit research network, supported by the telecom firm MCI, became a reality.

In the early 1990s, an Englishman, Tim Berners-Lee, invented a exceptional technology that would completely change how the Internet was used. While working at CERN, the high-energy physics lab in Geneva funded by European governments, he devised ways to identify unique documents, store them for retrieval on demand, and link them to related documents. That required complex programming; a new transmission protocol; new standardized, cyberspace formats; and more. Berners-Lee called this intellectual and programming tour de force the World Wide Web – and it was another critical step forward in the Internet's development.

But it was difficult to navigate this World Wide Web. To make that easier, Marc Andreessen and Eric Bina, two University of Illinois seniors working as part-time programmers at the Champaign-Urbana supercomputer center, created a much-improved graphical browser that made it possible to simply click on a Web address or other link with a computer mouse. In 1993, when they put their new browser, MOSAIC, on the Web for free downloading, more than one million users downloaded it in less than six months.

Jim Clark, a former Stanford professor and the restless founder of Silicon Graphics, became aware of MOSAIC as he was leaving the company. Impressed, Clark hired Andreessen, who had since graduated, and the two of them recruited Bina and six other student programmers to rewrite the MOSAIC programming code, this time for commercial sale. After another frenzied round of programming, the former students produced the first version of Netscape Navigator, the world's first commercial graphical Web browser and the killer app of its day.[7] Now even non-techies could access the Web easily.

Making technology a priority

On their many bus rides during the '92 campaign, Bill Clinton and Al Gore, two policy wonks, sometimes discussed information technology and the role it could play in boosting the lackluster economy, creating high-paying jobs, and transforming people's lives, particularly in rural areas such as their home states of Arkansas and Tennessee. According to Roy Neel, Gore's chief of staff at the time, it was Gore who educated Clinton about IT's extraordinary possibilities and, as he was able to do with many complex subjects, Clinton quickly grasped its potential.

Their ideas on information technology first appeared in print during the heat of the Presidential campaign, in September 1992. The two men published a small book called *Putting People First: How We Can All Change America.*[8] In a chapter called "Rebuilding America," they set forth an economic approach, paralleling their bus-trip discussions, that would guide their administration. It emphasized the direct links between high-tech research and development, improved economic performance, and more and better jobs.[9]

These ideas were spelled out further in a September "position paper" on technology, no doubt the first issued as part of a Presidential campaign. Drafted for a group of high-tech supporters in Silicon Valley, Clinton and Gore went beyond their pledges to refocus federal R&D programs on critical civilian technologies and create a world-class environment for innovation. They promised to build information superhighways to homes, offices, and schools. And they vowed to establish training programs for a highly skilled workforce.[10] It was, the candidates said, "an agenda for the 21st century."

That paper also signaled that Gore would not be a typically inconsequential vice president. According to the campaign document, he would "head efforts to implement the Clinton-Gore national technology strategy."[11] In early December, with the election won, Clinton agreed that Gore would be a "managing partner," have a White House West-Wing office near his own, and lunch with him weekly. In addition, Clinton approved Gore's request for special "spheres of influence," areas in which Gore would lead the administration: the environment, science, the Internet and high technology, communications, space, reinventing government, and several more.[12]

For the first time perhaps since Thomas Jefferson, America's technology policy now had top-level political interest and leadership. Over the following eight years, Gore would play a critical role in extending America's digital lead, especially as it related to the Internet. It was Gore who offered a vision of what America's cyber future might be; who pushed several bold, new, Internet-related initiatives; who chaired biweekly meetings of some 40 key players from across government to insure a consistent approach to technology issues. And it was Gore who made the decisions needed to resolve bureaucratic conflicts and keep moving ahead. In short, he provided the type of political leadership, decision making, and momentum that can only come from the top.

But a telling disagreement over the information super-highway arose before Clinton and Gore even took office. In late December 1992, the President-elect invited a group of the nation's top business leaders to a day-long "economic summit" in Little Rock. During the morning session, Robert E. Allen, then chief executive of AT&T, welcomed federal encouragement of an expanding information infrastructure and networks, but made clear that he didn't think govern-ment should build or operate them. The private sector, in Allen's view, could and should be "incented" to do so. The government's role should be limited to funding research on "pre-competitive" technologies, backing their transfer to the private sector, and establishing critical technical standards.

Gore countered that government ought to play a part in deploying the superhighway's backbone by supporting networks such as the advanced, high-capacity National Re-search and Education Network – the NSFnet backbone. He added that "most people" thought that this new "very broad-band" network ought to be built by the federal government and transitioned to the private sector. Gore wondered aloud if Allen would disagree. He did.[13]

That basic division over the federal role in creating a na-tionwide information superhighway continues to this day. Allen was, of course, speaking for all entrenched telephone (and cable) companies, which feared competition from a fed-erally supported network made public. But others agreed with him for different reasons. Some, like the advisers to the elder President Bush (and his son), were opposed as a matter of ideology: government should not adopt an "industrial policy" approach, pick technology winners – in this case a nationwide fiber-optic backbone – or support an ultra-fast broadband network financially. Matters of that sort should be left to market forces. Others, misinterpreting Gore, had practical objections: the government, they thought, couldn't afford the tens of billions of dollars a comprehensive supernetwork would cost. Still others believed a viable network could be fashioned from the existing telephone network.

For their part, Gore and others in the administration repeatedly said that the private sector would build and run "virtually all" of the new infrastructure, but the federal government had a "key leadership role" to play in its development.[14]

Getting down to work

In February 1993, just a month after their inauguration, America's new top leaders journeyed back to Silicon Valley to present a more-detailed version of their campaign position paper: *Technology for America's Economic Future, A New Direction to Build Economic Strength*. The high-tech executives were delighted. They had received more attention from newly elected Democrats in four weeks than from George H.W. Bush in four years. But the new document went beyond payment of a political debt. According to Michael Nelson, a Gore staffer at the time, it was a policy blueprint that set clear goals to be pursued by the Administration – and it served to get everyone in the administration on the same page.[15]

The blueprint underscored the new, Clinton-Gore technology premises and priorities: investment in technology was essential not only to boost the economy and create jobs, but also for other reasons: to clean up the environment and produce a more competitive private sector; and to create an educational system "where every child is challenged" as well as an "inspired scientific and technological research community" focused on the quality of American lives, not just on national security. Investment in technology was the key to all of those advances, and government could play a critical role in helping private-sector firms develop and profit from innovation.

In his speech outlining the blueprint, Clinton stressed three priorities. First, to encourage innovation, his administration would refocus federal research funding on technologies important to industry, such as information technology and communications. It would do this by shifting federal research funds away from purely military technologies, which then accounted for 60% of the federal research budget, toward civilian projects until an equal amount was spent on each. No longer would government rely on what Clinton called the "serendipitous application of defense technology to the private sector." Gore would coordinate this and the government's IT programs. And, symbolizing the new approach, DARPA, renamed in 1972 to underscore its relevance to the Vietnam war effort, would revert to its original name and acronym, the Advanced Research Projects Agency (ARPA).

Government, Clinton continued, would also "promote" a national information infrastructure that could have the same positive effect on the economy that the railroads had in the 19th century. By promotion, he meant funding the research necessary to produce faster computers and networks and underwriting network pilot projects to test them. But industry would deploy the infrastructure. Third, Clinton said, the federal government would bring the Internet to America's community colleges and schools.

Some months later, Clinton institutionalized this new approach and further underscored the importance of science and technology. He established the National Science and Technology Council, along side his newly created National Economic Council and the well-known National Security Council,. He followed that up by appointing a Presidential advisory council on science and technology to bring academic experts and business leaders into the policy-making process. Later still, he created a Presidential advisory group on information technology. But it was Gore's obvious interest that made it clear to all that technology policy would play a central role in the Clinton administration.

At this juncture, Congress, too, played a vital part. Within weeks of the new administration's arrival, it created the conditions for the next step in the Internet's evolution. By the early 1990s, there were already dozens of private networks in the United States. But the nation's largest network by far was the NSFnet, which was dedicated to *research* and composed of the regional academic networks and others connected to the NSF Backbone. By then, many private-sector researchers were using the national network, because their employers were helping to fund it. But the NSF's ban on commercial activity, established at its birth remained in place, hampering the Internet's growth and threatening private-sector funding. Something had to be done.

One of Congress' most tech-savvy members provided the solution. In the early 1980s, along with fellow Representative Al Gore, Rick Boucher, who represented a rural district in the southwest corner of Virginia, had developed an interest in high technology and the Internet. In the process, Boucher became convinced of the Internet's great potential to bring education and greater prosperity to rural districts such as his. His district was, he said: "poor...with inadequate transportation and communications. It was impossible to upgrade the highway system, but we could do something about communications. And improved communications would permit outside corporations to take advantage of the district's surplus labor, dedicated workforce, and high quality of life."[16]

In the late 1980s, about the time Gore was holding his Senate hearings, Boucher got to know Stephen Wolff, then head of the NSF's computer and networking division. Wolff told Boucher there were no good reasons to keep NSFnet in government hands – or to restrict its use to research. Moreover, if the private companies were to end their support, the federal government might end up having to underwrite the entire network. To avoid this possibility, Boucher, with the NSF's blessing, introduced legislation to open up the NSFnet Backbone to the public – and commercial use. Widespread industry support for the nationwide network was then assured.

Eventually, both the House and Senate passed Boucher's bill, and newly inaugurated President Clinton signed it into law in early 1993. The Internet was now open to all[17], and when Netscape Navigator appeared the following year, usage soared.

"America's destiny is linked to our information infrastructure"[18]

The Clinton administration's first major information-technology initiative came in September 1993, when high-tech executives and association representatives, academic computer scientists and engineers, lobbyists and interested government officials crowded into the small auditorium of the Eisenhower Executive Office Building next door to the White House. Two White House staffers guided them through the science and technology portions of the administration's first (fiscal 1994) budget. Then Gore and Ron Brown, the charismatic Commerce Department secretary, took the stage to present a concept that would resonate around the world: the National Information Infrastructure initiative.

Gore's new vision was bold but vague. The "NII," as it came to be known, would be a "seamless web of communications networks, computers, databases, and consumer electronics that will put vast amounts of information at the user's finger tips," in Gore's words. And it would "help unleash an information revolution that will change forever the way people live, work, and interact with one another."[19] Although the private sector was already deploying the new infrastructure, Gore asserted, "carefully crafted" government action was also necessary to "complement and enhance" those efforts.

The federal government, he said, would:
- promote private-sector investment through tax incentives and regulatory policy;
- extend the universal-service policy to the new network, so that all Americans would have access to it;

- provide research funding and standards to insure network security and reliability;
- better manage use of the radio spectrum for wireless communications; and
- offer the public far better access to government information.

This vision of a national information superhighway – and the principles that should guide government action – was one of Gore's greatest contributions to the Internet's advance, and it continues to inspire Internet proponents to this day. But because it was a vision, people interpreted differently what the nation's information infrastructure would finally look like. Some thought it was the telephone-wire infrastructure that was mostly in place. Others imagined a nationwide, fiber-optic network sometime in the future. And still others thought it would be something in between.

Despite these different American points of view, however, news of Gore's NII initiative was picked up around the world. The following year, as we shall see, Japan launched its own version of the NII, and eventually 63 more countries followed suit. Gore encouraged those steps. Addressing an International Telecommunications Union meeting in Buenos Aires in March 1994, he said: "I have come 8,000 kilometers from my home to ask you to help create a Global Information Infrastructure." He urged his listeners to build networks to homes in their countries and cooperate in putting together a global network infrastructure. And he pledged America's "vigorous, continued participation in achieving this goal...."[20] Reactions to the speech were mixed: some saw it as an important and visionary statement; others, more cynical, suspected it was simply a means of selling American telecommunications equipment overseas.

But no one doubted that America was the world's leader in developing the Internet, in spreading it across the United States, in deploying the new, faster, broadband technology, and in encouraging the global community to join in an even wider effort.

A critical part of this effort was a high-level Information Infrastructure Task Force headed by Commerce Secretary Ron Brown. The group, formed to "articulate and implement" the administration's NII vision, focused on framing a consistent telecommunications policy and universal Internet access, intellectual property rights and online privacy, and promoting new online applications, online government information, and extending the Internet throughout the government.[21] Most importantly, it spurred high-level official interest in promoting IT and Internet issues across the federal government.

Yet in the United States, where deployment of the information infrastructure was the orbit of the private sector, it was hard to imagine when and what kind of infrastructure might emerge. Seeking to clarify these issues, an NII working group turned again to the National Research Council – this time for a study of anticipated technology deployment over the next five to seven years, that is, through 2000. The working group specifically wanted to know the extent to which the private sector shared a vision of the infrastructure and what government might do to speed its deployment. After the study, chaired by Harvard's Lewis Branscomb, got underway, Gore asked the group to take a special look at broadband: How much capacity was enough? How should it be deployed? And how could the Internet user be assured that he or she would be able to upload material to the network as quickly as they could download it?

The title of Branscomb's report, *The Unpredictable Certainty*, summed up the study's findings – and, in the absence of any national plan, remains true today. There would eventually be a national information infrastructure, but when and how it would develop were unpredictable. Judging solely from history, the authors thought the nation's information infrastructure would emerge incrementally, driven by profit-seeking investment, consensus-based public needs, and countless entrepreneurs seeking their niches and riches.

But, the Branscomb group reported, the telephone and cable companies already felt stymied by the high cost of deploying infrastructure at a time when profits were dropping. And the most difficult investments for them to justify were network connections to homes and small businesses. As a result, the prospects for future private-sector infrastructure investment had dimmed markedly in the years since 1990. In fact, the vision of an America rewired within a few years had been replaced by the likelihood of incremental experimentation and upgrades only if driven by proven market demand. That approach would make the timing, as well as the direction, of infrastructure deployment uncertain.[22]

Al Gore, however, didn't wait for the Branscomb study. He was determined to do what he could with what he had.

Telecoms turned upside down

Gore greatly clarified the information infrastructure he envisioned, as well as his plans to encourage the private sector to build it, in a National Press Club speech in late 1993. "We need to rethink the role of government in telecommunications," he said. It was now technologically possible to communicate richly, with detailed images, to every home and office. But doing so required overcoming the legal, regulatory, and financial hurdles that stood in the way.

The national information infrastructure, Gore said, should be thought of as a network of highways – with broad interstates, concrete or asphalt feeder roads, and smaller gravel roads. Similarly, the information infrastructure would be made up of fiber-optic cable (the interstates), coaxial cable and wireless (the feeder roads), and the familiar telephone lines (the gravel roads). For the video and interactive applications of the future, however, all of these existing information avenues needed to be wider; they also needed to permit two-way communication and to employ far-greater transmission speeds. Fiber avenues, he added, would also permit equally fast uploads of video and other material to the Internet, as well as downloads.

The administration, Gore said, intended to create an environment that encouraged the private sector to provide just such broad, new information avenues, as well as the hardware and software to make them work properly and the innovative new material – or "content" – that would traverse the new avenues. In some ten to 15 years (2005-2010), that would provide an environment where consumers could choose their own "content" from competing sources at a reasonable cost. The key question for government was how to create that environment.

Gore likened this transition to the new information infrastructure as a "phase change" akin to the transformation of ice to water. The United States, he said, would soon enter a transitional telecommunications phase, a "slush" of part monopoly, part franchise, and part open competition. And because this slush was the most complex part of the change, government must manage it. Then came the big news: Gore announced that "the administration would support removal, over time and under appropriate conditions, of judicial and legislative restrictions on all types of telecommunications companies: cable, telephone, utilities, television, and satellite."[23] In other words, the existing telecommunications order of separate and regulated monopolies, which had existed for a century, would be turned on its head.

The administration, Gore quickly added, did not want to design the new telecommunications market. Its goals were to encourage private investment to spur economic growth and stimulate competition to create consumer benefits. In fact, he and his policy team thought competition was the key to reaching both goals. But it should be the broadest possible competition: cable companies against telephone companies; regional telephone companies against other regional telephone companies, newly created telephone companies, and Internet service providers; and wireless against all the others. And the administration, Gore made clear, intended to forbid the regional phone companies from entering the long-distance market until there was local telephone competition.

Although controversial, these ideas were not new. Academics had been discussing them for years, according to one participant in the process, and the idea of introducing competition into telecommunications had been shared by many Republicans and Democrats since the early 1970s. But the legislation to accomplish that would take three years. Indeed, Gore and the administration ran head-on into powerful telecom interests that had different goals in mind. Finally, working with key Congressional allies, such as Edward Markey in the House and Jay Rockefeller and Olympia Snowe in the Senate, and threatening to veto bills that did not permit competition, Gore and his allies succeeded in shaping a bill they considered acceptable. President Clinton signed the Telecommunications Act of 1996 into law late that year in a grand ceremony at the Library of Congress.

Although filled with contradictory provisions, the new telecommunications law had competition at its core. The basic idea was that the final link between an information service provider, such as a telephone or cable company, and a home resembles a natural monopoly. To compete, potential competitors would have to build their own expensive telecommunications networks before they could begin to do business. So access to this final link between the network and a home should be decided by the homeowner, not the network owner. If the homeowner chose a company other than the network's owner, that company would have to compensate the network's owner. Beyond that, there was little guidance – and only two mentions of the Internet – in the entire law.

That left the most difficult political and practical inter-pretations of the new law to Reed Hundt's Federal Communications Commission (FCC). As Hundt has jokingly written, he was ideally suited to chair the commission: he was Al Gore's high-school classmate and Bill Clinton's law-school classmate. More important, he was also a savvy lawyer who knew exactly where Al Gore wanted to go with his competitive regime.

Nonetheless, Hundt had tough choices to make. He later wrote: "The more my team studied the law, the more we re-alized our [FCC] decisions could determine the winners and losers in the new economy."[24] The new FCC rules would either favor the telephone companies by holding off would-be competitors or hurt the companies by encouraging competition. There was, he said, no middle ground. Reflecting this zero-sum situation, many of the commission's initial decisions favoring competition were quickly challenged in court by the telephone companies. Not infrequently, the decisions were modified or overturned, often because of vague or contradictory language in the 1996 Telecom Act. But the principle of competition had been established by law and the FCC's rulings, and competition would predominate until the end of the Clinton-Gore administration.

Looking back in 2002, Hundt thought his competition policy had "worked well," even though "[t]his approach was probably a little less efficient than the government-subsidy approach. The smartest means would have been to put money in the hands of the municipalities or communities to have them contract for fiber to the home – pretty much the way roads are built. As a practical matter, an information road is like a regular road. Demand must be aggregated, but private markets can't do that. So they won't pay for a fiber infrastructure." Such an infrastructure would eventually be built in the United States "if we return to Clinton-Gore-like fiscal policies." In the meantime, fiber networks would be developed in "almost every other country in the world."[25]

"Reinventing" government

In early 1993, soon after Clinton and Gore took office, the vice president began the extensive project of "reinventing" government, which essentially meant providing more (and better) government services with fewer people and less money. After countless meetings of many task forces, Gore announced 384 separate recommendations for improving government. A baker's dozen dealt with information technology. The most important of those called for the integration of IT into government operations.[26] That was easier said than done, however. Most top bureaucrats knew little about IT and generally distrusted it.

But Gore sought and, in 1996, gained passage of an information-technology management act that went a long way toward integrating IT into the operations of the vast federal enterprise. Later, to provide badly needed IT expertise to the government's top managers, Clinton issued an executive order requiring each department to have a chief information officer.[27] Those CIOs, as they were called, would later be directed to form a council to suggest ways to improve the use of information technology throughout the government.

By and large, Gore and his allies in the principal government departments succeeded in using information technology to drive his wider goal of reinventing government. IT became a major management concern. Congress granted more money – if not enough – for hardware, software, and training, and networked computers were increasingly made available to government officials at all levels. The chief information officers provided the technical expertise to put all this together effectively. Along the way, the government did become significantly smaller and more efficient.

In Clinton's second term, Gore zeroed in on "electronic [e-] government" – another major initiative. This project moved beyond using IT to connect government elements and simplify procedures. Here the centerpiece was making government information and services available to the public and the private sector online. To accomplish this, Gore laid out 18 large and complex IT goals. Improving the public's online access to government services was a primary one, and it led to the creation of a new, government-wide website, "firstgov.gov" (now "USA.gov"). From that site, a user could easily go to any other federal government site, and extraordinary amounts of information – from animal regulations to visa information – became available online. For the first time, businesses could look up environmental, safety, and health regulations with computers in their own offices. Most federal payments were soon being made by electronic transfer. And federal offices put more and more of their intended purchases on a common website for competitive bidding.

Individuals and businesses could now quickly find government services, in some cases interactive ones, on the government's website. Federal procurement became much more transparent, and the number of bidders increased greatly. Moreover, with IT tools, the government handled many costly and time-consuming tasks – financial transactions, registrations, procurement tenders – far more efficiently. In e-government, too, the U.S. government led the world.

Connecting the schools and the less privileged

Time and again during the 1992 campaign, Clinton and Gore had promised to bring the Internet to the nation's schools. Coming from poor, rural states, both men saw it as a way to bring the same resources available to well-to-do students in cities to poor students in rural areas. Throughout the campaign, Gore described his vision of a young girl in Carthage, Tennessee, the Gore family seat, consulting books in the Library of Congress via the Internet. He occasionally spoke grandly of connecting all of the nation's *classrooms* to the Internet; but connecting at least the *schools* was a firm policy priority from the outset – and still another major initiative. Congress authorized – though it did not fund – school and library Internet connections in a 1993 computing and communications act.

The cost of connecting all of America's schools was, of course, a large number. McKinsey consultants estimated it at $10 billion over five years; it would be the largest K-12 educational outlay in America's history, and Commissioner

Hundt began to consider where to find the money. According to Hundt, a friendly Republican Congressman warned him that Congress would never approve the outlay; instead, the Congressman said, Hundt's FCC should tell industry to come up with it. This money would return to industry through competitively awarded contracts – supplemented by state and local matching funds – to make the connections.[28]

Following the Congressman's suggestion, Hundt and his staff devised a five-year plan to link the schools – public, parochial, and private – as well as the nation's libraries. Hundt proposed to take roughly $2 billion a year from the telephone companies to create an "e-rate communications fund." Local school districts would contribute according to their ability: poor school districts would pay 10% of the connection cost, and the wealthiest districts 60%. The rest of the money needed would come from the e-rate fund. When Hundt discussed the idea with President Clinton, the latter, weighing the politics, decided that the schools should be connected during his next four-year term, rather than the five Hundt proposed. The four-year version of the Hundt plan became the basis for Clinton and Gore's 1996 campaign pledge to connect all the schools by 2000.

On the heels of Clinton's overwhelming reelection, Hundt easily persuaded his fellow FCC commissioners and their state counterparts to approve his plan. The FCC then required the telephone companies to direct $2.25 billion – about 1% of their revenues – in each of the next four years to the e-rate fund, and the local school districts nearly matched this with $2 billion annually. For its part, the U.S. government provided $766 million for computers and staff training.

The plan worked, and by the end of 2000, as scheduled, 95% of all U.S. schools – plus 60% of their classrooms and most of the nation's public libraries – were connected to the Internet. The young Carthage girl of Gore's imagining could now reach the Library of Congress from a seat in a Tennessee school.

The e-rate fund also served as the administration's approach to reducing the "digital divide," the gap between those who had Internet access and those who didn't, and eventually providing universal Internet service. The e-rate fund did, in fact, give poorer citizens something like the access their wealthier fellow citizens had. Nearly all children had Internet access through their schools, and most adults could access the Internet at libraries if they wished. In principle, at least, students would receive a richer education, young adults would approach technology more naturally, and even senior citizens might maneuver in the new online world.

Promoting electronic commerce

In the mid-1990s, the advent of Netscape Navigator and Microsoft Explorer – easier-to-use Internet browsers – and rocketing Internet use led to a surge in (dial-up) online shopping. Large corporations, too, began to use the Internet to buy materials for their operations. "E-commerce" was beginning. At about this time, too, the administration's health-care initiative ended in failure. As a result, the man who directed that effort, Ira Magaziner, yet another law school classmate of Bill and Hillary Clinton, was looking for a different project. President Clinton obliged by asking him to develop a strategy to extend the high-growth economy into the next century.[29] Soon after Magaziner began work, he understood that the centerpiece of such a strategy must be a framework for electronic commerce.

In early 1995, Magaziner assembled a team of people from 18 government offices interested in e-commerce. Over the next year and a half, those officials hammered out a road map to a new, global electronic marketplace. They concluded that the marketplace should be subject to no more than minimal government intervention. But government would have to act on a few matters to set the stage for private-sector leadership. Those included some deregulation; some new legislation (to make "electronic signatures," such as clicking on a "purchase" button online to authorize a credit-card charge, legally binding); and the application of existing commercial law to electronic commerce as well. To create a global marketplace, the government would also have to persuade other countries to adopt a similar minimal government role in e-commerce.

In July 1997, with Ira Magaziner by his side, President Clinton announced a new "framework for global electronic commerce." Because of the Internet's "explosive potential for prosperity," Clinton said, "it should be a global free-trade zone." Governments needed to refrain from imposing taxes or tariffs, unnecessary regulations, or approval requirements. Instead, the private sector should be encouraged to regulate itself. Clinton also suggested approaches to several e-commerce issues – among them, electronic payments, intellectual property protection, and privacy and content concerns. In each case, he favored market solutions wherever possible.

Government, the President made clear, should intervene only when it was absolutely essential.

By the end of 1998, just eighteen months later, the administration had achieved remarkable success with its e-commerce initiative. Congress had passed a three-year moratorium on e-commerce taxes; well over 100 nations had pledged not to impose duties on electronic transactions; Japan, the European Union, and many other nations had sub-scribed to Clinton's market-driven approach. All of that had the desired effect. By the end of 2000, e-commerce transactions topped $1 trillion in the United States alone.

Advancing the Internet itself

Yet another major initiative of the Clinton-Gore years drove the development of the Internet itself. To provide university researchers with faster network access, the National Science Foundation pushed ahead with its earlier goal of developing a vastly faster *research* network, one that could transmit data packets at one gigabit (billion bits) per second – the entire Encyclopedia Britannica in three seconds – by 1999. NSF officials expected the new giga-bit network to follow the same path the NSFnet had taken earlier: an experimental phase, then broad research use, and finally open access for the general public and the private sector.

The plan proceeded on that basis. Following the model it had used in creating NSFnet ten years earlier, the NSF in 1993 solicited bids for a "very high-speed Backbone Network Service" (vBNS). After signing a cooperative agreement with MCI to build the new backbone, the two organizations activated the "vBNS network" two years later. But many university researchers who connected indirectly to the new network complained of slow connections. So, to speed their access, the NSF subsidized direct fiber connections to the much faster backbone for some 100 research universities. Meanwhile, the NSF continued to ramp up the network backbone's speed until, in early 1999, it reached 2.4 gigabits (billions of bits) per second, vastly surpassing the one-gigabit goal set ten years earlier. And a year later, as planned, the NSF opened vBNS to public – and commercial – use. At this point, the network backbone had been renamed the "vBNS+."

But the NSF's plan to open the vBNS network backbone to public and commercial use was opposed by many academic researchers. They felt they were being forced to use a network that, however fast, would soon become as overcrowded as NSFnet had been. In 1996, just a year after vBNS was launched, the critics took matters into their own hands. A group of 180 research-oriented universities, and their recently recruited corporate partners, formed a new corporation called "Internet2." Their purpose, they said, was to create a leading-edge network for the national research community, "a parallel and complementary initiative" to vBNS. With $300 million, the consortium launched its own ultrahigh-speed backbone network called "Abilene" in 1999. Although the universities' initiative vexed government officials who felt vBNS was adequate, the NSF yet again agreed to provide grants so the major research universities could connect directly to Internet2 as well. Now the country had two ultra-fast backbone networks: vBNS+ for public and commercial use and Abilene for research use only.

In addition to backing the research networks, the government continued its support of *experimental* networks, which represented the future. In his 1997 State of the Union address, President Clinton announced a Next Generation Internet (NGI) initiative aimed at making a quantum leap in network speeds. As Clinton put it, the initiative would create the foundation of the 21st century's networks: research for a terabit backbone, 1,000 times faster than its gigabit counterpart, capable of transmitting one trillion bits per second or more – the Encyclopedia Britannica in *three-thousandths* of a second. And the initiative included testing of a 100-gigabit network backbone – much larger in scale, but slower – and "revolutionary" new network applications. Most of the NGI project tasks were completed by the end of 2000, although DARPA – again renamed, this time by the George W. Bush administration in 2001 – continued to work on the terabit experimental network.

Finally, Clinton sharply increased federal spending on IT research and development. The increase was prompted by an early 1999 warning from the President's Information Technology Advisory Committee, comprised of 25 leading academic and industry specialists. In a widely circulated report, the committee expressed alarm that U.S. technological leadership might be undercut in the near future unless long-term federal investment in fundamental research was greatly increased.[30] The administration responded in mid-1999 with a "bold investment in America's future" as part of its fiscal year 2000 budget proposal. As a result, federal research spending on IT jumped from $1.3 billion in fiscal 1999 to $1.9 billion in fiscal 2001 (Clinton's last budget proposal).

At century's end, a double blow to Gore

As the second Clinton-Gore term wound down, and Gore became increasingly involved in his own Presidential campaign, two unexpected events occurred. The first made it impossible for Gore to take credit for the administration's remarkable technological achievements. The second called into question the information-technology-based "new economy" itself. Together, they may well have cost Gore the 2000 election.

The first event occurred in March 1999 on CNN's "Late Edition" news program. Wolf Blitzer, the host, asked Gore how he differed from fellow Democrat Bill Bradley, who was also running for the Democratic Presidential nomination. In the course of his meandering response, Gore volunteered: "During my service in the United States Congress, I took the initiative in creating the Internet." Soon Gore was a laughing stock. The media had a field day ridiculing his statement, with several pundits noting that the Internet had been invented in the late 1960s, when Gore was still in high school. He became the butt of recurring monologues by late-night comics Jay Leno and David Letterman. Republicans piled on, too: then-Senate majority leader Trent Lott claimed to have invented the paper clip, and former Vice President Dan Quayle, who had famously misspelled "potatoes" at a school spelling bee, said he had invented SpellCheck. Throughout the entire Presidential campaign, whenever the Internet was mentioned, it would prompt someone to laughingly or caustically recall Gore's misstatement. It was, as Gore would later tell a Dartmouth College audience, the worst political mistake he ever made.[31]

The second event, the "dot-com bust," began in March 2000, when technology stocks led a stunning stock-market descent. Millions of Americans lost a substantial portion of their investments, and talk of a "new economy" or future technological marvels died down. In fact, the real economy, as distinct from the stock market, had made remarkable gains during the Clinton-Gore years – the best in American history. But the final report of Clinton's Council of Economic Advisors, which spelled out the economy's remarkable growth, rapid productivity gains, rising incomes, low unemployment, and moderate inflation of the Clinton Presidency, fell on deaf ears. And few noted the report's estimate that (mainly private-sector) spending on information technology accounted for fully one-third of all U.S. growth from 1995-1999 and produced hundreds of thousands of new jobs.[32]

So it was not surprising that, during the 2000 campaign, Gore did not dwell on his remarkable technology-policy record during his vice presidency. He did form a "digital cabinet" of high-tech luminaries called the "Gore techs." And he made campaign promises: he would double federal information-technology research funding over five years; make permanent the existing tax credits for private-sector IT research; and create "at least" ten million new high-tech jobs over ten years. But mostly he talked of other things.

His opponent, George W. Bush, also made some Internet-related promises on his website. But when asked about the "digital divide" at a New Hampshire debate in early 2000, he said that, given quickly changing technology, "...I worry about government funding and government programs that are haphazard and will be obsolete before they're even funded."[33]

America's pre-eminent position

As the Clinton-Gore administration came to a close, the United States was the globally acknowledged Internet leader. U.S. government officials had offered a vision of the Internet and led its advance from the outset. In the 1960s, the Defense Department's Advanced Research Projects Agency had designed, funded, and managed ARPAnet, the Internet's forerunner. In the 1970s, ARPA underwrote the breakthrough research of Vinton Cerf and Robert Kahn that made it possible to connect dissimilar networks and set the stage for the Internet's emergence. In the 1980s, the National Science Foundation planned and funded the Internet's spread across the country, and a small group of information-technology bureaucrats charted its progress through the early 1990s.

In 1993, Clinton and Gore, in the firm belief that technology was a prime driver of economic growth and a creator of new jobs, made information technology a national priority and provided top-level political leadership for the first time. And through a new vision of our communications future and a series of widely publicized, Internet-related initiatives, they captured the national imagination and the interest of the world.

Government leadership and funding were essential, but not sufficient to assure Internet leadership. From the outset, university researchers were deeply involved in the Internet's advance, and later, when the technology was proved, industry became interested. As the small group of computer scientists and electrical engineers working on networking problems gradually expanded, they moved in and out of government, academic, and private-sector positions. Aiding their effort were thousands of talented foreign experts and students who came to America to join the exciting new project. Together, they created a global industry second to none and made Intel microprocessors, PCs, the Microsoft Windows operating system, and Cisco routers, along with many other products, the global standard.

But the dot-com bust and Gore's election defeat left the Internet's future progress in doubt. What happened next would depend on George W. Bush and the people he chose to develop and carry out his policies.

When the Bush administration took office, in January 2001, everything changed. There was no apparent interest in the Internet, information technology, or even broader technology issues. In President Bush's view, economic growth would be stimulated by tax cuts and defense spending, not technology investments. Moreover, the market, not the government, should lead the Internet's advance. Government's role was simply to take the deregulatory steps needed to free up the private sector. Missile defense, not the information superhighway, became the priority. And a few months later, 9/11 and the decisions taken in its wake completely absorbed the administration.

America had laid down the Internet leadership baton.

Chapter 4.
Japan takes on the world

Japan's powerful trade and industry ministry has monitored and analyzed scientific and technological developments
around the globe since the late 1950s. In the early 1970s,
as part of that process, the ministry designated information
technology as a "critical emerging industry." But it didn't
build Japan's first computer network; it was only responsible for the "computer" part. The "network" part was the
domain of the ministry of telecommunications. That ministry didn't build Japan's first computer network either; it
saw its role as simply overseeing Japan's national telephone
company, Nippon Telephone and Telegraph (NTT). Neither
did NTT build the network, despite its extensive research
laboratories, nor did one of Japan's several large computer
makers. Rather, Japan's first computer network grew out of
a project at Tokyo University that was funded by the ministry of education.

The professors who designed the large chemistry
database project at Tokyo University, Japan's preeminent
university, were aware of ARPAnet, launched three years
earlier. They realized that their database would be much
more useful if it could be accessed remotely. So in 1972,

Hiroshi Inose, the university's internationally known professor of electronic engineering who would dominate Japanese academic computing for nearly three decades, and Toshiyuki Sakai, a Kyoto University professor, added a small computer network to the database proposal and submitted it to the ministry of education for funding. A short while later, their proposal was approved by Atsuko Toyama, a rising star at the ministry who would later become Japan's first female minister of education.[1]

Inose and Sakai proposed a network of seven mainframe computers: three at national (public) universities, Tokyo University, Kyoto University, and Tohoku University; one at the telecom carrier, Nihon Telephone and Telegraph (NTT); and three at large computer makers, Hitachi, Fujitsu, and NEC. But instead of using a subnetwork of identical IMP computers to connect the network, as ARPAnet did, Inose and Sakai decided to connect each mainframe directly to the network. This worked (and was less expensive), but it made each computer connection – and network expansion – much more difficult. The two professors also created a unique transmission protocol to transmit data files. Later, the government insisted they replace their transmission protocol with a complex and clumsy internationally approved one. But despite these problems, the *Nippon 1* network (N1) was up and running in 1974, less than five years after ARPAnet was launched.

As planned, the Japanese researchers used the N1 network to transfer files and consult databases. They didn't know that their American counterparts now used ARPAnet mainly to exchange e-mail messages and participate in electronic group conversations called news groups. But even if the Japanese had known, they couldn't have created e-mail. It was illegal then for non-NTT employees to use the telephone lines to *transmit* data packets (although they could access databases). In addition, no satisfactory way had yet been developed to transmit Japanese-language messages that use both Chinese[2] and Japanese characters. Moreover, the academics who controlled the network were understandably cautious about unplanned network uses. Such departures might cause the education ministry to end its network funding.[3]

During the late 1970s, the education ministry expanded the N1 network by adding to it several more national universities. In this way, the ministry increased the number of Japanese engineers and computer scientists with networking experience, just as ARPA had done. But neither the ministry nor the N1's creators made any attempt to form a broader networking community in Japan, significantly limiting the influence of the N1 networkers. In the mid-1980s, however, when the education ministry became aware of the NSF's critical role in expanding the Internet to colleges and universities across the United States, it decided to fund a nationwide academic network in Japan as well.

To do so, the ministry established a new National Center for Science Information Systems and appointed Inose, the N1 network pioneer, its first director general in 1986. His new center now had a much broader mandate: to coordinate academic computing, provide database services, and guide academic networking research. The center would also manage a new (mainframe) academic network, along with the older N1. This new Science Information network was modeled in part on the NSF's supercomputer-center backbone. Over the next five years or so, the education ministry underwrote the connection of more than 100 national (public) universities and 100 private universities to the new SI network.

NTT's alternate approach

The telecom giant NTT set forth another approach to networking in its "vision" for the 1980s. The vision, drafted by NTT executive vice president Yasusada Kitahara, was based on reports from France and Britain.[4] To meet Japan's future needs, it called for a digital network made up of fiber-optic cable and digital-switching equipment in urban areas and satellite service in more remote districts. The vision also offered a loose timetable: NTT would begin laying fiber to connect Japan's larger cities in the early 1980s, smaller cities would be tied in by the late 1980s, and by the mid-1990s, the entire country would be connected – at a cost of nearly $200 billion. NTT clearly meant to be the world's telecommunications leader by the end of the 20th century.

In 1984, after fully rebuilding the nation's copper telephone network destroyed in World War II, NTT turned to the new digital network approach outlined by Kitahara. The company began by laying fiber cable between Tokyo and Japan's second great city, Osaka. That same year, NTT was among the first telecommunications firms in the world to offer data (but not voice) services over its new Integrated Services Digital Network (ISDN). But despite some imaginative service offerings, such as a videotext service called "Captain" and related cable and satellite services, there was little demand. Unfortunately, by the time demand did emerge, around the turn of the century, the ISDN system was nearly obsolete. Its top transmission speed, only 168 kilobits per second, a mere three times the dial-up rate, was too slow to be competitive, and the company never recovered its investment.

Top NTT executives had argued from the start over the wisdom of launching the ISDN digital network. Those who prevailed believed that the firm should lead by moving to a digital infrastructure and offering imaginative digital services. Demand would follow. Those who disagreed contended, much as their counterparts in the United States do today, that supply should follow demand. Moreover, the critics said, it was an obvious mistake – a heavy bet on a technology soon overtaken by a superior one. But there were also benefits to Japan: NTT had begun the transition to digital technology, had gradually expanded its fiber backbone, and had replaced its analogue switches with digital ones.

At the time, however, the top NTT executives were more concerned about the public corporation's pending "privatization." After considerable debate in Japan's Diet (parliament), a new law was passed requiring that 40% of NTT's stock be sold to the public in 1985. A little-noticed provision allowed outsiders, as well as the company's employees, to use NTT lines for packet-data transmissions. That opened the door for yet another approach to networking in Japan.

The "Internet samurai"

In 1979, about the time NTT was readying its 1980s vision, Jun Murai received his bachelor's degree in mathematics from Keio University, a leading private institution. He then pursued a computer-oriented doctoral program at Keio, but he found academic computing boring. Keenly aware that his country lagged behind the United States in networking, Murai, along with two professors and a group he formed, began building a local-area network. When the LAN project was finished and his doctoral coursework completed, he launched an "experimental" network in October 1984.[5]

To create the network, Murai put into service two telephone modems and a "borrowed" Keio University telephone line. Then, using dial-up connections and a Unix transmission protocol common in the United States, he linked computers at Keio, Tokyo University, and the Tokyo Institute of Technology. Techies at the three universities soon began transferring files on the "experimental" network. This was the beginning of Japan University/Unix Network, or JUnet. Murai was then 29, and soon dubbed the "Internet samurai."[6]

Murai's fledgling network was an initial success. When the use of non-NTT data on NTT telephone lines was legalized the following year, the number of network participants grew quickly. Soon they included not only universities but industry research labs as well. This hadn't happened before because of the education ministry's jealous control of academic computing. But now academic and industry researchers could work together on Murai's JU network. And the scope of the network's operations was limited only by the voluntary contributions that funded it.

But to Murai's surprise, very few were actually using JUnet. The reason was simple: e-mail still had to be sent using Latin-alphabet letters, literally in a foreign language. This was frustrating for the Japanese researchers, because Japanese-language programs for stand-alone word processors had existed for some time. So the Murai group tackled the e-mail problem. After much discussion and two substantial technical fixes, the group developed a way to send e-mail messages in Japanese. During this process, the Murai group also adapted the then-popular "C" programming language to Japanese. Thus the group not only created the Internet's most popular application for Japan, it also made it possible for Japanese programmers to create other new applications in their own language. With these advances, the use of JUnet ballooned. Within two years, IBM Japan started yet another network, and soon both networks were linked to others in the United States.

But Murai, about to receive his doctorate in computer science, had still larger ambitions. He wanted to greatly expand JUnet. In 1987, he began discussing a wide-area network in Japan that would be underwritten by private industry. That same year, working with graduate-student programmers and corporate money, he launched the Widely Integrated Distributed Environment. WIDE was the first Japanese network to use the ARPAnet's increasingly universal TCP/IP Internet protocol.

WIDE was soon linked to NSFnet via Hawaii, and by fall 1991, the new network had an annual budget of $1 million and 57 networking researchers. Five years later, 250 researchers were using WIDE, and 80 companies were supporting it. Although obviously impressive, WIDE was dwarfed by the NSFnet of the day, which linked over 2,000 colleges, universities, and companies. The difference, of course, was that NSFnet was initially guided and heavily subsidized by the U.S. government; WIDE, on the other hand, was mainly the creation of one talented individual.

In his blue jeans and his determination to go it alone, Murai stood out in the staid Japanese academic world, according to Haruhisa Ishida, an Internet pioneer, where group enterprises and caution were the custom. Murai was able to make these remarkable networking advances in such an unpromising environment, according to one of his collaborators, because he really knew his stuff. By the end of the 1980s, he was no longer considered an unpredictable maverick. He was idolized by his graduate students and envied by his peers, and he had won the reluctant respect of his seniors.[7] As WIDE continued to expand, it became generally thought of outside Japan as the Japanese segment of the global Internet. And Jun Murai became known as the father of the Japanese Internet.

Slow progress in the early 1990s

Those three approaches to networking – academic, NTT's ISDN, and WIDE's relative eclecticism – persisted in Japan through the early 1990s. The education ministry, following the NSF's lead, expanded its SI network and funded four new academic networks devoted to physics, science, and other research concerns. But they continued in splendid academic isolation.

NTT pursued in its own approach to networking. Its vision for the 1990s, called "VI&P" (for "visual", "intelligent", and "personal"), was published in book form by

NTT chairman Haruo Yamaguchi in March 1990.[8] Based on what NTT staffers thought customers might want, the "visual" element included video telephones, video-on-demand, and video conferencing. The "intelligent" dimension featured an answering service, daily schedule maintenance, and simultaneous interpretation/translation services. And the "personal" theme consisted of person-to-person communications by telephone, online connections, mobile phone, or even "pocket telephone." The Japanese consumers could be connected at low cost and have access to whatever they wanted – voice, data, images. In retrospect, Yamaguchi seems prescient.

But the vision's main focus remained infrastructure, as it was in the earlier vision. The new VI&P services Yamaguchi foresaw would stream over NTT's rapidly expanding ISDN network. After laying fiber-optic cable between Tokyo and Osaka in the late 1980s, NTT had aggressively rolled out the service to 2,000 locations around the country. But few Japanese were ready for the new services, such as digital fax transmission, floppy disk transfers, and at certain locations, videoconferencing. In fact, only 60,000 customers signed up for NTT's expensive new ISDN service.

Despite this, Yamaguchi was determined to press ahead with the ISDN network. And it wouldn't be cheap. In all, the conversion would entail replacing 54 million subscriber telephone lines, four million local switching lines, 1.6 million long-distance switching lines, and 10,000 switching stations at a cost of $192-$230 billion.[9] That, it turned out, was overly ambitious. As Japan entered its economic "lost decade" of the 1990s, Yamaguchi's bold plan was thwarted.

He had to expand NTT's ISDN network with only the modest funding he was able to set aside.

As NTT pursued it own path and WIDE continued to expand, three more industry networks were launched, following IBM Japan's example. One of these linked smaller (refrigerator-sized) "mini-computers," rather than mainframes, and was named after its U.S. counterpart, VANnet. In the mid-1990s, the government, too, created an interministry network called IMnet. Its name was misleading. The ministries themselves were not, connected, just their research institutes and laboratories.

Besides the onset of economic doldrums , several things slowed the Japanese Internet's advance in the early 1990s. Ishida described some of them in a mid-1992 report. The dominance of mainframe (rather than personal) computing was the main reason, he believed. Moreover, each of Japan's mainframe manufacturers – IBM, Fujitsu, Hitachi, NEC – had their own proprietary networks, and it was difficult to connect them. There were too few local-area networks and routers with Japanese-language software, needed to send message packets on their proper path. Restrictive regulations were still in place, difficulties in using Japanese text persisted, and the telephone lines needed to connect the mainframes and local area networks were overpriced. Finally, Ishida reported, Tokyoites still preferred older ways of communicating: by telephone, by fax, and face to face.[10]

Japanese who wanted to connect to the Internet at home encountered another set of problems. PCs were very expensive, because Japanese manufacturers typically marked up prices by 200%. Dial-up Internet access time was also costly: NTT charged its regular voice rate of about 10 cents for every three minutes of use. As a result, many Japanese parents were amazed to discover their children had run up a $300 or $400 telephone bill simply surfing the net. With that in mind, many parents decided against a home computer.

But most off-putting was the difficulty of using a keyboard – what the Japanese then referred to as their "keyboard allergy". Only the limited number of people who had used word processors had ever tried a keyboard. So when personal computers began to show up in offices, most Japanese were forced to use a keyboard for the first time. It was a frustrating experience. Unsurprisingly, the older the user, the more frustrating it tended to be. As a result, many senior executives and officials simply relied on junior staff members to print out their e-mail messages and send responses in their name. For all of these reasons, Japan lagged well behind the United States in network use.

Yet there *was* progress. The telecom ministry eased its regulations sufficiently to allow commercial use of the Internet in 1993, the same year public use of the Internet began in the United States. Soon residential Internet service providers began to spring up, and enterprises – including Jun Murai's Internet Initiative Japan – began offering Internet access to businesses.

Aside from the education ministry's academic computing networks, the government's role in all of this was very modest. A "war" had erupted in the 1980s between the powerful trade and industry ministry, responsible for computers, and the equally powerful telecommunications ministry in charge of NTT and telecommunications, and the combat spilled over into the 1990s.[11] Cooperation between the two ministries on something as minor as networking was therefore out of the question, and broader government direction of the Internet's advance was impossible.

The government makes a start

But things soon began to change. In 1993, shortly after Clinton and Gore took office, Mickey Kantor paid a visit to Japan as the new administration's trade representative. As the visit was coming to a close, the Japanese, according to a former senior NTT official, were casting about for a suitable farewell gift for Kantor. U.S. officials, by law, were not permitted to accept gifts costing more than $25. To meet this condition, the Japanese finally settled on giving Kantor a book, *Telecommunications: NTT's Vision of the Future*, NTT chairman Yamaguchi's 1990s vision statement that had been translated into English two years earlier.

As the story goes, Kantor didn't pay much attention to the book, but he did pass it along to someone on Gore's staff when he returned to Washington. Gore, some Japanese believe, took the book seriously, mistaking what was clearly described as a "vision" for a Japanese blueprint. The result was furious work on an American counter plan that Gore announced just months later as the National Information Infrastructure initiative.[12] The delicious ending of this story is that after Gore made public his infrastructure initiative, Japanese officialdom took Gore's vision as an *American* blueprint and quickly began planning their own response. (One well-placed Gore aide at the time, however, doubts this and points out that the NII was previewed in the February policy outline before Kantor went to Japan.)

In any event, Gore's Washington announcement *did* galvanize parts of the Japanese government. The telecommunications ministry quickly argued that because the United States planned to roll out a fiber-optic network to American homes, Japan should do the same. When Japanese journalists pointed out to the ministry spokesman that the U.S. government intended only to encourage the *private* sector to build the new network, the ministry retreated, but only slightly. It then suggested setting up a new public corporation, reporting to the ministry, to lay the fiber. At this point, NTT joined in, saying *it* should construct the new network, at a cost of $400 billion over twenty years. But the cabinet would not go nearly that far. It could only agree on a new fiber-optic network – the aforementioned IMnet – to connect some 50 government research labs at a cost of $40-$50 million over three years..

Pressing on despite this decision, a standing telecommunications-ministry advisory council released yet another broad vision statement in May 1994. It called for Japan's transformation into a creative information society. To reach this goal, the council said, the government should encourage the private sector to lay fiber-optic cable to every Japanese home by 2010, support the development of basic technologies and high-speed network applications, and reform the telecommunications regulatory framework.

Not to be outdone, the trade and industry ministry that same month advanced its own plan. It specified that the private sector should lead the way to an "advanced information society," with government "supplementing and reinforcing" private sector initiatives. Instead of infrastructure expansion, the trade ministry urged the development of educational software and the placing of computers in all Japanese schools by 1999. In addition, the government should purchase ten massive new supercomputers for research, create an *actual* inter-ministry network, and use information technology more broadly.

Seizing on Al Gore's April 1994 call for a *Global* Information Infrastructure, then Prime Minister Tomiichi Murayama established an "advanced information and telecommunications society headquarters" in his Cabinet Office four months later. With the PM himself at the helm, the new headquarters soon issued a "basic policy" to achieve the desired new Japanese society. So in early 1995, for the first time, Japan put forth an ostensibly coordinated, government-wide effort.

The plan the new headquarters crafted was an amalgam of the goals of the competing ministries. There were five aims: creation of a nationwide fiber-optic network, greater government use of information technology, government funding of information-technology R&D, government support for development of new IT applications, and revision of the regulations hobbling Japan's telecommunications sector. The goals were supported by few specifics, no deadlines – and no money. Nonetheless, they marked the beginning of Japan's government-wide commitment to information technology, and the government *had* laid out a basic direction. Equally important, a consensus began to form – among those who understood this new world – that information technology could be used as a means to encourage government reform and deregulation. Steps toward those goals, the proponents believed, would also help lift the ailing Japanese economy, now stagnant for four years.

Throughout the remainder of the decade, members of the "advanced information and telecommunications society headquarters" continued to meet and devise implementation plans. But there was little progress.

A burgeoning Internet

Yet while the government was planning, Japanese Internet growth exploded. In the two years after its commercialization in September 1993, the Internet in Japan went from zero to "overcrowded."[13] Several developments produced that astonishing growth. Compaq, the American computer firm, entered the Japanese market forcing down markups (to about 25%), and sales of personal computers grew by 70%, more than a third of them for home use. The Windows operating system arrived, and the Internet itself became easier to use, more interesting, and less expensive. The language-related difficulties were largely overcome, people became accustomed to using keyboards, and Netscape Navigator, the first easy-to-use web browser, reached Japanese shores in 1995. At the same time, Japanese-language websites expanded exponentially, making the web a more interesting place to visit. And after much prodding, NTT began offering a low, flat rate for Internet access between 11 p.m. and 8 a.m. in 1995, which tens of thousands took advantage of.

Meanwhile, NTT, following its own infrastructure-centric vision, rapidly expanded the fiber (ISDN) infrastructure. International University of Japan's Center for Global Communications, headed by Professor Shumpei Kumon, encouraged NTT to embrace the Internet and strongly supported Internet use elsewhere. Thousands of companies invested in local-area networks, and as more people used the Internet at the office, home use grew as well. Responding to this new demand, Internet service providers mushroomed throughout the country, and by the mid-1990s, it was possible to connect to the Internet from virtually anywhere in Japan. In addition, in 1996, the government finally broke up NTT into a holding company and six subsidiary corporations. The breakup freed the telecom hierarchy to think of other things, a precondition for forceful government action. By 1998, a knowledgeable observer described the Japanese Internet as "mature."[14] The stage was set for a major new means of access – wireless telephones.

The i-mode Internet garden

NTT's new wireless company, NTT DoCoMo – usually called just DoCoMo, a play on the Japanese words *doko de mo*, meaning "anywhere"[15] – faced tough competition in the wireless voice market almost from its birth in 1996. DoCoMo and its two competitors had extensive nationwide wireless networks and offered excellent service. The only way to compete was on price, and harsh competition forced nonstop price cuts. Soon, it seemed, none of the companies would be profitable.

In 1997, to avoid this downward spiral, DoCoMo executives offered data services, such as e-mail, to businessmen, along with wireless voice. The new data service didn't attract many subscribers, but the experiment convinced DoCoMo senior vice president Keiichi Enoki that a potentially large market existed for a mobile-phone with Internet access. When a rival mobile-phone company's short-messaging service became popular, Enoki decided to push ahead.

With the earlier failure in mind, Enoki knew he must find a new approach. In mid-1997, he hired Mari Matsunaga, a young woman who worked at Recruit, a well-known personnel firm, where she edited a magazine filled with classified ads for various jobs. What appealed to Enoki was the connection he saw between the limited text in a classified ad and the text limitations of a mobile-phone screen. Otherwise, Matsunaga was a far-from-obvious choice. A French literature major in college, she described herself as a technophobe and didn't even own a mobile telephone. She was put off, she said, by people who used them in public. Moreover, when she accepted the DoCoMo position, she had never used the Internet. She did, however, have one very firm idea: the new mobile-phone service should appeal to the average person – not just technology buffs.

Shortly after her arrival at DoCoMo, Matsunaga hired Takeshi Natsuno, who had already launched an Internet start-up. Together they developed the critical concept of the new service: easy access to a "walled garden" of Internet websites in cyberspace. Each of the garden's websites would be designed with a mobile phone's small screen in mind. To enter the garden, subscribers would have to sign a contract with DoCoMo, receive a garden-access pass-word, and purchase a specially designed handset that would provide access by pushing just one button. Most important, the new service would be aimed at young people and offered at a price they could afford.

To put her concept across, Matsunaga fought ferocious battles with DoCoMo's outside consultants, who favored tar-geting businessmen again, and with the company's engineers, who were skeptical about the proposed technology. But her boss, Enoki, backed her, and she and Natsuno pushed for-ward. They began marketing, offering firms that might ap-peal to young people an opportunity to create content websites in the new DoCoMo garden. After some larger firms signed on, others soon followed, and by the official launch of the new service, 67 had agreed to host content sites. In keeping with Matsunaga's guidelines, the firms agreed to charge 100, 200, or 300 yen (roughly $1, $2, or $3) a month for unlimited visits to their website. DoCoMo consented to do this micro-billing for 9% of the website revenues and added a small charge for using the service. Monthly bills, they thought, would average about the yen equivalent of $30 or so.

With the nervous approval of DoCoMo's top executives, the new mobile-phone Internet service – "i-mode" – was launched with a big marketing push in February 1999. At first, there were few takers, mainly because of the handsets. The only one available at the outset was far too big and too expensive ($350), and its batteries lasted only an hour or so. But DoCoMo worked closely with a small group of hand-set makers, and within six months, they produced several smaller versions and began charging customers only $50 for a phone, burying the remainder of the price (about \$450) in a two-year usage contract. By the end of the year, the handset makers had also upgraded the black and white screens with color, sharply improved battery life, and developed easy-to-use search engines to replace an awkward early version.

Despite the growing pains, DoCoMo's i-mode service was stunningly successful. I-mode subscribers went from zero in February 1999 to nearly 5 million in April 2000 to over 23 million in April 2001. And as Matsunaga foresaw, more than 60% of the i-mode subscribers were under 30 at the end of 2000.[16] By April 2003, after DoCoMo's two rivals had set up their own Internet gardens, more than 60% of the entire Japanese population had mobile phones – and three-quarters of them could reach the Internet with the press of a button. Matsunaga and her DoCoMo colleagues had created one of the most successful business ventures of the late 20th century, and in so doing, they gave Japan a lead in mobile-phone Internet access that continues to this day.

The government takes the lead

In 1998, yet another colorless conservative politician, Keizo Obuchi, became prime minister. As *The New York Times* reported shortly before Obuchi's selection, he had all the charisma of "cold pizza."[17] But whatever he lacked in charm, Obuchi did know telecommunications. He had been minister of post and telecommunications, and he had led the ministry's support group in parliament. Now, as prime minister, he strongly favored revising the 1994 advanced information and telecommunications society plan to emphasize e-commerce. E-commerce, he thought, would revitalize the

Japanese economy, which had failed to grow for *eight* years at that point.

In fall 1998, the revision Obuchi wanted was approved. The new plan called for the government to create a favorable environment for e-commerce, while the private sector would demonstrate leadership by setting de facto e-commerce rules. A year later, in December 1999, he announced that promotion of IT in education, in government, and as part of a broader "IT 21" plan would be one of the nation's three Millennium Projects.[18] Five months later, however, as he was preparing to host a G8 summit meeting in Okinawa, Obuchi died unexpectedly. His successor, Yoshiro Mori, had had no experience with telecommunications, the Internet, or technology generally. This lack of knowledge was demonstrated most memorably shortly after his selection as prime minister when he referred to IT as "it."

The Mori government made little headway. Five days after Obuchi's death, the new PM dutifully chaired the *eleventh* meeting of the advanced information and telecommunications society headquarters group and its advisory council. In a short, formal statement, clearly prepared by others, Mori simply said he would work to advance projects that were so important to his predecessor. In the meeting that followed that tepid endorsement, the group approved the "first follow-up program of the basic guidelines' action plan to promote an advanced information and telecommunications society." Six years after the government had come together to promote information technology, that was how far they had come. Without funding, the bureaucrats were mostly talking to one another, and not much was happening.

But sometime during the next seven weeks, Prime Minister Mori was persuaded of the critical importance of information technology to Japan's future. One old Mori friend claims to have personally persuaded him to adopt information technology as a priority.[19] It is also possible that Japanese officials pushed the head man because Japan was falling further behind the United States – and even South Korea. It is also likely that the private sector urged him to focus on information technology as a means of improving the long-stalled economy. For a few weeks later, Prime Minister Mori told *Washington Post* columnist Jim Hoagland that "a *kamikaze*, or divine wind, of information technology would blow Japan back on [economic] course."[20]

But many are convinced that Mori's experience as host of the 2000 G8 summit that issued the Okinawa Charter on a Global Information Society swayed him. The very month of the summit, July 2000, Mori replaced the advanced society headquarters group he had addressed so formally two months earlier with a new "IT Strategic Headquarters" situated in his Cabinet Office. The prime minister himself directed the new headquarters group; it included all 19 cabinet ministers and was supported by a staff of senior bureaucrats. This marked an important turning point: the beginning of serious top-level Japanese political involvement in information technology and its high-priority treatment.

At the same time, and underscoring this new priority, Mori named a blue-ribbon "IT Strategy Council," headed by the dynamic Sony Corporation chairman, Nobuyuki Idei, to develop the actual strategy. The future was Idei's obsession; in May 1997, for example, he proclaimed the "Age of

Networks" at the annual Sony corporate conference.[21]   The remainder of the IT Strategy Council was made up of six academics, including the Internet samurai, Jun Murai, and an IT-savvy Keio University economics professor, Heizo Takenaka;   12 businessmen;   and the governor of Gifu prefecture.   This high-powered group was one of the few, it was said, that the bureaucrats did not control.

The council members were well aware of the enormous benefits information technology had brought to the U.S. economy (although, ironically, the dot-com bust had begun four months earlier).   Yet the consensus view was that Japan lagged about five years behind the United States – and behind Europe as well.   It was, in the council's view, past time for Japan to replicate the American "Internet miracle."

The council made public its final report, the "basic IT strategy," in late November 2000.   It centered on a daunting goal: the government will strive to create an environment where the private sector, utilizing market forces, can make Japan the "world's most advanced information technology nation within five years."   But based on the elements of the IT strategy itself, a more accurate reading of what the council really intended was: to make Japan the world's Internet leader by 2005.

Why was that necessary?   The new information-technology revolution, the council said, was comparable to the industrial revolution in 18th century Britain.   In the same way, information technologies – "primarily the Internet" – would revolutionize relationships between individuals, between individuals and organizations, and between individuals and society by drastically reducing the cost and time required to distribute information. To maintain its economic prosperity and improve the national quality of life, it was vital that Japan promptly establish a new legal and communications infrastructure.[22]

The IT revolution, the council continued, would determine world leadership in the 21st century. Japan was way behind, and it might not be able to catch up. To catch up, the council members said, Japan must quickly adopt institutional reforms. The central government should end its top-down administrative approach and cooperate with local governments to create an environment that would encourage prompt deployment of an Internet infrastructure based on market forces. If that was done, the private sector could become the driving force of a *new* revolution, which would create an ideal information-technology society in which all Japanese would be technologically literate and able to access the Internet from any location. Japan's economic structure would be reformed through "free and disciplined" competition, and the nation would attract talent from around the world.

The strategic priorities

The council set forth strategic priorities similar to those in the government's 1998 plan. Most observers did not recognize it at the time, but this new strategy differed markedly from its predecessor. First, over the protests of the government officials, Idei and his fellow non-government council members added bold, quantitative targets for each of the priorities. Second, and again over resistance, they set deadlines for reaching each of the targets. Third, the new strategy was a top government priority, as indicated by the establishment of the IT Strategic Headquarters for implementation of the strategy and Prime Minister Mori's September 2000 announcement of the overall goal: making Japan the world's Internet leader by 2005. There was also the promise of funding to achieve these targets implicit in the entire strategy planning process. Taken together, these differences made the new strategy a new animal.

The government officials charged with implementation were deeply skeptical about becoming the world's leader and about hitting the challenging targets. They knew Japan was well behind the global Internet leaders, and some of the targets seemed quite impossible to realize. But they were compelled to make the best of an unfamiliar situation, and the targets forced them to come up with new approaches. As they succeeded, strategic planning was carried forward to new levels. The officials gained confidence: not only could the targets could be hit; the overall goal – Internet leadership – could be reached.

As part of its IT basic strategy, the council urged the acceptance of four strategic priorities, each with specific targets and deadlines:

- **Establish one of the world's most advanced Internet networks within five years**. This the council defined as "high-speed" broadband access – DSL, cable, satellite, wireless – for at least 30 million Japanese households, and "ultra-fast" access – fiber-optic cable – for an additional 10 million households. Together, this covered most of Japan's 47 million households. The council also described how to achieve these aims. The private sector should lead the broadband deployment, while the government promoted "free and fair" competition among the private-sector players. To insure fair competition, the government should impose asymmetrical regulations – greater restraints on NTT, the dominant carrier, and greater freedom for its competitors – until a competitive market where NTT's market share was 50% or less was achieved. Next, the government should set out clear rules to encourage the private sector to deploy fiber-optic cable. And, finally, to insure universal broadband service, the government should study ways to bring high-speed Internet access to rural and isolated areas.

- **Create an IT-literate nation and sharply increase the number of IT specialists.** To achieve the first of those goals, the council urged the government to promote IT-driven education in elementary schools, high schools, and colleges. To reach the second, the government should increase the number of students receiving M.S. and Ph.D. degrees in IT-related fields – and admit approximately 30,000 "outstanding" foreign IT experts into Japan by 2005. Taken together, the number of home-trained and foreign IT specialists, the council said, should exceed the number of such specialists in the United States. This was essential to undergird Japan's industrial competitiveness, because nations would compete globally for valuable intellectual capital in the 21st century.

- **Promote electronic commerce.** This was essential to improve the economy. Business-to-business (B2B) e-commerce should grow tenfold from its 1998 level to $610 billion by 2003; business-to-consumer (B2C) e-commerce should grow by the same magnitude, to $27 billion, over the same period. Again, the private sector should be primarily responsible for expanding e-commerce. But the government should reduce regulation to a minimum, protect consumer privacy, and create a non-judicial means of settling e-commerce disputes.

- **Achieve e-government.** The council saw that as a means to completely reform Japanese public administration. The council urged the government to bring its internal communications online, along with information for businesses and citizens, and most government services. As an overall goal, the council suggested that electronic information be handled just as information on paper by 2003 – and that all documents be digitized within five years to create "paperless" government offices.

When the IT basic strategy was announced, with its startling goal of global Internet leadership in five years, few Japanese paid any attention. Most of the Japanese who noticed viewed the strategy as simply a ploy to shore up support for an unpopular prime minister. IT specialists, too, were skeptical; they found the whole project too centralized and top-down in its emphasis. They were particularly dubious about the goal of deploying fiber to ten million households, which would cost billions of dollars. No one seemed to take seriously the goal of Internet leadership. Even Japanese officials downplayed the idea. And because nothing about Japan's new IT strategy appeared in the U.S. media, Americans were completely unaware of it.

Launching the five-year plan

On January 22, 2001, two days after President George W. Bush was inaugurated, the government announced an "e-Japan strategy." There were no surprises: it was the same – word for word – as the council's "basic IT strategy" made public two months earlier. But the goal – global Internet leadership by 2005 – was now official. The government was committed. The pressure was on. Whatever the doubts and misgivings, the government got down to work.

In March 2001, the strategic headquarters added a fifth priority goal – **ensuring the security and reliability of the contemplated advanced networks** – and laid out a comprehensive implementation plan. The plan made public hundreds of implementation tasks, each assigned to a specific ministry, each with a deadline for completion. The strategic headquarters also asserted a special role for government: funding basic information technology and coordinating the networking advances of the universities, industry, and government itself. At that point, for other reasons, the Mori government fell.

The following month, in April 2001, a new prime minister, Junichiro Koizumi, and his new cabinet took over. Pledging himself to dramatic reform, Koizumi firmly committed himself and his government to the e-Japan strategy. Surprisingly, he gave the economic and fiscal affairs portfolio – along with information-technology policy – to a non-politician, Keio university economics professor Heizo Takenaka. A graduate of prestigious Hitotsubashi University, Takenaka had lectured at Harvard and been a visiting fellow at the Institute of International Economics, a Washington think tank. He had also been a member of the original IT Strategy Council and, consequently, was an enthusiastic and knowledgeable proponent of the e-Japan strategy.

But pursuing it would not be easy. A *Financial Times* reporter concluded that "the pace of implementation [of the e-Japan strategy] has been traditionally slow as incumbent players seek to protect their advantages and politicians remain under the sway of vested interests."[23] Despite that glum assessment, Takenaka soon made his influence felt. Some fresh blood was brought into the IT strategic headquarters, including Mari Matsunaga, the i-mode creator. A few weeks later, the augmented strategic headquarters announced slightly revised priorities for the following fiscal year. Thus began an annual planning cycle that has continued up to the present.

In mid-2003, at the half-way point of the original strategy's five year push, the strategic headquarters announced a substantially revised plan, called the "e-Japan strategy II." The original priorities remained the same but, because the high-speed network infrastructure was now mostly in place, the plan's focus shifted from promoting the deployment of the infrastructure to encouraging its use. Among the uses suggested were: providing medical services remotely, tracking the food supply, extending services to those living alone, and encouraging telecommuting.

As more of the original strategy's goals were met, the communications ministry announced in mid-2004 yet another five-year plan – "u-Japan." u-Japan promised "ubiquitous networks," seamlessly connected ultra-fast broadband and wireless networks throughout Japan, permitting anyone to communicate anywhere, anytime with anyone or anything by 2010. In early 2006, the strategic headquarters announced yet another plan, a "New IT Reform Strategy." Proclaiming that "Japan has become the world's most advanced IT nation," the Reform Strategy called for structural reform of healthcare, creation of the world's safest and most secure society, and a more competitive business sector – all through expanded use of information technology. Moreover, "...by 2010 – ahead of all other nations – ..Japan will achieve a complete transformation of itself through the utilization of IT...."[24]

So there we have it: two approaches to global Internet leadership. The Japanese government launched the e-Japan strategy, the first of four major plans, aimed at global Internet leadership within days of the younger President Bush's inauguration in January 2001. At that same time, the Bush administration, with other priorities, turned its back on IT, leaving America's Internet lead to the market – and chance. And now, eight years later, the results are in: Japan has overtaken the United States in the two most important dimensions of Internet leadership. We turn now to a closer examination of those two, broadband infrastructure and wireless progress.

Chapter 5.
The landline broadband dimension: getting to fiber

Broadband – more specifically , the landline broadband infrastructure – is the prime dimension of Internet leadership. It determines who has access and how fast that access is. In this sense, broadband infrastructure is to the 21st century what the railroads were to the 19th and the interstate highway system to the 20th. It lies at the heart of the information revolution that will continue to transform our lives.

The best way to understand this infrastructure is to liken it to a highway system. The pre-broadband Internet infrastructure that permits *dial-up* Internet access simply uses the existing telephone system that reaches well over 90% of the population in both the United States and Japan. Permitting Internet access speeds of only 56 kilobits (thousands of bits) per second, these telephone lines are the pokey, unpaved, gravel roads that remain in today's highway system.

Broadband Internet access can be divided into three categories, based on the speed of access: basic, high-speed, and ultra-fast – the paved local roads, state highways, and interstates.[1] The infrastructure that provides *basic* broadband – ranging in access speed from 768 kilobits to 10 megabits (millions of bits) per second – consists of the telephone and cable company infrastructure with certain upgrades, the satellite system, and newer, fixed wireless Internet services. Infrastructure for basic broadband (excluding slow, expensive satellite service) is now available to something over 75% of all American households, but very few of those can choose anything faster. In other words, nearly all Americans are using *basic* broadband, in effect, driving on paved local roads.

High-speed broadband can also be provided by DSL, cable, or fixed wireless with further upgrading and closer proximity of the Internet users to the nearest telephone, cable-company, or wireless access equipment. This high-speed Internet infrastructure, with access speeds of 10 to 70 megabits per second or so, now covers almost all of Japan. Therefore, 98.3% of Japanese households have high-speed Internet access, that is, travel on state highways that are five to ten times faster than the local roads now used by most American households. High-speed access to the network has significant advantages: almost any Japanese household can, for example, view real-time, high-definition television over their Internet connection, while most Americans can only get the small, jerky figures of streamed digital television.

Finally, there is the *ultra-fast* Internet infrastructure: a fiber-optic cable network, linking the Internet backbone to individual households. With speeds of 100 to 1,000 megabits per second and even higher, this fiber-optic infrastructure comprises the interstate highway system of the Internet, but with no upward speed limit. It is the gold standard of Internet access, and sooner or later all developed countries will adopt it. At the end of 2007, this fiber infrastructure – called fiber to the home (FTTH) – was already available to more than 85% of all Japanese households, while the corresponding figure in the United States was a mere 7%.[2] These fiber connections permit a wide range of interactive video applications, such as multiple streams of high-definition TV, realistic "live" videoconferencing, telemedicine, six-minute movie downloads, interactive Internet game-playing, and connected sensor networks that can track a child's whereabouts or a senior's vital signs.

All of this raises the question of how much speed is enough. Here, reasonable people – and governments – disagree. Some, like the Japanese government, believe that faster is better; thus fiber is the network of choice and, although expensive, Japan should deploy a nationwide fiber infrastructure as quickly as possible. Others, like the Canadian government, think that given today's applications and infrastructure costs, universal *basic* broadband is adequate for the time being. Still others, like the officials in the Bush administration, were content to let demand drive the market, no matter how slow and expensive Internet connections remain or how long it takes – it took electricity 50 years – for high-speed broadband to reach the countryside and inner cities.

All of these strategies carry risks, but the Bush strategy carries the greatest risk. Lagging deployment of landline broadband infrastructure means lower economic growth, reduced productivity, fewer new jobs, and lessened global competitiveness. It means doing without advanced IT and Internet help in solving the nation's problems. It means diminished quality of life for many of the nation's inhabitants. And it means second or third crack at innovating for the new Internet markets: high-speed, ultra-fast, and ubiquitous. Those are the consequences of setting the bar too low.

The question, then, is how to encourage these huge broadband infrastructure investments?   Nearly everyone agrees the private sector should do most of the work, but should government take the lead – and provide incentives? Or should it rely on market forces? In Japan, the government led; in the United States, after 2001, market forces did. The results of these two approaches are strikingly different. Let's take a closer look.

Japan plays catch up

In early 2001, Japan lagged well behind the United States in Internet access. About half of all Americans and Japanese had home computers. But more Americans (42%) had dial-up Internet access than Japanese (34%), mainly because NTT charged ten cents for every three minutes of telephone or Internet use, and Internet service providers tacked on another ten cents a minute. When it came to broadband access, America's lead was far greater. Many American households could choose between DSL access from a telephone company or independent service provider, or a cable-modem broadband connection through a cable-TV company.[3] As a result, 5.2 million American households (and small businesses)[4] subscribed to something like basic broadband at the end of 2000. In Japan at that time, only 635,000 had broadband access, nearly all from cable-TV companies. In fact, there wasn't a single DSL connection in Japan until March 2000, and there were only 10,000 at year-end.

But in April 2001, shortly after George W. Bush took office, Junichiro Koizumi became Japan's prime minister and made the e-Japan strategy a national priority, as noted earlier. To direct the strategy, he selected Heizo Takenaka, an Internet-savvy Keio University professor who had been a member of the IT strategy council.

The first aim was broadband Internet access for most Japanese: DSL or cable "high-speed" broadband for 30 million of Japan's 47 million households and "ultra-fast" (fiber-optic) broadband for an additional 10 million.[5] The IT strategy council also described how this should be done: through competition – creating a highly competitive market for high-speed Internet service providers. But the communications ministry officials couldn't pit regional telephone companies, providing DSL, against the cable companies, providing cable-modem Internet access. The cable-TV networks, mostly mom-and-pop operations in rural areas, covered only a fraction of the country.

Instead, if they were to create competition and meet the 30-million-household target, the officials concluded that they would have to compel the existing regional telephone companies, NTT East and NTT West, to open their residential telephone lines to outside companies willing to provide DSL service. The hope was that this new competition would force lower prices, increase the number of subscribers, and quickly encourage wider DSL availability.

To create this competitive marketplace, the officials rewrote the regulations that made it difficult for outside competitors to enter the DSL market. Then, using the asymmetrical regulatory authority parliament had given them – stricter limits on the existing (NTT) telephone companies and more freedom for their competitors – they ordered the two NTTs to open their local home and business telephone lines to qualified outside competitors. The DSL market would be considered "competitive" when the NTTs had half (or less) of the market. At that point, but only then, the ministry would completely deregulate the DSL market.

To spur outside competition – and encourage the NTT companies to build next-generation fiber networks – the ministry set a very modest charge (about $2 per line per month) for outside competitors to connect to the telephone companies' residential lines. The officials also required the NTTs to permit outside competitors to place their equipment in the NTTs' local-exchange facilities.[6] In addition, the officials forbade the NTTs and the outside DSL providers to screen Internet content or slow its transmission. In doing so, they established at the outset the principle of "net neutrality."

NTT East and NTT West resisted this new competition. First, they offered only a limited number of local lines to competing DSL firms, and they opened only 11 of tens of thousands of local exchanges to competing companies' equipment. They also restricted the space available in their local exchanges for "outside" equipment and sat on applications from would-be competitors. But two of the latter, Tokyo Metallic and e-Access Japan, complained to Japan's Fair Trade (antitrust) Commission about the heavy-handed treatment. After a two-month investigation, the commission ordered the NTT companies to comply with the new regulations or face antitrust action. Compliance quickly followed, opening the way for prompt, inexpensive, competitive access to the NTTs' local exchanges and telephone lines.

At about this time, in June 2001, "Yahoo!BB," an offspring of the Softbank investment bank, unexpectedly entered the market, offering basic broadband for $20 a month – $5 cheaper than e-Access' *wholesale* price, and at the time, the lowest price in the world. This disruptive competition came from Softbank CEO Masayoshi Son, a Japanese of Korean ancestry, a former UC Berkeley student, an early Yahoo stockholder, and one of the world's boldest businessmen. According to e-Access CEO Sachio Senmoto, $20 a month was the amount Son thought customers would like to pay, never mind the cost to the company – a revolutionary way of pricing in any country.[7] A few months later, ACCA Networks, a wholesale firm, introduced broadband service five times faster (8 Mbps) than any of its Japanese competitors – for about $22 a month. Soon, e-Access and Yahoo!BB matched this offer. The freewheeling competition so prized in the United States had transformed the Japanese market.

Japanese living in cities could now subscribe to 8 megabits-per-second (Mbps) broadband for about $20 a month, the cost of ten hours of dial-up service. By the hundreds of thousands, customers responded to this bargain, and by the end of 2001, Japan's "year of broadband," 1.5 million of them had subscribed. Within less than a year, the Japanese government's competition policy and Japanese entrepreneurs led by Masayoshi Son had given the country's city dwellers high-speed broadband at the world's lowest prices.

But that was just the beginning. The following year, young Japanese men and women wearing red-and-white "Yahoo!BB" uniforms were on street corners throughout Japan offering 8-Mbps broadband service for about $20 a month and 12-Mbps broadband for about $27 a month – and a free modem to connect to the service. Moreover, for an additional $5, a subscriber could have unlimited Internet telephone service throughout the country. The NTT companies soon offered their own 12-megabit service at somewhat higher prices, and the number of Japanese high-speed subscribers continued to skyrocket.

By June 2002, high-speed broadband connections were available to 33 million Japanese households, surpassing the e-Japan strategy's 30-million target three-and-one-half years ahead of schedule! Less than a year later, Japan blew by the United States in broadband usage, when a greater percentage of Japanese than Americans subscribed to broadband. Japan's world-class policy on competition, as well as its daring entrepreneurs, "accommodating" telecommunications giants, and adventurous consumers, had combined to surpass the U.S. effort in just 30 months. Nearly a quarter of all Japanese households were now using high-speed broadband,[8] and one of every 25 telephone calls was being made over the Internet.

In July 2003, having exceeded the original high-speed target, the IT strategic headquarters announced the "e-Japan strategy II." Aimed at boosting the actual use of the new broadband infrastructure, "e-Japan II" called for 30 million high-speed broadband *subscribers* by 2005. By December of that year, when the original e-Japan strategy ended, high-speed (DSL or cable) or ultra-fast (fiber) Internet access was available to nearly every Japanese household.

But with only 17.7 million *high-speed* broadband sub-scribers, government officials had fallen well short of their 30-million e-Japan II target. Yet connection speeds then *av-eraged* 26 megabits per second and the price was still $20-$30 per month, restrained not only by competition in the high-speed market, but also by the sharply declining price of *ultra-fast* fiber connections which had already attracted nearly five million subscribers. As more Japanese switched to fiber, the number of *high-speed* subscribers, having reached 17.9 mil-lion in the last quarter of 2006, began to decline.[9]

The United States falls behind

During the latter half of the 1990s, the United States, too, sought to create a competitive Internet service market. Fol-lowing passage of the 1996 Telecommunications Act, Presi-dent Bill Clinton's FCC compelled U.S. regional telephone companies to open their residential lines to competing In-ternet service providers and eased regulations to encourage them. The FCC capped the price the telephone companies could charge for access to their residential lines (at about $15 per line per month), and it required the telecoms to provide competitors with equipment space in their local exchanges.

But the regional phone companies fought this enforced competition tooth and nail. They used delaying tactics with would-be competitors; they went to court repeatedly to challenge the new requirements; they lobbied for more favorable legislation; and despite earlier assurances to the contrary, they refused to compete in one another's territories. They mounted a two-pronged argument: the new competition was unfair; and if their networks were opened to competitors, they would have no incentive to improve their networks – or build next-generation fiber networks.

Faced with this stiff resistance, the Clinton FCC did what it could to prevent the telephone companies' delaying tactics, meet their court challenges, and blunt their lobbying. This effort ensured modest competition, but a deep-pocketed, disruptive competitor did not emerge. Even modest competition lowered the price of dial-up and broadband, although the latter was slow (around 1 Mbps), expensive ($45-$60 a month), and somewhat unreliable. And the United States, at the end of 2000, did become one of the world's leaders in broadband usage.

All of that changed when the Bush administration took office in January 2001. President Bush had other priorities: lowering taxes, missile defense, and after September 11, the "war on terrorism." The new administration sought economic growth through tax cuts and deficit spending, not advances in information technology. During his first three years in office, Bush mentioned broadband only twice and only in passing.[10]

The administration's commentary on broadband came from the second echelon. The new FCC chairman, Michael Powell, the son of Secretary of State Colin Powell, spoke eloquently about the benefits of the coming "digital broadband migration." But in a December 2000 speech, he backed away from the modest DSL broadband competition that already existed. Powell told his listeners that competition through innovation is "perhaps more important than price competition;" competitive markets should not be sub-ject to "intrusions and distortions from inapt regulations;" and, consumer protection was no excuse for "engaging in industrial policy."[11]   Nancy Victory, the administration's broadband voice at the commerce department, was more di-rect: she insisted that the market, not government, should drive the rollout of broadband.[12] Beyond more deregulation, the new administration clearly saw little need for govern-ment action.

Pursuing its minimalist strategy, the Bush administra-tion proceeded to ignore broadband during its first two years except for responding to two court cases. In the first, a Cali-fornia appeals court set the stage for additional broadband competition by raising the issue of opening cable-TV compa-nies' residential lines to outside competitors. To thwart that possibility, the FCC issued an order that exempted those com-panies from any external competition whatsoever.[13]   When the appellate court, predictably, questioned the commission's action, the administration decided to appeal the court deci-sion to the Supreme Court, leaving the matter in limbo. In the second case, the regional phone companies persuaded the District of Columbia appeals court to require the FCC to jus-tify its regulations allowing competitors' access to residen-tial telephone lines. Unless the FCC justified its competition rules, the court would likely rule out that access.

In early 2003, as required by the telecommunications act, the FCC carried out a formal review of the now-unsettled broadband situation. Instead of creating clarity, the com-mission proceeded to issue controversial new rulings based on internal disagreements and trade-offs related mostly to telephone issues of the past. The confusion was further compounded when FCC chairman Powell ended up partially opposing a majority of his fellow commissioners. The commission's initial pronouncements were interpreted to mean that companies investing in "next-generation" (fiber) networks would not have to share them with competitors. Moreover, companies then leasing residential lines from the regional phone companies to provide competing DSL service would have that option for only three more years. Those controversial rulings were confirmed six months later, when the commission finally issued its formal, 576-page written ruling.

The FCC justified these decisions by finding that the high-speed Internet sector was already "competitive" and therefore needed little regulation. Noting that the cable industry controlled about two-thirds of the nation's broadband market, the commission found no need to handicap the phone companies with outside DSL competition for much longer. And when the administration decided in June 2004, five months before the presidential election, not to appeal the DC appeals court's insistence that the FCC justify its regulations forcing competition on the telephone companies, the administration's goal of complete deregulation of the broadband market was within sight.

During these years, the number of American broadband subscribers continued to grow, from 5.2 million U.S. homes and small businesses in 2000 to 20.6 million in June 2003. But American Internet service was still too slow, expensive (at $40-$55 a month), and unreliable.

The first signs of broadband competition between the telephone and cable companies appeared in 2004. Earlier the cable companies had extended higher speed networks closer to their subscribers' homes. That permitted 3-megabit-per-second Internet access and reliable Internet telephone use, and the cable companies began offering "triple-play" – TV, Internet, and telephone – service. This proved a popular combination, and by the end of 2004, more than 7 million American households had signed up. To compete, the telephone companies, which were slower to upgrade their infrastructure, began deploying fiber networks in 2002.

Meanwhile, as the presidential campaign gained momentum in 2004, John Kerry, the Democratic candidate, announced a wide-ranging broadband deployment plan.[14] It attracted little notice, but rumors of the emerging policy did prompt President Bush, running for reelection, to promise "affordable broadband for all Americans" by 2007. Although Bush himself was vague on the details, the White House website spelled them out. The ambitious goal would be achieved through broadband competition among four kinds of companies – telephone; cable; electric power, with their own fiber-optic networks; and wireless, with their promising new technologies. At this point, America's de facto "hands off" broadband strategy was clear. But despite the optimism, during those four years of Bush's first term, the United States dropped from 4th to 16th in international broadband-usage rankings.[15]

Bush's campaign promise was his final word on broadband. But his new FCC chairman, Kevin Martin, described broadband deployment as the commission's highest priority. It would be achieved through the promised "platform" competition among DSL, cable, power line, and wireless. So in early summer 2005, the Supreme Court, at the administration's urging, freed cable companies from any threat of competition from rival broadband providers.[16] To level the playing field, Martin then persuaded his fellow Republican commissioners to end, after a one-year grace period, the FCC's requirement that telephone companies open their residential lines to DSL competitors as well.[17] America's broadband success was now up to the market, but the market has been slow to deliver.

Dissatisfied with market-led broadband deployment, several cities decided to launch citywide wireless initiatives based on WiFi (Wireless Fidelity), the short-range wireless technology commonly available in coffee shops, hotels, and airports. Many of these projects, particularly in large cities, involved partnerships in which private entities would own and operate the networks on city-owned facilities. Philadelphia was one of the first with plans to allow Earthlink to place WiFi equipment throughout the city to provide all of its citizens with broadband. That seemed a good, cheap solution. But problems began almost immediately. First, Verizon, using its exceptional political muscle, sought to block the project. In the end it persuaded the Pennsylvania legislature to ban similar WiFi experiments elsewhere in the state in exchange for permitting the Philadelphia initiative to proceed. Second, the city's lead technological partner, Earthlink, ran into financial difficulties and pulled out. Third, there were problems with the technology itself: WiFi signals travel only 50-100 yards and don't penetrate walls easily. This means that users farther away from the WiFi signal or inside their homes may get unreliable broadband – or none at all.

As a result of these kinds of problems, the WiFi projects in virtually all large cities, including Philadelphia, Chicago, and San Francisco, are now on hold or have been abandoned. The only exception is Minneapolis, where a small, determined, local company appears to have succeeded in building a citywide WiFi network.

One of the few broadband success stories occurred at the state level. In 2004, Kentucky governor Ernie Fletcher, fearing that broadband might not reach Kentucky's rural areas, launched the "Connect Kentucky" project, a public-private partnership. By bringing (basic) broadband to all Kentuckians, Fletcher sought to improve the lives of those not already online, bring hope to withering rural communities, entice high-tech industries and jobs to Kentucky, and create an environment for lifetime (distance) learning, better healthcare, and an improved quality of life. The Connect Kentucky organization first mapped the availability of broadband within the state, then developed strategies to advance broadband deployment and use, as well as general IT literacy. "eCommunity" teams in each county set about implementation, and the results have been impressive.[18] In July 2008, broadband was available to 95% of all Kentucky homes, and 44% of all households were using broadband, up nearly 50% from 2004.[19]

The "Connect Kentucky" program was successful as far as it went, but its goal was too modest. What is needed, not only in Kentucky but throughout the country, are ultra-fast networks capable of carrying the vast data flows of the near future. Showing the way, more than 40 municipalities have launched successful *fiber* broadband initiatives.

Fiber – the 21st century network infrastructure

For all the talk of basic and high-speed broadband, it is already clear that ultra-fast fiber is the unmistakable Internet infrastructure for the 21st century. Fiber networks are the only Internet infrastructure that can meet sharply increasing demand for additional speed. In the United States, demand for speed is increasing fivefold every five years: from 1.5-megabit broadband in 2000 to 7.5 megabits in 2005. If that pattern continues, it will generate demand for nearly 40 megabits per second in 2010 and nearly 200 megabits in 2015. Only fiber can provide those speeds, because it has virtually no upper speed limit.

In addition, fiber is more reliable and more secure than competing technologies – and the essential underlying infrastructure for high-speed wireless Internet access, mobile phones, and WiMax long-distance wireless. Moreover, fiber is the only mode of Internet access that enables a user to *upload* data at the ultra-fast speeds he or she can download it, a critically important advantage in an interactive video age.

Most important, a fiber Internet infrastructure is critical to solving the major issues now facing the United States: increased productivity and economic growth (through job creation and retention, improved industrial efficiency, and innovation), better and less expensive health care (telemedicine), improved education (distance learning), reduced energy use and environmental protection (telecommuting, teleconferencing, and transport control), and homeland security (connected sensor networks). Without that infrastructure, those issues will be more difficult to manage, if they can be managed at all.

Making those kinds of issue-technology connections led Japan's IT strategy council to insist, way back *in 2000*, that fiber Internet access be made available to more than one-fifth (10 million) of Japan's households by 2005. The council was convinced that fiber is the essential communications infrastructure of the 21st century. But laying fiber to 10 million households was a daunting target. When the e-Japan strategy was launched in January 2001, the regional NTT telephone companies were experimenting with pokey, 10-megabit fiber service. But two months later, Japan got lucky: an unexpected competitor to the NTT companies again came out of nowhere. Usen Broad Networks, a little known background-music company with an expansive fiber network, began offering blazing fast, 100-megabit-per-second direct fiber service to apartment and office buildings in the Tokyo area. The cost was just $48 per month plus a few hundred dollars for installation.

With little fanfare, the world's first commercial fiber-optic service had been launched. The event concentrated NTT-corporate minds. They scrapped their plans for 10-megabit service and launched 100-megabit service later that year – for about $80 a month.

As Usen was signing up its first customers, communications ministry officials began wrestling with the question of how to entice the private sector to make ultra-fast fiber broadband available to 10 million Japanese households by

2005 – and how to open the fiber network to outside competitors. With some funding promised for this top-priority
project, the officials decided to offer tax incentives. Companies could depreciate about one-third of their cost in the
first year, and they could obtain low-interest loans[20] and loan
guarantees if they were willing to lay fiber. But the government decided where the fiber would be laid by requiring government approval of company proposals. And to overcome
certain resistance from those companies to opening the fiber
networks to competitors, the officials set a *high* interconnection charge (nearly $50 per month) for leasing them. That
meant potential competitors would make little, if any profit
after paying the interconnection charge. The government
also declared that the networks would be open to all content,
devices, and so forth.

As it turned out, these incentives alone were enough to
encourage the private sector to lay fiber to more than 10 million Japanese households. But the communications ministry
officials also worried that, even with tax and loan incentives,
the private sector wouldn't include smaller cities and towns.
To encourage fiber networks there, they offered subsidies
worth about one-third of the entire cost to any municipality
willing to build its own network. The officials also required
that all of the fiber networks created with either tax incentives or subsidies be open to all outside applications, services, and content without discrimination – again, network
neutrality.

The officials' fiber strategy worked: NTT East and NTT
West began laying fiber. They did so in response to the ministry's tax-incentive offer and because they were losing the

battle for high-speed DSL customers. Because of the low interconnection charge to provide DSL service, Yahoo!BB and others could quickly go toe to toe with the NTTs for DSL customers. To regain their competitive advantage, those companies began their transition to fiber networks. Many municipalities also took advantage of the ministry's subsidy offer, further expanding the availability of fiber service.

As a result, ultra-fast fiber service was available to 13 million Japanese households, well above the 10-million e-Japan goal, by June 2002, just 15 months after the ministry announced its implementation strategy. But demand for the fiber service increased only slowly. People wondered whether the additional speed was worth the money, as fiber at that time cost at least twice as much as slower high-speed connections.

Yet starting from zero in March 2001, the number of ultra-fast fiber subscribers grew to 9,000 by the end of that year. Usen soon dropped its price for 100-megabit service to $42 a month, NTT East reduced its to $52 – and two large electric-power companies entered the ultra-fast fiber market promising more competition and even lower prices.[21] By the end of 2002, Japan, with 210,000 fiber subscribers,[22] had easily overtaken the United States. Six months later, the original e-Japan strategy's midpoint, the IT strategic headquarters announced a new e-Japan strategy II target: 10 million fiber service *subscribers* by 2005.

Without tackling the demand side, there was little the ministry could do other than extol the benefits of 100-megabit service. The hope was, as one knowledgeable communications ministry official put it, that the cost of fiber service would continue to fall and when it was roughly the same as high-speed DSL service, many would shift to fiber. That is exactly what happened. But it would take until September 2007 for Japan to top the e-Japan II target of 10 million fiber subscribers. Moreover, the NTTs' goal of 30 million of them by 2010 had to be revised downward to 20 million[23] – even though over 90% of the country is expected to have fiber access at that time. Yet the trend was clear: fiber subscribers exceeded DSL subscribers in June 2008, becoming the mainstream of Japanese broadband.

Meanwhile, in 2004, the Ministry of Internal Affairs and Communications announced yet another plan, the *u-Japan strategy*, which called for making the fiber network available to nearly all Japanese households by 2010 (and combining the fiber network with ultra-fast wireless networks).

America slowly embraces fiber

When the U.S. cable companies began offering popular "triple-play" packages – TV, Internet, and telephone – in 2004, their telephone-company competitors faced an awkward choice. Should they get into the triple-play game by upgrading their DSL networks to provide the 25 megabits-per-second access speed[24] needed for high-definition television, the next obvious "new thing" for broadband? Or should they lay ultra-fast fiber directly to the home – or near it. Verizon chose direct-to-home which permits superb triple-play service with all of the potential speed needed for decades to come. But laying fiber to the home is expensive. Verizon now claims to spend an average of $700 to connect a home (mainly by stringing fiber on telephone poles in suburban areas), but that average is misleading. It can run much higher, in the $1,300 range.

That expense and a belief that household connections don't need to be that fast led AT&T[25] to choose a cheaper route: laying fiber to a neighborhood "node," which means bringing fiber-optic cable to within 3,000-5,000 feet of a large group of homes and using the existing copper phone lines for the remainder of the distance. That reduces the per-home cost to roughly $300-$500, but there is a notable downside. Even using advanced DSL technology (ADSL2+), the copper telephone lines sharply limit the household's connection speed, typically to 16-20 megabits per second or so. AT&T CEO Randall Stephenson thinks this is fine for now.[26] Many observers don't.

Spurred on by the cable companies' $100-per-month triple-play offers, both Verizon and AT&T announced ambitious targets for laying fiber. At the end of 2007, Verizon had made it available to nine million households (with over one million subscribing), and it plans to offer fiber to an additional nine million by 2010, in all about half of Verizon's subscriber base.[27] But Verizon's FIOS fiber service is pricey: $43-$90 per month for 5-50 Mbps Internet service alone. AT&T, on the other hand, had made its slower (6-10 Mbps) "U-verse" service available to nine million "living units" by March 2008 (with 380,000 subscribing), and plans to reach 30 million households by 2010.[28]

AT&T may reconsider these plans, however, because two of the largest cable companies, Comcast and Time Warner, are introducing a new technology. Known as DOCSIS 3.0, it will offer Internet access speeds of 5 to 50 megabits per second, depending on the number of users online. Comcast has introduced the service in Minneapolis/St. Paul at a price of $150 a month and the company claims that it will offer similar service to all of its customers by 2010. In all of these cases, however, it will be interesting to see whether those services reach into neighborhoods where there is no comparable competing service. Even if the deployments take place as scheduled, the access speeds that AT&T and the cable companies intend to offer are far too slow for future needs.

For its part, the Bush administration's fiber "strategy" has been limited to assuring the telephone and cable companies that they will not have to open their "next-generation" networks to outsiders unless they wish to – and, if they do, the companies themselves, not the government, will decide the cost of interconnection. So far, the broadband competition the administration envisioned from electric power companies and wireless companies has not emerged. With several minor exceptions, the power companies, one of America's most regulated and least adventuresome industries, have shown no interest in using their existing fiber networks[29] to offer residential broadband. They won't become significant competitors.

Meanwhile, the high-speed (and eventually ultra-fast) wireless-technology companies have run into technical problems. For example, the highly touted WiMax (Worldwide Interoperability for Microwave Access), which promises access speeds up to 70 megabits per second or so, has yet to be deployed widely except in South Korea (where it is called "WiBro"). Proponents continue to say deployment is just over the horizon. Eventually, WiMax, or another wireless technology, will be put in service, but its best use is likely to be for remote areas where the cost of laying fiber is prohibitive.

The way forward

As we have seen, the U.S. government and the Japanese government have pursued sharply different broadband strategies over the past eight years. The U.S. government let the "market" lead, with government action confined to a bit of deregulation. The Japanese government, by contrast, oversaw a bold plan to bring high-speed and ultra-fast broadband to nearly all Japanese households. While the private sector did the work, the government created a highly competitive broadband environment and offered tax write-offs, low-interest loans, loan guarantees, and municipal subsidies to achieve its goals.

These strategies produced sharply different results. Starting well behind, Japan has overtaken the United States in nearly every dimension of broadband leadership. The most important of these dimensions is the availability of broadband, where Japan has a very substantial lead. The service– including fiber, DSL, and cable – is available throughout 95% of the country. In the United States, no one is sure of broadband availability, but a 2008 Pew Internet Project survey suggests it may be something over 75%.[30] In fiber broadband, the 21st century infrastructure, Japan's lead at the end of 2007 was dramatically greater: fiber extended to 85% of Japanese households, compared to 7% in the United States.

Much has been made, and justly so, of America's rapid descent in global broadband *usage* rankings since George W. Bush took office in 2001, when the United States stood in 4th place. By the end of 2007, the United States had dropped to 15th position among the world's 30 most industrialized nations, according to the Organization for Economic Cooperation and Development (OECD). Japan, however, having overtaken the United States in 2003, dropped slightly behind the United States in mid-2007 and ranked 17th at the end of 2007.[31] This may be explained by Japanese dropping their fixed broadband connections in favor of mobile ones.

But Daniel K. Correa at the Information Technology and Innovation Foundation, a Washington think tank, has devised a more comprehensive and realistic "ITIF index." This index measures not only the percentage of a nation's households using broadband, but also the speed and cost of that broadband. According to the index, Japan ranked 2nd (behind Korea) and the United States 15th among the 30 most industrialized nations as of June 2007.[32] While South Korea had the largest share of broadband users, Japan had the fastest average download speed (63.6 Mbps, 12 times faster than the United States) and the lowest monthly broadband cost (13 cents per megabit, compared to the U.S.' $2.83). Indicative of just how far behind the United States is, fewer than 100,000 American homes had Internet access faster than 25 megabits per second in mid-2007;[33] in Japan, nearly all broadband subscribers did.

The United States also leads Japan in its total number of broadband subscribers, where America's far greater population (300 million to 127 million) is decisive. But here, China surpassed the United States in December 2007.[34]

Yet the trends favor Japan. By 2010, Japan expects to make broadband available to the entire country and fiber to over 90% of it. In the United States, an estimated 80-90% are likely to have (far slower and more expensive) broadband available in 2010, but fiber-to-the-home will reach only about 15% of the nation (unless AT&T in the meantime decides to lay fiber to the home). Japan may continue to trail the United States slightly in broadband usage, but it will certainly lead in average download speed and average monthly cost. Moreover, Japan plans to connect its ultra-fast fiber and *wireless* networks by 2010, making Internet access possible any place in the country, anytime, with any device.

Critics of these kinds of comparisons are quick to point out that Japan is a much smaller country (about the size of California) than the United States. But Canada, the country with the second-largest area in the world, has consistently led the United States in global broadband rankings. Others say the differences between the United States and Japan are due to Japan's far-greater population density. But Canada, Norway, Sweden, Iceland, and Finland, which are less densely populated than the United States, have greater percentages of broadband users, and Australia, the least densely populated country in the OECD, ranked just behind the United States in that organization's 2007 broadband rankings.

A better explanation is that the United States is the only developed country without a national strategy to extend and improve broadband. And if the United States continues to let the market lead, one current model indicates that all Americans will not have fiber (or the equivalent) Internet access until 2025,[35] ten to 15 years after Japan, Korea, and the Scandinavian countries complete their fiber infrastructures. Given the stakes, is that acceptable?

The way forward for America

At least in broad strokes, the road seems clear:

1. Think realistically: declare affordable, nationwide, *fiber* broadband (to the home) a national priority. Determining the broadband goal is the most critical digital decision facing the United States. As things stand, sharp disagreements exist. Some, content with current progress, favor letting the market determine the goal over time. Others, have in mind a nationwide, "high-speed" broadband network – that is, existing basic DSL and cable broadband in the 1.5-10 megabits-per-second range – along with wireless broadband (WiMax) down the road. Still others, observing today's Internet leaders and gauging future needs, believe that only ultra-fast fiber will provide the network capacity Americans will need when the networks are completed several years from now. How this infrastructure question is resolved will determine America's digital future for the next decade or two.

The case for fiber to the home is compelling. It is the gold standard of broadband networks, the network that almost everyone agrees the United States will need in the next decade. Fiber has virtually no upper speed limit and will accommodate all foreseeable future digital needs. Just as canals and railways were the essential infrastructure of the 19th century, and electricity, telephone, and superhighway networks that of the 20th century, nationwide fiber-optic networks will be the essential infrastructure of the 21st century. Recognizing that, today's leading Internet nations are rapidly moving to fiber.

For those unconvinced that fiber's speed is necessary, recall that U.S. demand for broadband access speed has increased roughly fivefold every five years. If that pattern holds, demand will rise to nearly 40 Mbps in 2010, nearly 200 Mbps in 2015, and nearly 1,000 Mbps in 2020. While DSL, cable, and wireless technologies have or will eventually reach speeds of 100 Mbps or more, it's highly unlikely they will reach 1,000 Mbps. Fiber, on the other hand, is already delivering 1,000 megabits per second to homes in Japan and Hong Kong, and it can provide much higher speeds.

If the infrastructure decision is left to the market, the result, in a decade's time, will be a patchwork of networks – ultra-fast fiber in the most profitable areas, basic or high-speed DSL or cable broadband for most of the country, and dial-up for a significant part. If the decision favors universal basic broadband, considerable political and financial capital will be consumed in spreading today's obsolescent basic networks across the country. It would take another decade or so to summon, again, the political will and additional funding needed to deploy fiber networks. Instead, the incoming U.S. President should set a national goal of affordable, nationwide fiber networks.

2. Extend fiber to 80% of U.S. homes by 2012 and 100% by 2016. In setting the goal of nationwide fiber networks, the incoming President should also set specific targets for achieving that goal. These targets would be a stretch, but bold objectives have a way of concentrating people's minds and calling forth the best possible thinking. Linking the targets to Presidential terms isn't coincidental.

3. Name a Supernetworks Task Force to develop a strategy to reach those targets, encourage an 80% usage rate, and recommend ways to fund the new networks. The Supernetworks task force will need three subgroups to chart strategies for nationwide and ultra-fast fiber, wireless, and ubiquitous networks. The fiber broadband subgroup is described here; the latter two are described at the end of the next chapter.

The fiber group should include all the stakeholders: high-level federal, state, and local government representatives; the CEOs of the leading telephone, cable, wireless, and satellite companies and their union; the CEOs of the leading equipment makers and application, service, and content providers; and top representatives from the medical, educational, library, and consumer communities. Including all of the stakeholders will lead to a better strategy – and avoid sabotage. Top-level representatives are needed to make the difficult choices and compromises necessary.

In developing the fiber deployment strategy, the task force will no doubt set apart the profitable areas of the country where the private sector will want to deploy fiber; the potentially profitable areas where public-private partnerships will be needed; and the unprofitable areas where public funding will be required. Here, regional and municipal fiber networks should be encouraged. But this framework shouldn't preclude other approaches, such as laying fiber along the interstates and permitting any company, regional entity, or municipality to connect.

The task force should also consider ways to increase consumer demand to reach the 80% usage goal. (In this context, "usage" means that 80% of the households subscribe to fiber service where it is available, not use of 80% of the network's capacity.) Reaching this target will require educational campaigns, describing the benefits of Internet access: communication, education, shopping, entertainment, and so on. It will mean putting hardware – cheap new PCs, used PCs, and other less expensive or less complex Internet access devices (especially for the elderly) – into the hands of those without. It will call for new software applications and content aimed at bringing specific demographic groups online. In addition, it will entail widespread IT literacy programs, especially in rural and central city areas, perhaps offered by school and library e-rate beneficiaries. On top of that, it will involve readily available coaching and troubleshooting, ideally from volunteer, tech-savvy, high-school students.

The toughest challenge will be designing the mix of funding to underwrite the new fiber networks. John Windhausen, Jr., in an EDUCAUSE White Paper, "A Blueprint for Big Broadband," estimates the cost of taking fiber past virtually all U.S. households by 2012 at $100 billion, about $1,000 each to pass the roughly 100 million households still without fiber. Windhausen has a well-thought-out plan for funding this project. He suggests that the federal government, state governments, and the firms laying the fiber each cover one-third of the cost. Over the next four years, the federal government and its partners would each contribute about $8 billion a year to complete the universal fiber network.[36]

But whatever the approach, the fiber network will certainly require additional private-sector investments, public-sector incentives and subsidies, reformulation of the Universal Service Fund and the Rural Utilities Service Broadband Loan and Grant Program to support the fiber deployment, and perhaps additional user fees. But designing the funding package should also call forth creative thinking about how money now being collected for use of existing telephone and cable networks can be reallocated to build out fiber networks; and how the coming transition of television "broadcasting" to fiber-network distribution can be utilized to finance the new networks themselves.

4. Call on the National Research Council to study ways in which these new networks can be used to resolve pressing national problems. Construction of new fiber networks and their widespread use will add to the nation's economic growth, productivity, and job inventory. It will also fundamentally change the lives of the Americans who subscribe. That will happen naturally. But these new networks can and should also play a major role in resolving the nation's current problems: energy, health, education, security. That, however, will not happen automatically. Making this linkage will require careful study by issue experts and IT specialists working side by side. When these groups' recommendations demonstrate the exceptional contribution these networks could make to resolving the nation's challenges, that , too, should add to support for deploying the fiber networks themselves. The National Research Council, related to the National Academies of Science and Engineering, has carried out these sorts of projects successfully in the past.

5. Learn from others. Political leaders, members of the task force, and experts assembled by the NRC should look carefully at the experience of other nations. During the past eight years, many approaches have been tried, some successful, others less so (see, for example, Chapter 11). It would be foolish to ignore that useful history.

With that in mind, let's move on to the second major Internet leadership dimension, wireless.

Chapter 6.
The wireless dimension:
anytime, anywhere

Japan has an even greater lead over the United States in mobile-phone technology, mobile-phone Internet usage, and wireless infrastructure. It is developing fourth-generation (4G) mobile phones and ultra-fast wireless networks. A far greater percentage of Japan's population has mobile Internet access (although the percentage of mobile phone users is roughly equal in both countries). And its wireless infrastructure is almost complete.

Does that matter? It certainly does. Soon most of us will access the Internet wirelessly most of the time. Stop and think for a moment. There are only three reasons you really need a big desk-top or laptop screen. First, a big screen is necessary for serious office work: word processing, spreadsheets, presentations, database creation. Second, a computer screen is handy for certain sorts of web searching and graphics editing: heavy-duty web research, downloading graphic displays, such as a Rembrandt portrait, or selecting, editing, and displaying photos in your online photo scrapbook. Third, certain types of multimedia will always look best on a computer's bigger screen: for example, videoconferencing; downloaded movies; complex, interactive games.

A small, wireless handset should be perfectly adequate for voice and video calls, global positioning, sports scores, stock quotes, brief movie and restaurant reviews, taking digital photos, watching television, getting news headlines, and playing simpler games, as well as dealing with e-mail, checking the time, your daily agenda, telephone list, and address book, paying for most things, and keeping track of your expenses. In short, a wireless handset should be adequate for nearly everything. Some in Japan are even writing novels on them. True, hapless road warriors may continue to drag around their heavy laptops, handheld devices, and extra batteries, along with mobile phones. But for the rest of us, a small, simple, easily portable handset should do quite nicely.

As the usefulness of mobile phones grows, so will their economic benefits. Although more difficult to measure than with landline broadband, more extensive use of increasingly sophisticated wireless devices will contribute to economic growth, increase productivity, and add jobs. And as with landline broadband, large, new wireless markets will spur innovation. One of them, the third-generation (3G) mobile phone market already exists in Japan, and it has spurred the development of scores of new applications, products, services, and content unknown in the United States or Europe. Moreover, the Japanese (and Koreans) have two more markets for innovation – 4G and ubiquitous networks – in the offing. Americans continue to innovate, of course, but they often find ingenious new products for today's limited 2G mobile phones rather than 3G, because in mid-2007 only 5.5 million Americans subscribed to Internet-related mobile-phone services.[1] The new 3G iPhone, introduced in mid-2008, is changing this, but 3G market expansion will take time.

But if those innovation benefits are hard to measure, Japan's current lifestyle gains are obvious. Life is certainly simpler and more convenient with advanced mobile phones. In addition to the obvious voice calls, most of the applications Americans associate with personal data assistants – schedules, lists, expense registers, address and telephone "books," along with e-mail, instant messaging, and instant multimedia exchange (a video clip, for example) – are now available on Japanese 3G phones.

Huge numbers of Japanese access the Internet through their mobile phones: 73 million in April 2008. On top of that, commuters are able to move through Tokyo's complex system of subways, buses, and trains without tickets or even smartcards, simply by waving their mobile phones over a scanner. The phones can serve as payment at vending machines or in stores. Global-positioning systems incorporated in mobile phones remind their owners that they are in the neighborhood of certain restaurants, retail stores, theaters, or tourist attractions. Those owners have also been able to download TV programs to their handsets since early 2006.

Fiber-optic cable provides the backbone for wireless. But wireless can provide Internet access nearly anywhere as well as fill many gaps. With its range of 100 yards or so and typical speeds from 5 to 40 megabits per second, WiFi (Wireless Fidelity), for example, provides not only "hot spots" at hotels, airports, and coffee shops but also convenient home and office networks. WiMax (Worldwide Interoperability for Microwave Access) can send a wireless signal over 40 miles at higher speeds (70 Mbps and more, point to point). Combined with other wireless technologies, it seems ideally suited for taking broadband to sparsely populated rural areas. (For remote areas, satellite broadband may be the only solution.)   So wireless, like landline broadband, is also a primary dimension of Internet leadership.

In assessing all of that, let's look first at the main use of wireless: for mobile phones.

Already ahead in 2000

In December 2000, Japan had a substantial lead in mobile phones that provided Internet access,[2] and in the past seven years, that lead has gotten much larger. At the end of 2000, 53% of all Japanese subscribed to mobile phone service. Of these, almost three of four could access the Internet with their mobile phones. More important, all-digital (second-generation) cellular networks covered 98% of the country.[3] This meant calls went through, and they weren't dropped. There had been keen competition among the three mobile carriers since the mid-1990s. The government had set a common standard, so all of the phones could communicate with one another. Moreover, the government's stated goal was universal service, and to protect consumers, it required the mobile-phone companies to meet coverage and quality of service standards.

In the United States in 2000, by contrast, a mere 40% of the population was using mobile phones – and doing so almost exclusively to *talk* with someone. The cellular infrastructure was an ongoing problem: only three-fifths of the limited analog infrastructure had been converted to digital, and the entire infrastructure covered only 57% of the nation's land area. Competition among carriers was keen, but no governmental consumer protections were in place. Then as now, calls didn't go through and dropped calls were commonplace. Road warriors and others needing to access the Internet used laptops, not mobile phones, from the late 1990s on. Even at that, access was painfully slow and pricey. The mobile phone companies were just beginning the transition to third-generation (3G) mobile technologies in 2004, and the U.S. government was seeking ways to free up additional spectrum for 3G use.[4]

Unlike broadband, where the Japanese government led the way, Japan's substantial lead in wireless was mostly the private sector's doing. But the Japanese government set the stage for the private sector effort. The government made timely allotments of spectrum for mobile-phone use; encouraged a comprehensive infrastructure build out; shaped a competitive market; and insisted on consumer protections and the goal of universal service. As we shall see, the U.S. government did a far worse job. But it is also true that, contrary to conventional wisdom, the Japanese mobile-phone companies were more innovative and less risk-averse than their American counterparts.

With Uncle Sam's help

When NTT DoCoMo, the wireless arm, was spun off from NTT in 1991, its prospects were bleak. Meant to benefit the parent firm's bottom line, DoCoMo's mobile connections to NTT's wired network were expensive. The hefty connection charges made mobile service so expensive that only corporate executives could afford it. Mobile phone handsets were then so bulky that they were used mostly in cars. That fact determined the configuration of DoCoMo's limited infrastructure: its cell towers ran only along main thoroughfares in large cities and major highways. As a result, there were vast areas of Tokyo, to say nothing of other parts of the country or its subway systems, where the phones could not be used. And the entire mobile-phone business was circumscribed by government regulations: what services might be offered, their price, and so on. As a result, although mobile phones had been available for 13 years, only one million people had chosen to subscribe.

Then Uncle Sam lent a hand. During talks between the U.S. and Japanese governments in the early 1990s, the Americans insisted that Japan allow foreign competition in the mobile-phone market and reduce the regulations that stifled any possibility of growth. After some resistance, the Japanese reluctantly agreed. This opened the mobile business not only to Motorola, on whose behalf the American officials had made the request, but also to numerous new Japanese competitors. Prices fell, and Japanese mobile phone subscriptions burgeoned. Also encouraging the boom were the cost to consumers of Japan's expensive regular telephone service and the government's early adoption of a "calling-party pays" system. (In the United States, perversely, both the calling *and* receiving parties pay.)

Japanese officials made several other far-sighted decisions. They encouraged the 40-odd providers of mobile service to use *one* nationwide infrastructure, which almost all did. They set one standard for service that permitted interconnection throughout Japan, so that calls could be made and received with any handset. And they gave the mobile phone companies the radio spectrum they needed – without charge (so that the government continued to control the spectrum). That set the stage for the private sector.

In the mid-1990s, DoCoMo named an extraordinary leader to the post of chief executive officer. Kouji Ohboshi graduated from Tokyo University's prestigious law faculty and went up the NTT ranks at the normal pace, but he was unusual. Even when he became CEO of DoCoMo, his thinking was anything but conventional. Intensely focused, he was also exceptionally energetic and a believer in immediate action. Further, unlike most Japanese managers, he had a powerful need to control and was obsessed with details. His staff described him as "something of a character."

Ohboshi referred to himself as the *gokiburi shacho*, or "cockroach president." He liked to explain that as follows: What does a cockroach do? He scurries around and gets into everything. He doesn't network to find out what other people are thinking. He doesn't wait for agreement. He finds out what's happening, and then decides in a flash what should be done. Then he starts to make things happen immediately. The key to management is speed.[5]

One day, in typical fashion, Ohboshi took home to read 700 complaint forms about DoCoMo's mobile service. The complaints fell into three main categories: the networks were made for cars not pedestrians; the handsets were too big and didn't work properly; and the service was much too expensive. Ohboshi immediately saw what to do. DoCoMo would have to spend more on infrastructure to extend the network well beyond main streets and major roads. He talked directly with the handset producer, offered some incentives, and soon received smaller, more reliable models. Then he simply halved the subscription cost, eliminated handset deposits, and cut the cost of airtime by two-thirds (to U.S. levels). DoCoMo subscriptions skyrocketed. The company added 30 million new subscribers between 1995 and 2000.

But as DoCoMo lowered its prices, so did competitors. Moreover, because everyone was seeking corporate customers, DoCoMo's market share actually fell. Mobile phone service was rapidly becoming a commodity business with a limited customer base. Ohboshi needed to find a way out of this profit squeeze.

In his unconventional way, he did so by seeking to create an emotional bond between DoCoMo's mobile phone customers and their mobile phone handset and service. Ohboshi had seen young Japanese women buy a $500 Louis Vuitton handbag when a $25 bag would have done just as well. Using similar analogies, he came up with the idea of mobile phones that could be used not only for voice calls but also to link instantly to the Internet. This meant adding a packet-switching system to digital voice handsets. Ohboshi's DoCoMo subordinates thought differently. As Ohboshi light heartedly explained it: "Some people thought I had too much time on my hands. Others figured I was getting old. There was speculation that I must have a rare blood type that was making me unpredictable and giving me stupid ideas."[6]

Whatever the reason, this was the beginning of one of the most successful business products in history: DoCoMo's "i-mode" mobile phone service.[7] In the process, DoCoMo became the most valuable company in Japan – bigger than its parent NTT and one of the largest companies in the world.

Third-generation service takes hold

By that time, DoCoMo had taken another major step. Earlier, in October 2000, Japan's telecommunications ministry had approved the launch of third-generation (3G), multimedia, mobile phone service. (First-generation was *analog* service; second was *digital* service; 2.5G represented upgraded digital service capable of Internet access, such as i-mode.) That summer, the ministry allocated spectrum for the new service (120 megahertz divided among three carriers). In so doing, the ministry assured continuing competition among Japan's three main mobile carriers – DoCoMo, KDDI, and (then) J-Phone (which had introduced the mobile-phone camera).[8] That set the stage for the introduction of 3G mobile service, but it would take someone supremely confident to actually make the attempt. The someone was Keiichi Tachikawa, who by early 2001, had taken over from Ohboshi as head of DoCoMo. A graduate of Tokyo University's engineering department, Tachikawa earned an MBA from MIT's Sloan School of Business before returning to Japan and joining NTT. By all accounts, he was a difficult man to work for. Sharing Ohboshi's sense of urgency, Tachikawa was nicknamed "machine" and "computer" by his colleagues. Now he was determined to push ahead with 3G service.

Several top executives favored a slower pace. DoCoMo had chosen a completely new technical standard for its 3G service: W-CDMA. It promised download speeds of 2 megabits per second, more than 200 times faster than i-mode connections. But Tachikawa planned to start with much slower speeds, about 64 kilobits per second, and work up to 2 megabits by 2005. In addition, the new standard required a completely new cellular infrastructure. That required an investment of tens of billions of dollars, and the government would not provide any financial help. There were also handset-design problems. Until the new 3G infrastructure was completed, handsets would have to shift to the older (2G) network when necessary. This meant larger and more expensive handsets than the Japanese were used to. New software was also needed to make these new elements work together. Most troubling, demand for the new service was uncertain. There wasn't yet a popular or "killer" application that might propel a shift to 3G.

None of that deterred Tachikawa. After reluctantly postponing a scheduled April 2001 service test in the Tokyo area, he placed huge newspaper ads announcing the formal launch of 3G service several months later, on October 1. There was no turning back, and DoCoMo's FOMA (Freedom Of Multimedia Access) 3G service was introduced as scheduled in Tokyo within an area 15 miles across. i-mode's success, Tachikawa said defiantly, taught him that even though "everyone says there is no demand, you can create demand."[9] DoCoMo planned to spend $25 billion over three years to roll out 3G nationwide.

Takeharu Mita bought a 3G "videophone" in Tokyo the day they went on sale. But none of his friends did, so he ended up talking with strangers. Mita told the *Financial Times* that he was surprised by their behavior. Some people asked if they could smoke during the video call, he said, and "everyone bows before hanging up, because this is Japan."[10]

In addition, there were 3G teething problems. Even six months after launch, service was available only in portions of Japan's three largest cities. Just as in the i-mode days, handsets were clunky, expensive (over $300), and unreliable – and their batteries lasted only about two hours. But the main issue was why anyone should use 3G phones; video calls were fun, but hardly essential.

Nonetheless, Japan's second-largest mobile carrier, KDDI, entered the 3G market six months later. KDDI chose a less expensive path: a simpler standard (CDMA2000) with a slower download speed. Although the speed was too slow to produce good video, KDDI needed to make only modest infrastructure upgrades and could redesign for 3G the small, light, clamshell handsets the Japanese prefer. Furthermore, KDDI undercut the DoCoMo price and threw in an on-phone digital camera and a global positioning service option. Demand quickly swelled for KDDI's 3G service, because the price was right and the small phone could be used in more than three-quarters of the country.

The third large mobile carrier, J-Phone (later Vodaphone and now Softbank Mobile) brought its 3G service to market in December 2002. The delayed entry proved advantageous. It chose the tougher, faster W-CDMA standard DoCoMo used and was able to use DoCoMo's costly infrastructure that then extended to all major cities. J-Phone could do so, because the telecom ministry, intent on boosting competition, allowed access to that costly infrastructure at an exceptionally reasonable price. On top of that, the handset problems were now mostly over, and the price had dropped to about $100 with a two-year contract. So with very little investment, J-Phone could offer a competitive product almost immediately and take part in the mass migration from 2G digital service to 3G multimedia service.

In spring 2003, nearly two-thirds of the entire Japanese population, or 81.5 million, had mobile phones, and nine out of ten subscribed to Internet data services as well.[11] Moreover, the number of 3G subscribers was climbing rapidly: in mid-2003, there were over 9 million subscribers, up from 27,000 in December 2001.[12] By the end of 2005, DoCoMo's new 3G infrastructure covered the entire nation. This permitted Japanese 3G subscribers anywhere in the country to download realistic video at world-class speeds of 2 megabits per second, significantly faster than most Americans could download data to their immobile desktop – or laptop – with broadband connections.[13]

The Japanese private sector deserves the credit for taking the risks that led to these remarkable successes (although the government had provided free spectrum). DoCoMo's leader, Keiichi Tachikawa, maintained his nerve even as predicted difficulties came to pass – and he *did* create demand for the new service through marketing. His courage and that of his competitors, which soon marketed their own versions of 3G service, stand in sharp contrast to the risk-adverse American mobile-phone companies.

Japan's adventurous consumers deserve credit as well. Many paid a premium to try the new 3G technology in its frustrating early stages. The Japanese government could also claim some credit. It provided timely allocations of essential spectrum and created a competitive market that not only benefited Japanese consumers but accelerated the migration to 3G. And it set quality-of-service standards that encouraged universal mobile-phone use.

"The most out-of-date cellular systems in any developed country"[14]

Logically, the United States should be the world's mobile phone leader. Bell Laboratories developed the cellular phone[15] concept in 1948, and Motorola's Martin Cooper made the first wireless telephone call in New York City in 1973. But in 1983, when the first mobile phones were ready for market, the FCC made a colossal blunder.

In fairness, the blunder was based on a spectacularly wrong estimate by the McKinsey management consulting firm. McKinsey predicted (for AT&T) that the mobile phone market would be very limited: an estimated 1 million users worldwide in 2000. (There were, in fact, over 730 million.) Based on that judgment, U.S. regulators attempted to reduce competition and increase the profits of those willing to offer mobile- phone service. They did so by creating 734 tiny "cellular market areas" across the country and awarding two mobile-phone licenses in each area: one to the regional

Bell company and the other to the winner of a lottery. As intended, little competition emerged among these artificially created duopolies.

The FCC protected the mobile phone companies in several other ways. It refused to release additional spectrum, the life blood of wireless. It allowed the regional Bells to charge enormous fees to connect mobile calls to their regular telephone networks and permitted all companies to bill steep "roaming charges" for calls made to another carrier's network. The FCC did set a single analog (first-generation) mobile-phone standard for the entire country. This meant that, for a time, all mobile phone handsets could connect with one another. But the commission did nothing to encourage a nationwide mobile network, insuring that expensive mobile phone service would last for more than a decade. As former FCC chairman Reed Hundt would later put it: "The FCC served its characteristic, if unwitting, historical purpose: it had precluded vigorous competition, discouraged innovation, handed out wealth to a few, denied price competition to the many, hampered the creation of national businesses, and guaranteed that the U.S. would lag in promoting this new technology."[16]

In 1993, after being named FCC chairman himself and getting Congressional approval, Hundt tried to work around this mess by making additional spectrum available for mobile-phone use. To maximize revenue, the FCC decided to award the spectrum through a two-month-long, online auction that attracted bids from six companies and eventually netted $7.7 billion for the U.S. treasury. At long last, the United States had six "nationwide" mobile networks, and they slowly began to compete with one another.

But there was a long way to go. The auction winners decided to construct new digital (second-generation) networks, which took time to complete and were understandably thin at the outset. Worse, because the FCC had declined to set a common 2G standard for the entire country, as was done in Europe and Japan, the six carriers chose four *different* standards for their networks. As a result, it was uncertain whether a call would go through unless the caller was trying to reach someone using the same mobile carrier's network. So, although the price of mobile-phone service dropped 75% over the next four years (to 2001), the quality was awful. Predictably, many subscribers (18%-36%) changed their carrier every year.[17]

In mid-2003, the U.S. cellular infrastructure was still spotty. Although the FCC claimed 97 of 100 Americans lived in a *county* with access to 2G service, those numbers did not tell the real story: the 1G analog infrastructure still existed in nearly one-third of the country's land area, and much of the country had no wireless infrastructure at all.[18] There were some positive developments: more than half of all Americans (53%) now had mobile phones, and nearly 90% of them were 2G digital. But in sharp contrast to Japan, only an estimated 8% of those Americans subscribed to data services at the end of 2002. And mobile-phone service was still bad by European, let alone Japanese, standards. Many calls never reached their destination; many others were dropped. On top of that, American mobile-phone users were frustrated by complicated calling plans, clunky handsets, baffling and frequently inaccurate bills, and inadequate customer and technical support.

3G comes to the United States

In October 2000, a year before DoCoMo launched 3G service in Japan, President Clinton warned that unless the United States moved quickly to allocate 3G spectrum, "there is a danger that the U.S. could lose market share in the industries of the twenty-first century."[19] There was indeed a danger, an alarming one. But it took *six years* for George W. Bush's FCC to auction the additional 3G spectrum Clinton had called for. In the meantime, the Bush FCC removed restrictions so that existing spectrum allocations could be used for 3G service, and it allowed wireless companies to trade and lease spectrum. Before additional spectrum could be allocated, however, the Defense Department had to be persuaded to give up some of its extensive spectrum, while TV broadcasters refused to give up their double spectrum allocations as they moved from analog to digital broadcasts. This led Bush's then-FCC chairman Michael Powell to declare that the spectrum allocation system was "broken," and, in 2004, a Presidential commission urged an overhaul of the entire system of allocations. In fact, it would take until 2006 before substantial new spectrum would be auctioned.

But despite this handicap, 3G mobile service came to the United States. In late 2002, Monet Mobile Networks, a little-known Midwestern company, launched America's first true 3G service in Duluth, Minnesota, a city of 85,000 people on the western shore of Lake Superior. Eventually,

Monet expanded to cover eight northern cities and signed up 3,000 subscribers – only to declare bankruptcy a year-and-a-half later when it couldn't raise additional funding. The major U.S. mobile-phone companies moved more slowly. In 2001, they began to upgrade their 2G networks and, as in Japan, they decided on two different 3G standards. Verizon and Sprint Nextel chose the easier (cdma2000) path used by KDDI in Japan. Cingular (now AT&T Wireless) and T-Mobile decided on the more difficult DoCoMo route (W-CDMA).

In late 2003, two years behind DoCoMo, Verizon introduced true 3G (EV-DO) service in two cities, Washington and San Diego. In 2005, Verizon claimed that half the American population could access its 3G network, then available in 181 cities, by phone, handheld, or laptop, but declined to provide the number of its 3G subscribers.[20]

Having also chosen the less difficult path to 3G, the smaller Sprint Nextel company (then Sprint) made a number of contradictory strategic choices. After completing its intermediate 3G network at the end of 2002, it hesitated to go further. But in mid-2004, it abruptly changed its mind and decided to advance to true (EV-DO) 3G as quickly as possible. By the end of 2005, Sprint Nextel said its 3G network was available to some 90 million people in 141 (mostly smaller) cities. Then a new CEO, faced with tough 3G competition, decided to make a risky bet on a new wireless technology, WiMax, rather than extend its existing mobile-phone infrastructure. But Wall Street and his board balked at the steep cost and uncertain profits of WiMax, and he was fired. Nonetheless, in May 2008, Sprint Nextel, along with Google, Intel, Comcast, Time Warner, and Clearwire, again announced its intent to build a nationwide WiMax network.[21]

Choosing the more difficult DoCoMo path to 3G, AT&T Wireless (then Cingular), launched 3G service in summer 2004. But download speeds were considerably slower than Verizon's, and infrastructure deployment was slow as well. At the end of 2005, AT&T service was only available in 16 metro areas with only ten percent of the U.S. population.[22] The company did, however, incorporate a new technology: HSDPA (High Speed Downlink Packet Access) that increased download speeds up to six times; when download speeds reached 2-3 megabits per second, 3.5G television service became possible.

Moreover, HSDPA service has three additional advantages over the simpler Verizon technology. You can talk and surf the web at the same time. You can *upload* data twice as fast. And eventually, the service will be compatible with European mobile phones (but not yet because U.S. and European phones use different bands of the spectrum). At the end of 2005, despite the new technology, AT&T's network could only be accessed with a laptop, download speeds remained slow, and – at $60 a month – the cost was still rather steep.[23]

T-Mobile, the remaining U.S. mobile phone carrier owned by Germany's Deutsche Telecom, is bringing up the 3G rear in the United States. Also taking the more difficult DoCoMo route, it waited until the FCC auction of 2006 to obtain the spectrum it needed for a national network. It plans to launch its new network in 2008.

Where matters stand

At the end of 2006, the last year for which we have FCC data, nearly the same share of the population in the United States subscribed to mobile phones as in Japan, around 80%.[24] And it was much cheaper to make a mobile phone call in the United States. But in every other way, the Japanese were far ahead.

Japan's mobile phone infrastructure was incomparably better. Upgraded infrastructure, capable of handling 3.5G broadband service, reached virtually the entire Japanese population and the entire country. In the United States, *advanced 3G infrastructure* reached only 80% of the population – and only 20% of the land area. Even the digital (2G) infrastructure reached only two-thirds of the U.S. land area. In terms of quantity – and reliability – the disparity is even greater: at the end of 2006, Japan, a country the size of California, had more than 150,000 cell towers, while the United States had fewer than 200,000. That explains why there are still problems with 15% of all U.S. mobile phone calls.[25]

At the end of 2006, nearly 60% of the Japanese subscribed to 3G service and 85% had mobile Internet access,[26] while a mere 9.2% of Americans subscribed to 3G service, and an estimated 10% of those were able to surf the web.[27] Japan's extensive 3G market spurred mobile-phone uses that can scarcely be imagined in the United States. For example, "one segu" (referring to one segment of spectrum) service that permits live TV reception, was introduced in April 2006. Other recent innovations include: mobile phones used as cash, credit cards, office keys and ID, car-navigation devices, medical records terminals, i-books, search engines, and smart-tag readers (to read bar codes, for example); for news, music, web access and video (such as YouTube), 3-D maps, online banking, railway tickets, shopping (online and in stores), medical services, GPS, eBay-like auctions, IP services (such as TV and VOIP calling), teleconferencing, tracking one's daily activities, and natural disaster warnings; and to control home appliances, "geotag" photos, and find addresses using GPS. And something new pops up every month or so.

Many of those uses rely on the greater speed of Japanese mobile networks. Japan's high-end 3.5G service, introduced in August 2006, transmits data at 3.6 megabits per second, nearly as fast as many home broadband connections in the United States. American's mobile phones are, on average, much slower, limiting not only how they can be used but also wireless innovation. Competition in the United States is still based mainly on price for mobile voice service, rather than on innovative, non-voice uses. As a result, voice calls in the United States are second cheapest in the world (after Hong Kong). But American customers are still dissatisfied with their mobile-service providers – 68 on a satisfaction score of 100.[28] Over one-fifth changed carriers yearly as of early 2007[29]; the comparable figure for Japan was less than 4%.

How have the Japanese carriers achieved this success? They have invested heavily in infrastructure, taken great risks to introduce improved mobile-phone service, and dealt conscientiously with their customers. The government delivered needed spectrum in a timely manner, set the conditions for a competitive market place, insisted on quality-of-service standards, and encouraged universal service.

In the United States, mobile-service providers, dealing with a much larger country, spent far less proportionately on infrastructure,[30] were slow in moving to higher levels of service, and treated their customers shabbily. The government, in the form of the FCC, has lagged in providing spectrum. In addition, it declared a competitive market place for mobile services without defining it, turned a blind eye to quality of service and customer dissatisfaction, and ignored the goal of universal coverage. In a nutshell, the Japanese carriers have been imaginative and bold, while their American counterparts have been defensive and cautious. The Japanese ministry of communications has been actively engaged, while the FCC has been passive, pleased with whatever progress the market makes. Each nation got the mobile-phone service it deserved.

Different approaches to the wireless future

The Japanese know where they are going. The communications ministry's goal, announced in 2004, is "ubiquitous networks. This is their most daunting goal of all, combining a nationwide fiber network with speeds in the 100-1,000 megabits-per-second range with a wireless network capable of transmitting data up to 1 gigabit (1,000 megabits) per second – by 2010. To reach the goal, the Japanese must begin to construct an entirely new 4G wireless network, start connecting it to the fiber network, and develop the hardware and software for a 4G handset.

They are hard at work on this, but they have had to push back the 2010 deadline. NTT DoCoMo continues to develop 4G telephones with specifications calling for data-transmission rates of 100 megabits per second when moving at high speed and 1 gigabit (1,000 megabits) per second when moving slowly or stationary. DoCoMo produced a 4G prototype in mid-2005, and in early 2007, the company hit 5 gigabits per second in stationary 4G tests (besting Samsung's 3.5 gigabits). But the cost of building out yet another entirely new 4G wireless network proved to be too much for even DoCoMo, which invested over $30 billion in 3G infrastructure and nearly $7 billion introducing its 3G service. Harsh competition and lower profits in the wireless market, plus less-than-expected demand for NTT's fiber offerings, added to the problem.

So DoCoMo and its competitors have decided to scale back their plans for the time being. Instead of attempting 4G by 2010, the wireless companies aim to create a stepping stone to that goal by that date, something DoCoMo calls "Super 3G" and the communications ministry refers to as "3.9G," one of a number of LTE (Long-Term Evolution) technologies. Super 3G will only require upgrades to the existing nationwide 3G infrastructure, and the handsets will eventually ramp up to download speeds of 300 megabits per second. The government's original goal of launching ubiquitous networks utilizing true 4G and a completely new wireless infrastructure could be met as early as 2015.

It is less clear what will happen in the United States. It is only certain that, without ambitious goals or deadlines, the

United States will trail well behind Japan, South Korea, and Europe. As of spring 2008, Verizon was the only carrier to announce its next technology upgrade: a version of LTE, comparable to Japan's stepping stone, that will be tested in 2008 and require only upgraded infrastructure; it is scheduled to be ready for commercial service in 2015. Verizon is calling this new service "4G," but it will be comparable to DoCoMo's "Super 3G" service – arriving five years later.[31]

More troubling, it will take years to build out truly na-tionwide 3G networks in the United States. At the end of 2006, Verizon reached 82% of the population (but only 19% of the land area) with its advanced 3G network (EVDO Rev. A). AT&T then reached 43% of the population (but only 2% of the land area) with its advanced network (WCDMA/ HSDPA).[32] The Sprint Nextel network was considerably smaller, and that of T-Mobile had yet to be launched.

Given America's limited *mobile-phone* (2G and 3G) in-frastructure, plans for a nationwide WiMax network con-tinue to surface,[33] as they do abroad. WiMax has certain advantages: coverage up to 40 miles, top speeds of 70 mega-bits per second, less expensive equipment, and compatibility with any Internet-access device. But as with WiFi, there are building-penetration problems (although a new technol-ogy, femtocells, may help), many base stations are needed to insure complete coverage, and the technology remains problematic. Still, the desires of equipment makers to sell WiMax gear and those of the cable companies to offer wire-less service may yet come together to produce a "nationwide" WiMax network. WiMax, however, may be better suited to serving rural and remote areas, not the entire country. So even if a nationwide network is attempted, it could end up as simply another patch on the U.S. wireless infrastructure quilt. And sooner or later, it will be outstripped – even in America – by faster LTE and 4G networks.

What is to be done?

1. Extend the ultra-fast wireless infrastructure to cover virtually all of America – 70% by 2012 and 90% by 2016. Unhappily, the United States is playing catch up in wireless as well as landline broadband. There is a way to join the wireless leaders, but it will require a move in the same direction as Japan and South Korea. To do that, the United States must build out an ultra-fast wireless infrastructure to cover nearly the entire country. That would require upgrading the existing (nearly 200,000) cell towers, more than doubling their number, and an order of magnitude of additional spectrum – all within the next eight years. Surprisingly, no one has estimated what this project might cost. But one thing is clear: the private sector will not be interested in building additional cell towers or bidding on spectrum to serve many rural areas. To assure rural coverage, government will have to create incentives and subsidies to encourage construction of the needed infrastructure and provide additional spectrum without cost.

A second subgroup of the Supernetworks Task Force should chart the extension of the ultra-fast wireless infrastructure, so that the fiber and wireless projects can be coordinated. The way forward is less clear than that for landline broadband, because the future of wireless technologies is murkier. But because most Americans will (soon) want fast, mobile access to the Internet, the wireless subgroup should work toward an objective of 70-300 Mbps (WiMax, LTE, or more advanced) wireless service throughout virtually all of the United States. Several steps will again be required: mapping existing service; determining how much of the country the private sector is likely to cover; and then developing ways – demand aggregation, incentives, and subsidies among them – for government at all levels, working with the private sector, to cover the rest. Again, the subgroup should recommend the funding mix to underwrite this project.

Beyond that, the contentious and time-consuming issues surrounding tower siting will have to be dealt with and provision should be made for sharing of the towers for different types of service (3G, Super3G, 4G, and WiMax). That means extensive wireless network leasing at reasonable rates. It is wasteful to have more than one wireless network outside densely populated areas.

2. Begin now to plan for the essential transition to a new Internet address system (IPv6) and R&D on 4G mobile service, linked sensor networks, and ubiquitous networks. A third Supernetworks Task Force subgroup would consider these transitional issues already on the horizon. Here the goal should be to transition, by 2012, to a new Internet address system (IPv6) that will provide the billions of Internet addresses needed to activate extensive sensor networks to monitor people and control things, provide geopositioning-linked information, and much else. The target for launching true 4G service and extensive sensor networks and for beginning to tie the ultra-fast fiber and wireless networks together should be 2016 at the latest. That 4G service and ultra-fast wireless and ubiquitous networks are likely to be the norm in developed countries by 2020 or so.

As those new U.S. networks are put in place, it would begin to give Americans the opportunity to communicate quickly (and more reliably) anytime, from any place – and to offer opportunities for innovations related to those new networks. It would also put the United States back in contention for Internet leadership, although it was roughly five years behind in mid-2008. On the other hand, unless the United States moves along this path, it will surely cede Internet leadership to Japan and its northeast Asian neighbors (and perhaps Europe) for the foreseeable future.

The U.S. government will, of course, have to guide the transition to a new Internet address system and specify the required standards. In addition, because of the uncertainties and risks – technological and economic – involved in moving to 4G and ubiquitous networks, the telephone, cable, and wireless companies are unlikely, in fact unable, to tackle them. They spend very little on research (reportedly less than on lobbying) compared to their overseas counterparts. As a consequence, much of the basic research will have to be underwritten by government, perhaps through the NSF, with the remainder funded by public-private partnerships.

Given the importance of this project and its complexity, the incoming administration should consider the desirability of a wireless innovation hub, as outlined in John Kao's *Innovation Nation*. In a nutshell, that would call for a federal investment of something like $1 billion to create a new, small Silicon Valley, perhaps in the San Diego area, to do the cross-disciplinary research and development needed to tap the full potential of America's wireless future – and ubiquitous networks..

3. Ensure that adequate spectrum is available for 4G service by 2012. Given the extraordinary difficulty of freeing up spectrum, the Commerce Department and the FCC should begin work now.

4. In the meantime, look hard at existing mobile-phone service. Mobile-phone service in the United States remains unsatisfactory. True, problem calls dropped from 29% in 2005 to 15% in 2006. But is that good enough? Shouldn't mobile phones work in buildings along K Street, N.W., one of Washington's main thoroughfares? In subways? In a host of other places? And shouldn't the mobile-phone companies be required to provide an acceptable level of customer and technical support? The early days are over, and the two major mobile-phone service providers, AT&T and Verizon, bought the largest blocks of spectrum in the 2008 auction. Now they should be held to a reasonable standard of service and responsiveness. In fall 2008, the FCC moved in the opposite direction by dropping requirements that mobile carriers report annually on problem calls, cancelled subscriptions, and so forth. Perhaps the task of bringing the carriers to account should be given to the Federal Trade Commission, which takes customer complaints more seriously.

Now let's turn to the next Internet leadership dimension, the human dimension.

Chapter 7.
The human dimension: computer scientists and IT research

Internet leadership depends on a nation's IT experts and the research they do. Without them, there can be no research breakthroughs, no innovation or progress. With a handful of exceptions, the Internet's advance has been led by highly skilled computer scientists and engineers. These men (and later women) not only designed and developed the Internet but also continue to determine the pace of its progress.

Since the Second World War, the United States has led the world in nurturing scientific and engineering talent. Much of that leadership was due to the war effort itself – the large numbers of scientists and engineers that were mobilized, the brilliant émigrés, and the enormous sums given them. But it was America's response to the *Sputnik* scare that produced the bulk of today's scientific and engineering talent. To produce this exceptional generation, the U.S. government in 1958 passed the National Defense Education Act that provided $900 million (about $6 billion in today's dollars)[1] in low-interest loans to graduate students in the natural sciences, engineering, and certain non-European foreign languages; and it created ARPA (now DARPA) and the National Aeronautics and Space Administration.

The U.S. government continued to pump billions of dollars into basic scientific and technological research during the final decades of the 20th century. At one point in the 1970s, the government invested nearly 2% of the nation's GDP in research and development. As part of this process, university computer-science and engineering departments were strengthened, new labs created, and thousands of graduate students educated. This in turn attracted large numbers of foreign students, many of whom stayed in the United States when their education was finished. All of that produced American technological leadership that was the envy of the world.

But times have changed. In his book *The Flight of the Creative Class: The New Global Competition for Talent*,[2] Professor Richard Florida reminds us that the number of highly talented individuals in the world is limited and that governments and corporations around the globe are now aggressively competing for them. Nearly a dozen studies produced in the United States since 2001 warn of America's eroding scientific and technological superiority. The most widely publicized of them, *Rising Above the Gathering Storm*, which appeared in 2006, warned that American leadership in science and technology could be lost abruptly and not be regained.[3]

Competing for talent

In 2001, at the outset of the first George W. Bush term, the United States had an unparalleled pool of IT talent –

computer scientists and electrical engineers with advanced degrees. The huge investments in IT research, the open door to foreigners, and the booming Internet of the 1990s led to an extraordinary increase in the number of highly skilled IT specialists, both American and foreign. The prospect of starting one's own firm or receiving stock options in someone else's startup encouraged many young Americans and students from overseas to study computer science or engineering in hope of becoming rich quickly.

Drawn by the allure of America's famous research universities and the extraordinary opportunities available, half of all the computer scientists working in the United States at that time were foreign-born. And many were risk takers. In the 1990s, entrepreneurs from just India and China accounted for nearly one-third of all Silicon Valley startups and 70,000 new jobs. Many of these foreign-born entrepreneurs are now household names: Sergey Brin, co-founder of Google, from Russia; Sabeer Bhatia, co-founder of Hotmail, from India; Jerry Yang, co-founder of Yahoo, from Taiwan; and Pierre Omidyar, founder of eBay, from France. Understandably, many Americans were persuaded that their technological superiority would never be challenged.

But an old problem persisted and new challenges emerged. The persistent problem: the abysmal state of math and science instruction (and learning) in the schools. Too few math and science teachers are qualified to teach those subjects,[4] and math courses are not demanding. Not surprisingly, American students do poorly on international math (and other) exams. A recent example: out of 41 nations, American 15-year-olds placed 24th in math literacy and 26th in problem solving.[5] Without remedial work, most American students can't study math, science, or engineering in college, even if they want to.

Two unexpected challenges further diminished the number of college students studying IT. First came the dot-com bust of 2000. Internet startups lost their appeal, and American students' interest in computer science and electrical engineering plummeted. Their interest was further lessened by a new business practice in the United States: the outsourcing of IT work overseas, often to India. IT degrees came to be widely considered "too hard" to acquire while maintaining an appropriate college lifestyle.

Under different circumstances, this deficit might have been made up by foreign students. But yet another challenge, 9/11, intervened. Following this tragedy, the U.S. government took draconian measures to ensure that terrorists did not enter the country. It became more difficult to study in America: all student visa applicants had to be interviewed personally, and the visas became difficult to obtain, with the process often taking months. After the U.S. invasion of Iraq, many foreign students decided they didn't want to study in America. Expense was another barrier. As a result, other countries began to recruit successfully. Between 2000 and 2006, the declines in American and foreign student enrollment reduced the number of university graduates who had specialized in computer science from 15,960 to 7,800.[6]

At the critical graduate level, the United States faces a different challenge. Although the Stanfords, MITs, and Carnegie Mellons are still the best places to study IT, roughly half of the students studying computer science and electrical engineering at the master's and doctor's level come from abroad.[7]

American Internet leadership therefore hinges on whether these newly minted Internet experts remain in the United States or return home. Although a 2005 survey by the National Science Foundation (NSF) indicated that more than 80% of those with Ph.D. degrees stayed on, it is more difficult to do so nowadays. The H1-B visas that permitted many to stay (for six years) were cut back from 195,000 a year to 65,000 in 2003, and China, India, and other countries are now actively trying to lure their IT graduates and professionals back home. In addition, U.S. corporations have responded by moving more IT work (and research) offshore to take advantage of overseas professionals.

So just as up to two-fifths of America's "boomer"-generation science and engineering workforce is scheduled to retire within the next ten years and demand for IT talent is expanding, the domestic replacement pool is shrinking. In his 2006 American Competitiveness Initiative, President Bush proposed modest steps to increase the number of Americans studying science and engineering, and he promised to make it easier for technology-oriented foreign students and professionals to come to the United States and remain. Happily, the NSF reports that the drop in graduate-level, computer-science students (14% from 2002 to 2006) nearly stabilized in 2006, due to a 21% increase in the number of foreign students compared to the previous year. Unhappily, the number of U.S.-citizen and permanent resident computer-science graduate students continued to slip slightly (−7%) from 2005 to 2006.[8]

Japan plays catch up

In 2000, members of the IT Strategy Council, well aware that the country had too few computer scientists and engineers, made education of more Japanese IT professionals one of the main pillars of the e-Japan strategy – but without setting a specific target. They also called for the admission of 30,000 foreign IT "experts" – those with master's or doctor's degrees – into the country before the end of 2005. The ultimate objective, the council members said, was for Japan to have more IT professionals than the United States by that time.

Japan is doing well with math and science instruction in elementary and high school. Japanese students, with better instruction, more memorization, and more hours devoted to those subjects, continue to place near the very top in international science and math rankings. So, while the educational establishment continues to worry about the right balance between rote learning and creative thinking, Japanese high-school graduates have the knowledge needed to study IT.

As you might expect, the number of engineering graduates climbed gradually to a peak of 104,478 in 2001. But by 2005, the number had declined by 6.3%.[9] Like their American peers, Japanese high-school graduates have lost interest in science and engineering. Some say there were early signs of this in the 1980s, when Japan reached first-world living standards. Whatever the reason, Japanese companies are now feeling the pinch just as the college-age population has begun to decline. More generally, Japanese worry about the nation's competitiveness, because China turns out more than four times as many engineers each year.

The shortage of engineers is especially acute in the "digital technology industry," where one ministry of internal affairs official estimated in mid-2008 that 500,000 additional engineers were needed.[10]   Within that broader context, Japan lacks more than 15,000 advanced-software engineers, the people who design entire systems or lead software-development teams.   This shortage is so critical that *Keidanren*, Japan's leading business organization, and 14 major electronics companies, such as Hitachi and Fujitsu, are providing incentives to universities to set up software-engineering programs taught by the companies' practicing engineers.   The goal is to establish programs at ten universities by 2009.   But that will still not produce enough engineers.

An obvious solution is to recruit abroad.   The government was able to attract well over 20,000 foreign IT experts – but still fell substantially short of its 2005 goal of 30,000. Companies have also developed their own strategies.   For example, beginning in 2003, Fujitsu began hiring about 30 foreign engineers each year, mostly other Asians who had graduated from Japanese universities.   But nearly 80% of Japanese companies say they have no intention of following suit.   They fear that foreigners will not be able to learn Japanese or adapt to the nation's work culture.   To combat these notions, the internal affairs ministry is launching a $30-million Asian Talent Fund to offer Asian students Japanese-language training and internships.   Some labor experts think this is too little too late.   But others assert that, like it or not, Japan must welcome foreign engineers, because its economy cannot survive without them.[11]

Another way to cope with the engineering shortage is to send some of the work overseas. But the Japanese take a more cautious approach to "offshoring" than their American counterparts. Generally, they prefer filling low-end IT jobs by employing less-costly workers in northern China and southeast Asia, while – to the extent possible – keeping higher-skilled IT positions at home. Following this philosophy, the e-Japan strategy II revised in 2003 called for *educating* Japanese for the high-end positions at home and training tens of thousands of lower-level IT workers in Southeast Asia via distance learning.

But at least one company, Hitachi Systems, has broken that pattern. Having opened an office in Beijing with 15 software engineers in January 2006, Hitachi planned to expand its staff to 450 by the end of 2008.[12] And even the government seems to be hedging by bringing 1,000 Vietnamese to Japan for doctoral training in IT, engineering, and science between 2008 and 2020.[13] Some of them will undoubtedly remain in Japan after graduation.

So how do the United States and Japan compare in the critical area of training qualified IT personnel? In 2000, Japan produced nearly twice as many engineers with less than half the population of the United States. But in the following five years, Japan's engineering graduates decreased 5%, while the American total edged up 10% due to foreign students. In both countries, native-born engineering school applicants have dropped precipitously – by one-third at Utsunomiya University, north of Tokyo.

At the graduate level in 2000, Japan produced over 15,000 IT experts with master's or doctor's degrees, some 5,000 fewer than the United States. But in Japan, foreign students accounted for only 5% of graduates at the master's level and 15% at the doctor's, while in the United States, more than half were foreigners. From 2000 until 2006, graduate computer-science enrollments fell in the United States, finally stabilizing thanks (again) to foreign students. The situation is less clear in Japan, where computer engineers and software engineers (known in America as computer scientists) are lumped into one total for engineers. But with the widely noted shortage of software engineers, and the recent recruitment of 2,000 Vietnamese doctoral students, it is reasonable to believe that the number of graduate IT applicants has fallen off in Japan as well. If that is true, the United States still has a significant lead in the number of IT experts it is producing each year – but only due to foreign students. The bottom line is that both countries are facing critical shortages.

The United States has also been more successful at recruiting foreign IT experts, the dot-com crash and 9/11 notwithstanding. While Japan sought to recruit 30,000 in five years, the United States probably adds more than that number *each* year, assuming that half of the 65,000 H1-B visas go to new entrants and the remainder to renewals. It is also virtually certain that far more IT specialists work in the United States than in Japan – although achieving the reverse was another of the e-Japan strategy goals. In 2006, according to government statistics, Japan had 157,719 foreigners working in "highly skilled professions," which is only a small fraction of the 7.8 million in the United States.[14] In addition, American firms are doing far more offshoring than their Japanese counterparts

What should be done?

Several studies have pointed out what the United States must do if it is to maintain – and in some areas regain – its technological advantage:

1. Dramatically improve math and science instruction in K-12 by bringing in knowledgeable outside instructors, offering algebra in the eighth grade and calculus in high school, and rewriting high-school science textbooks to make them simpler, interesting, and readable. According to some reports, only one-third of all K-12 math teachers are qualified to teach math. It is therefore urgent to bring outside resources into the schools (as President Bush proposed). But that is not happening: Norman Augustine, chairman of the committee that produced *Rising Above the Gathering Storm* and former CEO of Lockheed Martin, wanted to teach math in high school after his retirement. But because he didn't have appropriate educational credentials, he wasn't permitted to do so. Overcoming this problem will mean taking on the teachers' unions, but it must be done. A second point: nearly all other developed nations teach algebra in eighth grade and calculus in high school; the United States should as well.

Anyone who wonders why the United States isn't producing more scientists need look no further than current high-school textbooks in biology, chemistry, or physics.

Written by college professors who seldom see the forest for the trees, the textbooks are overly detailed, densely written, and deadly dull. They are, in fact, slightly dumbed-down versions of current *college* textbooks, filled with endless, mind-numbing detail. Surely the U.S. science community can do better.

2. Impress upon high schoolers the extraordinary importance and intellectual challenges of a scientific or engineering career. Science and engineering are tough disciplines; they require consistent hard work; and they are, at least temporarily, out of favor. What is called for is an imaginative public-relations campaign, sponsored by the National Academies of Sciences and Engineering and the private sector, dramatizing the exciting and vital work that scientists and engineers do.

3. Provide thousands of college scholarships for needy students majoring in science, technology, engineering, and math, targeting particularly women and minorities. This is the talent the United States needs, and the federal and state governments should make a healthy contribution in the form of tax-supported scholarships. Women and minorities provide the greatest potential untapped sources.

4. Underwrite thousands of new fellowships and low-interest loans for U.S. graduate students studying science, technology, engineering, and math. The incentives should be comparable to those of the 1958 National Defense Education Act that funded the education of the vast majority of "boomer"-generation science, technology, and engineering professionals, who are now retiring.

5. Reopen the United States fully to foreign students wanting to study those subjects at the undergraduate and graduate levels. To that end, visa requirements and procedures should be reviewed and adjusted where necessary. Student applicants should be welcomed and, with the fewest possible exceptions, their applications should be processed quickly and sympathetically. This may require some reeducation of the Congress and homeland security officials.

6. Encourage foreign students who receive graduate degrees in these critical subjects to remain in the United States. The government should automatically award a master's graduate in one of those subjects an H1-B (or comparable) visa and grant Ph.D. recipients permanent residence (a green card).

The American research model

Research and development (R&D) funding is the fuel that drives the technology engine. It is the source of innovation and growth, the foundation of international competitiveness. Without it, technological progress slows and once-dynamic economies stagnate. Industry, which carries out two-thirds of American R&D, can usually be counted on to take innovative new research ideas and make them marketable. But many new ideas–and new industries – come from risky, long-term, basic research that is shunned by the private sector. For this reason, most (though not all) informed observers believe that government should fund basic research in areas where success, let alone commercial viability, is uncertain. This is essential, many of us believe, to ensure continuing technological advance, economic growth, international competitiveness – and national security.

The U.S. research enterprise has been the envy of the world. The government spends more than twice as much on R&D as any other nation (although nearly 60% is now related to national defense). The country's research capacity, measured in numbers of researchers or facilities, is unparalleled. Federal R&D funding functions smoothly (although funding is not always adequate). Research collaboration among government, industry, and the research universities is taken for granted. Not surprisingly, government-funded research has produced many notable successes, among them the Internet itself.

The U.S. government's *information-technology* R&D program has been especially successful. And since the inception of ARPAnet in the 1960's, networking research has been remarkably well coordinated, first by ARPA (now DARPA), and later NSF and the interagency coordinating committee. In 1991, legislation sponsored by Al Gore created a National Coordinating Office for IT research and development that continues to guide and coordinate federal IT research. The office's formal mission is to ensure the U.S. lead in computing and information technologies, accelerate their deployment, and increase U.S. productivity and competitiveness. Day-to-day, the office does its best to coordinate the IT research efforts of the Departments of Defense and Energy, the National Institutes of Health, the National Aeronautics and Space Administration, the NSF, and seven other agencies.

Each year, the coordinating office proposes a research budget focused on seven IT research areas, including large-scale networking. The proposal is reviewed by the Office of Management and Budget and funded through the usual give-and-take with Congress. During the course of the 1990s, Congressional funding of *applied* IT research crowded out *basic* research, and the money approved for IT research gradually dwindled, too. In 1999, this trend was reversed, thanks to a landmark report of the President's IT Advisory Council that urged renewed emphasis on basic research and several hundred million dollars of additional IT research funding.[15] These recommendations were reflected in the last Clinton (FY 2001) budget that provided funding of $1.5 billion, nearly double that of five years earlier.

Well into the second Bush administration, top officials showed little interest in science and technology, let alone research and development. The president, vice president, and cabinet members seldom even mentioned science or technology. Eventually, a mid-level official, John H. Marburger III, director of the White House's Office of Science and Technology Policy, emerged as the administration's spokesman for them. But he couldn't produce a national research agenda or set federal research priorities. So although the IT National Coordinating Office soldiered on, it was not surprising when Marburger confirmed that the administration had simply "maintained" the federal IT research budget during the administration's first five years.[16]

Toward the end of President Bush's first term, concern about America's slipping global position in science and technology was growing. September 11-related concerns and the war in Iraq had changed research priorities; DARPA, in particular, shifted much of its substantial research funding from basic to applied research and from universities to the private sector. In 2004, reports began appearing that suggested the United States was lagging behind other nations in science and technology research funding. High-tech executives warned that the nation could lose its technology leadership and pointed to declining federal government R&D spending.[17] MIT president Susan Hockfield was quoted as saying: "We're falling behind. We're not keeping up with other countries in our investment in science and engineering."[18] The nonpartisan Council on Competitiveness called for restoration of the Defense Department's "historic commitment" to basic research and for increased support of physical science and engineering research.[19] A $100-million cut in the fiscal-2005 NSF research budget prompted widespread criticism.

In fall 2005, a Congressionally chartered group, chaired by former Lockheed Martin CEO Norman Augustine, issued the widely publicized report, *Rising Above the Gathering Storm*. It warned that "...the scientific and technological building blocks critical to our economic leadership are eroding...." and urged the government to double federal funding of long-term basic research and invest an additional $500 million in research facilities.[20] Responding in his February 2006 State of the Union speech, President Bush announced an American Competitiveness Initiative that included a promise to double funding for physical science and engineering research over ten years' time in three government agencies:

the NSF, the Department of Energy, and the National Institute of Standards and Technology.

Reflecting this, the administration's fiscal 2008 *IT research budget* jumped 15% to $3.3 billion. Yet even including this large boost, the federal IT research budget increased on average only 6.2% annually during the Bush administration's first seven years. Moreover, it should be remembered that over 60% of the budget supports military IT research projects, rather than civilian ones.[21]

Tokyo sets research priorities

Although the U.S. government spends much more on R&D than other governments, when private-sector expenditures are added, other nations invest a greater percentage of their GDP on research. For example, the Japanese government *and industry*, taken together, lay out 3.3% of GDP on research and development, compared to 2.6% in United States. Three-quarters of Japanese R&D is underwritten by industry, and as in the United States, most of that is applied research. But with less pressure from profit-minded shareholders, Japanese industry does a good deal of basic research as well. The Japanese government, provides only 17% of the overall research budget, compared to the U.S. government's 30%, but only a small amount of the Japanese government's R&D funding goes to military research.[22]

Until the mid-1990s, there was little central direction of the government's science and technology research budget. In stovepipe fashion, the education ministry, the Science and Technology Agency, and both the trade and telecom ministries each sought R&D funding in annual budget requests;

the finance ministry, in consultation with the ruling political party, decided how much each would be given. But in 1995, Koji Omi, a young Diet (parliament) member, changed this ad hoc approach dramatically. Concerned about Japan's slipping international competitiveness, Omi, a former trade and industry ministry official, drew up a new national science and technology charter in consultation with his country's scientific community. The Diet adopted Omi's charter as a basic law that required the government to strengthen Japan's research infrastructure and reform the R&D system itself.

In 1996, the government brought together government research directors, industry research leaders, and some academics to draft Japan's first five-year, science and technology research plan. The plan had three goals: to double the government's *1992* science and technology research budget by 2000; to expand the country's research facilities; and to increase cooperation between universities and industry. The government met the first two goals, investing $125 million in science research during the plan's five years and expanding related facilities. But it was less successful in improving university-industry collaboration, mainly because the academics were constrained by education ministry regulation and because most of them preferred their theoretical research to commercial pursuits.

In January 2001, a Japanese government reorganization combined the two main funders of science and technology research, the education ministry and the science and technology agency. Together, they accounted for two-thirds of the government's science and technology research funding. Fittingly, the prime minister named Koji Omi, the author of the 1996 basic law, Japan's first minister for science and technology. The reorganization also transformed the agency's advisory group into a National Council for Science and Technology. Three months later, the new council approved a second five-year science and technology plan, which would run through March 2006.[23] The new plan set four research priorities: life sciences, information technology, environmental science, and materials science. It also called for investing *half* of the government's entire science-and-technology research budget in those four areas and sharply increasing overall research funding to slightly less than 1% of GDP.[24]

The council laid out specific strategies for each priority research area and gave a letter grade – A, essential; B, desirable; C, can be postponed – to each research project proposed by the ministries. For information technology, the strategy called for upgrading the research networks, creating ubiquitous networks, and using IT to undergird the entire research effort. To achieve the most ambitious of these goals, ubiquitous networks, the government funded research on mobile Internet terminals and tiny, mobile-phone hard disks, as well as high-productivity software and information-retrieval technology.[25] In 2004, the research planners added yet another IT theme: Internet tracking using small, inexpensive, radio-frequency identification tags, or RFIDs. These tags are the key to tracking widgets in a supply chain, appliances in Internet-controlled homes, and even lost children.

Toward the end of 2005, the government announced its *third* science and technology plan, this one extending to 2010.

Spearheaded by a new minister of science and technology, Iwao Matsuda, the plan had two important components: it asserted the primacy of the National Science and Technology Council on these matters within the government; and it called for raising research spending to 1% of Japanese GDP, or $217.4 billion, by 2010. That would be as much as Japan spends on the country's defense – and about the same percentage of GDP as the U.S. government invests.

The third plan's major research priorities remained the same, but this time the council focused the research even more precisely; it endorsed 62 specific research projects, ten of them under the IT rubric, for funding. At the top of the IT list is work on world-class supercomputers that the government itself will lead, along with next-generation integrated circuits and networks, world-class software, and cyber-security – in short, the cutting-edge of IT.

To support these large ambitions, the Japanese government steadily boosted IT research funding. In fiscal 2001, the government invested $1.5 billion. In each of the following years, it increased funding by about $85 million until, in 2005, the budget was $1.8 billion. Adding up these five years of the second-plan period (which paralleled the e-Japan strategy), government IT research spending came to $8.3 billion, compared to $9.2 billion in the United States. The Japanese total underscores the extraordinary effort made by the government . It spent just $200 million a year less, on average, than the United States did with a GDP more than twice as large.

If you include *all* Japanese IT research spending, private-sector as well as government, Japan's totals have risen from $19.6 billion in 2001 to $25.4 billion in 2006.[26] Japanese corporations, however, have been less eager to invest in research facilities overseas (and foreign researchers there) than their American counterparts. The government, too, seems more intent on keeping high-end IT research at home. To encourage this, the science minister has promised to provide more opportunities for young researchers, especially women. As part of this process, the government plans to create 30 world-class centers that will pursue advanced, cross-disciplinary research.

This attempt to keep high-end research at home will surely bring consequences. To the extent it succeeds, the approach rules out the insights overseas researchers with different cultures and perspectives might provide. Moreover, if current warnings of a *global* shortage of highly skilled IT talent are correct, it may be a strategic mistake: Japanese corporations may not be able to move research offshore later on today's favorable terms.

Comparing the two research efforts

How do the IT research programs in the two countries stack up? Clearly, when the private sector is included, the U.S. enterprise retains a commanding lead. But when you look at government-funded IT research, the American lead is relatively small, and Japan could conceivably wipe it out. The IT sector in the United States has had nearly five decades of government attention and financial support – and extraordinary success – while the Japanese effort was badly served by the stovepiped research programs of individual government ministries until 2000. But since the 2001 government reorganization and the second research plan were announced, Japan has made remarkable strides. It has set research priorities and placed big bets on its priority areas, including IT; modeled its research funding procedures on America's successful practices; and significantly improved the country's research facilities. Moreover, the government is boosting IT research funding year after year, with nearly all of it going to non-military projects.

But Japan's top-down approach to the research agenda, while efficient, could prove problematic. Once priority areas (such as IT) and funding have been set, it might be better to give researchers more leeway. Japan may also come to regret its decision to try and keep high-end IT research at home. But one thing is certain: the government clearly understands the importance of IT research, and is moving as rapidly as possible to expand and improve it.

Until recently, the U.S. government has been complacent about its IT research effort. The administration's overall research priorities have been unclear, a "bottom-up" approach, as the science advisor has termed it. Until the president announced his 2006 competitiveness initiative, research policy guidance and funding recommendations were made by the science advisor and the budget director. Without high-level political support, IT research funding only nudged up during the Bush administration's first six years. Although the president's competitiveness initiative brought an initial boost, it may not last.

Still, the U.S. government has been funding IT research for nearly 50 years. During that time, it has built up a formidable IT research capacity and has achieved extraordinary results, not least the Internet itself. Unlike several of America's largest IT companies, however, the government has been slow to recognize the critical importance of IT research that not only drives the ongoing information revolution and the economy but also serves as an essential weapon to attack the nation's pressing problems. In fact, on the scale of federal spending, IT research comes after four other kinds: military, homeland security, medical, and space (although some IT research is included in these areas as well). As a result, the United States has merely maintained its federal IT research program while other nations, especially those in northeast Asia, have been racing to catch up. That won't happen for some years, but catching up is what Japan, in particular, is remarkably good at.

What is to be done?

The best path for the U.S. government to follow with its R&D program is less clear than what is needed to produce more computer scientists and engineers. Here reasonable people will disagree, but the following propositions make sense to me:

1. Broaden the current project to produce a strategic plan for federally funded, advanced networking R&D to include all networking and information-technology R&D. That would move beyond the present coordination of individual-agency research plans to create a federal IT research agenda. Given Congressional loyalties, it would not be an easy task, but this approach would better focus federally funded IT research and could attract more Congressional support and money.

2. Increase federal funding for *basic* IT research, including "blue sky" research. President Bush's American Competitiveness Initiative calls for a doubling of federal research funding for a handful of federal agencies over ten years, an increase of roughly 7% a year. That is significantly less than was recommended by the Augustine Committee that produced *Rising Above the Gathering Storm*; they urged an increase of 10% a year over seven years to double the amount invested. As pressures grow to reduce non-emergency federal spending, those moderate Bush increases, at least, should be preserved. In addition, a portion – say, one-fifth – of the basic research funded by those increases should be devoted to completely unstructured, "blue sky" research that could produce tomorrow's new industries.

3. Devote a significant portion of *all* federal IT research funding to ARPA-style projects. Perhaps one-fifth of federal IT research funding should be devoted to developing promising, but risky, existing technologies – and doing the research needed for 4G networks and tying together ultra-fast landline, wireless, and sensor networks. The Internet itself is an example of federal IT research funding used to solve a specific problem: the creation of a computer network to permit computer sharing. Similarly, federal research money now should be devoted to linking fiber, wireless, and sensor networks. The telephone, cable, and wireless companies can't do this research, because they spend very little money on R&D and are unlikely to spend more. For that reason, federally funded ARPA-style research projects seem the best approach.

Also, as the role of ultra-fast networks in solving the nation's urgent problems – energy, health care, education, security – becomes clearer, ARPA-style research projects should be developed to take advantage the networks' potential in those areas. An example: many small doctors' offices still refuse to digitize medical records because the software, costing several thousand dollars, is expensive and not standardized. Modest federal research funding of standards (for all Medicare and Medicaid patients) and open-source software solutions could save an estimated $2 billion in medical costs. Energy is another obvious example where use of information systems could encourage beneficial time-shifting of electrical usage and the like. Moreover, these networks are a key to innovation, the subject of the next chapter.

Chapter 8.
The innovation dimension: patents, tech transfer, venture capital

The United States is the most innovative nation in the world, Thomas L. Friedman wrote in a March 2004 *New York Times* column, due to a multitude of factors – "extreme freedom of thought, an emphasis on independent thinking, a steady immigration of new minds, a risk-taking culture with no stigma attached to trying and failing, a noncorrupt bureaucracy, and financial markets and a venture capital system that are unrivaled in taking new ideas and turning them into global products."[1] And the conventional wisdom is that Japan is one of the least innovative, in fact a copycat.

Today that conventional wisdom is only partly true. While the United States remains the global leader in innovation, that lead is slipping – and one of the nations closing the gap is Japan. Fearful of further slippage, *Rising Above the Gathering Storm*, a Congressonally chartered study, expressed deep concern: "We fear the abruptness with which a lead in science and technology can be lost – and the difficulty of recovering a lead once lost, if indeed it can be regained at all."[2] That fear is realistic. Governments around the world

– and the European Union – now realize the central importance of innovation and have developed strategies to improve their nations' competitive position. Nowhere is this
more true than in northeast Asia and in Japan.

Why does innovation matter? In today's global economy,
innovation – new ideas, products, services, and technologies
that emerge from new ways of seeing and doing things[3] – is
crucial to a nation's international competitiveness and economic growth. It is also critical to a business firm's survival.
As former Johns Hopkins University President William R.
Brody succinctly put it: knowledge drives innovation; innovation drives productivity; productivity drives economic
growth.[4] This is the thinking behind the much-sought-after
"knowledge economy" with its scramble for scientific and engineering talent, and the focus on basic research and development. It is also the justification for government strategies to
increase related elements of the innovation process: patents,
basic research to industry transfers, the number of entrepreneurs, and the availability of venture capital. The quest for
innovation also leads governments to encourage the creation
of innovation clusters – Silicon Valley is a prime example –
and invest in a world-class information infrastructure.

So far, attempts to measure and rank nations on the basis
of their innovative success have been interesting but unper-
suasive. The European Union's *European Innovation Scoreboard 2007*, for example, looks at 15 quantitative "innovation indicators": everything from science and engineering
graduates and broadband users to public and private R&D
investment, early-stage venture capital, and intellectual property. By the EU's 2007 reckoning, Japan ranked sixth (behind

Sweden, Switzerland, Finland, Ireland, and Denmark) and the United States ninth.[5] But innovation is too elusive a quality to be measured simply with statistics.

Using a more subjective approach, the staff of the World Economic Forum, which meets annually in Switzerland, produced *2007-2008 Global Competitiveness Rankings*. According to the WEF, Innovation, one of 12 pillars of global competitiveness,[6] consisted of eight indicators, ranging from the quality of scientific research organizations and university-industry research collaboration to the number of patents received and the capacity for innovation. But of those indicators, only the "number of patents received" was hard data; results for the other seven were based on a survey of "over 11,000 business leaders" in 125 economies worldwide. That process ranked the United States first in innovation (Japan was first the year before), followed by Switzerland, Finland, and Japan. Yet it is too much to expect that these business leaders have accurate views of, say, the availability of scientists and engineers and the capacity for innovation in more than a handful of countries, including their own. Better to examine directly the critical elements in the innovation process.

Innovation's building blocks

Patents are the basic elements of an innovation economy. A patent provides the inventor with tangible proof that he or she has exclusive rights to a new invention. It is the starting point for the steps that lead to a new product, service, or technology. Patent *awards* are therefore invariably a central measure of a nation's innovative strength.

Judged by patent activity, the United States and Japan are the two most inventive nations in the world. According to the latest (2005) statistics from the Organization for Economic Cooperation and Development (OECD), the United States accounted for slightly more than 30% of the triadic patents – patents taken at the U.S., Japanese, and European Patent Offices on the same invention – while Japan received slightly less than 30% (and the European Union slighter fewer than Japan).[7]   So it is fair to say that both countries are highly inventive – and Japan no longer fits the copycat stereotype.   In fact, judged on patents *per person*, Japan is the world's most inventive country.[8]

But when it comes to *information-technology* patents that overall picture is misleading.   In the IT sector – telecommunications, consumer electronics, computers, office machinery, and other IT – the United States has a commanding lead over the rest of the world.   Again, according to the OECD, the United States obtained more than one-third of all IT patents in 2005 and nearly twice as many as Japan which received the second highest number.   But the average growth rate of Japan's IT patents (25.5%) was more than twice that of the United States (11.8%) from 1995-2005.   And perhaps surprisingly, the Tokyo region produced slightly more IT patents than Silicon Valley did between 2003-2005.[9]

The Japanese are also certain to do better in the future. Now that they can patent their own discoveries, even those made with government funds, university researchers will obtain more patents.   Graduate schools of business are burgeoning, and young Japanese are more inclined to invent something and form their own companies.   In addition, the

Japanese government is working to improve Japan's weak software capacity, and that should lead to more patents. The big boost, however, is likely to come from Japanese corporate researchers. Until the late 1990s, those researchers, who account for more than 95% of all patent applications, typically received $100 or $200 when their company patented one of their discoveries. But as a result of two widely publicized court cases – one of which awarded $193 million to a corporate researcher – new legislation was passed. It requires employers to negotiate the compensation their employees will receive for new inventions, and it provides an appeals process for disputes.

In the United States, there are few disagreements about who owns a patent or how an inventor will be compensated, because these matters are spelled out in the corporate (or university) researcher's employment contract and the corporation's compensation rules. Even the handling of promising ideas has been formalized.[10] And U.S. high-tech corporations are pressing for more patents. Microsoft, for example, has set ambitious monthly goals for new patent applications. Other American corporations are seeking to patent not only traditional inventions but also software code and even "business methods," such as Amazon's "one-click" ordering process. And growing numbers of patent-infringement lawsuits may also encourage patent accumulation.

But patent growth is slowing for other reasons. Most U.S. corporations are spending far less than in recent years on corporate R&D due to Wall Street-related financial pressures and the uncertainty of federal tax breaks for corporate research. With the economic meltdown, matters will only get worse. Moreover, according to one study, patent litigation costs outstripped patent profits from 1976 to 1999, and patent cases are mounting – 3,075 cases were filed in 2004. Said one of the report's authors, "[P]atents don't work, for the information technology industry especially."[11]

On top of that, the U.S. patent system itself is in trouble, if not broken. Sharply increasing numbers of patent applications have overwhelmed patent-office examiners. Delays in patent awards are now common, and the examination process is far less rigorous than it once was. As a result, patent validity is now frequently determined through expensive law suits. Urgent calls for increased resources for the patent office and critical reforms began in 2004.[12] Two years later, those calls were echoed in the *Gathering Storm* report that also presented a sensible list of what needs to be done.[13] But nothing has happened so far, and U.S. innovation suffers.

From patent to product

With a patent in hand, the next step in the innovation process is transfer of the patented discovery to commercial channels. In most cases, this is simple. Corporations in the United States and elsewhere do most of the product-oriented *applied* research themselves. Corporations routinely make discoveries, patent them, and produce new products such as Apple's iPod and Nintendo's Wii game controller. But today U.S. corporations do little *basic* research, that is, research done without any commercial application in mind. The famous corporate basic-research centers of the mid-20th century, such as Bell Labs and Xerox PARC, have changed character or no longer exist, victims of quarterly shareholder scrutiny. Nearly all of America's basic research today is performed in university labs, mainly funded by the government. That shift created the problem of how to transfer university-lab discoveries to the private sector.

The United States solved that problem in 1980, with the Bayh-Dole Act, which granted universities patent rights to discoveries made during the course of government-funded research on their campuses. The universities then created Technology Licensing Organizations (TLOs) to license the patents to the private sector. For example, the University of Illinois licensed its MOSAIC software to a small company called Spyglass that was later bought by Microsoft which used the MOSAIC code to develop its Internet Explorer browser. At other times, the university or one or more of its faculty members use the patents to create their own private-sector companies, or spinoffs. The Bayh-Dole Act also permitted government labs to grant exclusive licenses to companies to use the labs' patented discoveries.

By the early 1990s, the transfer process was highly refined. Patented university or government-lab research was quickly transferred to the private sector, often after worldwide competitive bidding. The transfer process was so successful that in 2001, a RAND study described it as "one of our [America's] most important national assets, as important to present and future economic growth as the nation's natural resources, workforce, or stock of capital goods were in the past."[14]

In Japan, with far less quarterly stock-market pressure, many large corporations still do basic as well as applied research. For example, NTT's research labs are now testing fourth-generation (4G) mobile phones. The government also funds private-sector research. Throughout the 1970s and 1980s, MITI (now the Ministry of Economics, Trade, and Industry) and other ministries funded high-profile, private-sector research, such as the supercomputer project. Government labs, too, did commercially useful research. But the universities didn't begin to play a role in innovation until the mid-1990s. Until then, academic researchers at national universities were isolated from the marketplace by education-ministry regulations, and nearly all university researchers prided themselves on the theoretical nature of their research, unsullied by commercial concerns.

That began to change in 1995, when the Japanese government launched its first science and technology research plan, singled out the universities as key research players, and called for greater cooperation among the academic world, industry, and the national labs. In 1998, the Diet (parliament) passed its equivalent of the Bayh-Dole law, giving patent rights to government-funded research discoveries to individual university researchers and encouraging patent transfers to industry through technology licensing organizations. In 2001, the second science and technology research plan urged further university-industry cooperation. At the same time, the "Hiranuma Plan," named for then trade and industry minister Takeo Hiranuma, called for 1,000 university-originated startups within three years, a goal that was met.[15]

Those incentives had dramatic effects. Beginning in 1997, inventions at Japanese universities rose dramatically, nearly doubling in 2000 alone. A year later, estimated inventions on Japanese university campuses exceeded 9,000, compared with some 13,500 at American universities.[16] And by fall 2002, Japanese universities had created 27 new technology licensing organizations and signed over 500 licensing contracts. In addition, the number of university-based startups was up sharply, from 10 in 1996 to more than 70 in 2000 and to 190 in 2003.[17] The nearly 100 national (public) universities were given a final shove toward industry in spring 2004, when, as part of a broad-ranging university reform plan, they became "independent administrative entities" facing 5% annual reductions in government funding. In spring 2007, there were 1,590 university-based startups.[18]

The America-like technology-transfer pieces were now in place, and the incentives were clearly working. But all of this has taken time and will continue to do so. One knowledgeable Japanese observer believes it will take Japan ten to 15 years to completely overcome the decades of enforced university isolation from industry. But the Japanese have begun, and pressure for results will only grow.

The entrepreneurship gap

Large corporations usually win the university patents and may even have contributed money for the research. But entrepreneurs – young (and not so young) men and women working in their parents' garages and in small businesses – are much more prolific sources of innovation in the United States. There, successful entrepreneurs have long been idolized. In Japan, however, the culture traditionally frowned on solo performers. And there were other obstacles. Failure meant not only loss of face for the individual but also for his (or less often her) family, friends, and associates. An unsuccessful entrepreneur couldn't find a mid-career job in an economy based on lifetime employment. It was difficult to study entrepreneurship in Japan: in 2002, only 13 universities offered courses in the subject, and only single ones at that.[19] Moreover, a recent unscientific survey of young Japanese women revealed that the vast majority would not marry an entrepreneur.

One of Japan's leading entrepreneurs, e-Access chairman and CEO Sachio Senmoto, who taught a course in entrepreneurship at Keio University, believes that Japanese attitudes toward entrepreneurs, while improving, remain far from supportive. He thinks that the shortage of entrepreneurs will hinder Japan's IT progress and that the government can do little to encourage entrepreneurship.[20] Senmoto is undoubtedly right in saying that Japan now has many entrepreneurs, just not enough.

He himself is an excellent example of an older generation of successful ones who established a large, impressive, and growing enterprise. Among the younger generation are Masayoshi Son, the Softbank CEO who founded Yahoo Japan, Yahoo!BB and Softbank Mobile; and Hiroshi Mikitani, the founder of Rakuten, an enormously successful online shopping mall. Moreover, American IT managers in Tokyo agree that young Japanese are no different than young Americans in their zeal to strike it rich early in their careers.

Senmoto's skepticism notwithstanding, the Japanese government *has* cleared away major obstacles to starting a business. Until a few years ago, an entrepreneur needed $100,000 to register a new company, couldn't use stock options to attract new employees, and was personally responsible for all of the startup's financial and other liabilities. Today, as a result of governmental action, a new firm can be registered for one yen (about one cent), stock options may be used to recruit employees, and the entrepreneur's financial responsibility is limited.

Moreover, beginning in 1999, the government created nearly 60 startup "incubators," offering low rents, shared equipment, and environments congenial to entrepreneurs. The private sector, too, after nearly a decade of disinterest, established almost 30 incubators in 2000 alone.[21] These steps are paying off. The Japanese trade and industry ministry announced that some 93,000 startups were begun in 2003 – 10% of them under the new one-yen regulations – and the number continues to climb.

But Japan has a long way to go. According to the 2007 annual rankings of the Global Entrepreneurship Monitor (GEM), sponsored by America's Babson College and the London Business School, Japan placed 18th in the list of "early-stage entrepreneurial activity" in 23 "high-income" countries. Only 4.3% of the Japanese between the ages of 18 and 64 were engaged in some sort of early-stage entrepreneurial activity. The United States ranked third, with 9.6% participating in early-stage entrepreneurial activity, behind Iceland and Hong Kong among high-income countries. (In countries with lower incomes, 16.4% of the Chinese, 8.5% of the Indians, and 26.9% of the Thai engage in early-stage entrepreneurial activity.)[22] Interestingly, the 2006 GEM survey found that the most important barrier to entrepreneurship in Japan was the difficulty of getting a (mid-career) job if things went badly; in the United States, it was the cost of employees' health insurance.

How long will it take for Japan to catch up to the United States? No one knows, of course, but at a 2003 Tokyo entrepreneurship forum, an American participant guessed 15 years, because prosperity came to Japan 15 years later than it did to the United States. A Japanese thought 20 years. But Yoshito Hori, the 45-year-old Harvard Business grad who is dean of Tokyo's Globis Management School and founder of Globis Capital Partners, talking in early 2006, disagreed: "Japan had a very rigid, stable society [in 1996]." But "[t]he mentality now is so much different. Entrepreneurs are respected." All they need, Hori said, were two things: money and Western business savvy. That year, he had 2,000 enrolled in the Globis Management School, and 10% were already running their own businesses.[23]

Innovation's lifeblood

Innovation's lifeblood is, of course, venture capital – money invested in new enterprises by financial risk-takers in exchange for a share of ownership. Most new companies – startups – come into being with money raised from family and friends and, in the United States, through credit cards. But the rookie entrepreneur soon needs more money, if he or she is to succeed. That will come in ever increasing amounts – first tens of thousands and then millions – from wealthy "angels" and, later, venture capitalists. In exchange for their money, they will take ownership stakes in the new company. Both will also offer strategic advice, will probably sit on the fledgling company's board, and may recruit a top manager.

The angels and venture capitalists get their money out when the new enterprise is sold to a larger company or its shares are offered on a stock exchange as an initial public offering (IPO).

Angels have existed in the United States for decades. They are often successful entrepreneurs interested in helping the next generation. The first venture capitalist in California's Silicon Valley is thought to have been Arthur Rock, a New York investment banker, who arrived in the 1960s. By the mid-1970s there were more than 150 venture capitalists in that region. By the mid-1990s, there were dozens of venture-capital *firms* in the Valley, many clustered on Sand Hill Road in Menlo Park. But these venture capitalists showed little interest in the Internet until late 1994.

Then a small San Francisco investment bank sold shares in Netcom On-Line Services by persuading investors to ignore Netcom's lack of profits and consider only its large number of subscribers. The following spring, two more Internet stocks, PSInet and UUnet, were offered to the public.. And in August 1995, the legendary Valley venture-capital firm Kleiner Perkins guided the phenomenally successful Netscape Navigator Internet-browser stock offering, and the entire nation took note.

The dot-com boom had erupted. The end came in 2000. By that fall, investors had lost billions in the dot-com crash. The collapse lasted through 2001 and 2002, as IT venture capitalists sorted through some 8,000 startups that were still in limbo, not having been purchased, gone public, or bankrupt.

By early 2003, the venture capital market was showing new signs of life. But everyone was more cautious. Angels, instead of investing individually, created scores of investment clubs to spread the risk. Sequoia Capital, one of the Valley's three largest venture capital firms, put together a $385-million investment fund, its first since 2000. It, too, took a more cautious approach, investing only $3 million each – half its usual stake just two years earlier – in just 15 new companies.[24] And the venture capitalists were cautious in other ways: shifting their attention to less risky, later-stage startups; and specializing in discrete sectors, such as IT or biotech.

Today, the entire U.S. venture-capital process is very sophisticated. Dow Jones and other news services track new startups in different sectors through a series of investment stages, and conferences give entrepreneurs an opportunity to make their case to angels, venture capitalists, university and foundation endowment managers, and others. In 2007, angels invested $7 billion in IT *startups*,[25] and venture capitalists invested $8.7 billion in IT ventures at *all stages* of development.[26]

Japan, on the other hand, entered the late 1990s with a very small venture-capital sector. The sector was limited by a shortage of entrepreneurs, a dearth of venture capitalists, constraining laws and regulations, and stock exchanges unable to accept new-company IPOs. But in 1997, the Japanese government began a series of regulatory reforms, providing tax incentives for angel investors, permitting trust banks and pension funds to invest in venture-capital funds, and allowing venture capitalists to sit on startup boards. A year later, the government limited the liability of venture-capital partnerships and allowed stock swaps to ease merger-and-acquisition transactions. In 1999, the government relaxed stock-exchange listing laws to permit the listing of new companies on exchanges such as the JASDAQ over-the-counter market and the Tokyo Stock Exchange's "Mothers Market."

The government's new regulations fostered the creation of significant Japanese and foreign venture-capital funds. Seven of them focused on the IT sector; the three largest were Masayoshi Son's Softbank Fund with $435 million, Hikari Tsushin with $287 million, and Kyocera-Goldman Sachs with $261 million. Softbank and Hikari Tsushin, however, were new to venture capital. They had plenty of funding, but a host of difficult-to-assess requests for seed money from hundreds of entrepreneurs soon reduced their investment evaluations to what Tokyo journalists described as a "spray and pray" approach. Nevertheless, the dot-com bust was not as devastating in Japan as it was in the United States, and during the U.S. 2001-2002 "bust" period, the Japanese launched more IPOs than Americans did.

Although Japan's small venture-capital sector is growing in size and sophistication, the United States leads the industrial world by far, with Japan near the bottom of the list. The United States led all advanced nations between 2000 and 2003: Its venture-capital investment equaled slightly more than three-eighths of 1 percent of GDP, or $157 billion, while Japan languished at only three-*hundredths* of 1 percent, or $5 billion.[27] Even at the depth of the U.S. bust in

2002, U.S. venture-capital investment in computer and software companies at all stages of development totaled several times the amount in Japan.[28] This disparity stems from the dominance of risk-averse banks, insurance companies, and corporations, which control 85% of Japan's venture-capital sector; in the United States, by contrast, 70% of venture-capital funding comes from more flexible pension funds and individual investors.[29]

Although the 2008 credit crisis is now putting pressure on the sector, U.S. venture capitalists invested $8.7 billion in all stages of IT – computer and peripherals, IT services, networking and equipment, and software – in 2007.[30] During a comparable time period (April 2006-March 2007), Japanese venture capitalists invested just $217 million.[31] Japan's lack of venture capital remains a weak link in its innovation process chain.

Clustering for Competitiveness

The concept of an "innovation cluster" is an idea whose time has come. A 2001 study led by Harvard professor Michael E. Porter for the (U.S.) Council on Competitiveness found that "[t]he nation's ability to produce high-value products and services that support high wage jobs depends on the creation and strengthening of ... regional hubs of competitiveness and innovation."[32] This concept of hubs or clusters was a major focus of the Council on Competitiveness' fall 2005 "U.S.-Japan Innovation Summit." And in spring 2007 speaking to a Washington audience, former Harvard president and economist Lawrence Summers pinpointed support of "clusters of excellent performance" as "one of four actions the United States should take to assure its prosperity in the 21st century."[33] Noted Summers: "Clusters like Silicon Valley in information technology, New York City in finance, and Boston in life sciences can't be shifted overseas – and everyone will want to come."[34] "Innovation hubs" are also a central element in John Kao's persuasive 2007 book, *Innovation Nation*.

Silicon Valley remains, of course, the prototype for all innovation clusters. For nearly a half century, technology geeks have inhabited the 50-mile corridor running south from San Francisco, and for most of those years venture capitalists have been in the Valley looking for the next new thing. They have not been disappointed. Beginning with computer chips in the 1950s, PCs and storage devices in the 1970s, and more recently, software and Internet-oriented ventures, the Valley has produced. Yahoo, eBay, Google, the iPod, the iPhone, are just a few of its big-name successes.

Given this record, it is not surprising that, in 2007, more than one-third of all U.S. venture capital was invested in Silicon Valley, up from one-fifth at the height of the dot-com boom in 2000.[35] That venture capital attracts lots of newcomers with new ideas, and the newcomers soon connect with the existing network of technology veterans, who offer examples of success, valuable advice, and often startup money. According to AnnaLee Saxenian, dean of the School of Information at the University of California/ Berkeley and the author of *Regional Advantage*, the Silicon Valley network "isn't matched anywhere else in the world," a fact that "allows people to recombine technical ideas much more quickly here than anywhere else." Moreover,

Saxenian remains convinced that "[i]n terms of creativity, the Valley remains as far ahead of the rest of the world as ever."[36]

But Japan, along with many other nations, is trying to catch up. Its main IT innovation cluster, "Bit Valley," is located in the Shibuya district of Tokyo. Although the scale is dramatically smaller, Shibuya has several of the advantages enjoyed by Silicon Valley: excellent universities, an exciting city, a large domestic market, fledgling entrepreneurs with can-do attitudes, and a sprinkling of venture capitalists. But there are sharp differences as well. Venture capital, especially angel capital, is in short supply, foreigners are far scarcer (about half of those in Silicon Valley speak English with a non-American accent), too few examples of success exist, and failure remains unforgivable. Still, in a December 2005 ranking of regional "knowledge competitiveness," Tokyo came in number 22, up 16 places from the year before. (Forty-one of the 50 regions ranked – led by San Jose, Boston, and San Francisco – were in the United States.)[37] Moreover, the Japanese may hope that a few of the planned five "world-class research centers" become full-fledged innovation clusters, alongside other existing clusters in Kyoto and Sapporo.

In any event, these Japanese research centers won't be Silicon Valleys for many years, if ever. It is difficult for Europeans, Asians, and even most Americans to conceive the extraordinary array of intelligence, imagination, technical knowledge, ambition, self-confidence, venture capital, and startup experience that now exists in Silicon Valley. The Valley is the product of decades of extraordinary effort and success, and, as Summers says, it continues to attract thousands of very talented people from around the world.

Infrastructure and innovation

Japan does enjoy a substantial lead in one critical aspect of IT innovation: nationwide ultra-fast broadband and high-speed wireless infrastructure. That infrastructure is a significant advantage in permitting innovators and others involved in the innovation process to communicate quickly and test new products aimed at those with ultra-fast connections. Underscoring the importance of infrastructure, U.S. business executives rated communications infrastructure as the top precondition for making new investments in a 2005 survey.[38]

In the United States today, researchers at major universities, product developers in leading technology corporations, and those working in the large innovation clusters, such as Silicon Valley, Austin, Texas, or Boston, have ultra-fast broadband connections, if not high-speed wireless ones. But those at smaller colleges and universities, small and medium-sized enterprises, and especially those working in garages are unlikely to. That is a profound disadvantage for the United States, because innovative ideas (as opposed to basic research and product development) often come from small labs and garages. Japan, with its nearly complete nationwide fiber broadband network and its recently completed 3G wireless network, has a distinct advantage here.

Moreover, the expanding infrastructure itself creates opportunities for innovation. As a critical mass of users (around 10 million) begins using new networks, an irresist-ible new market is created for innovators. In the past five years alone, Japan has developed three huge new markets in this fashion: high-speed (DSL and cable) broadband, ultra-fast (fiber) broadband, and relatively high-speed (3G) mo-bile phones. Japanese corporations and entrepreneurs have taken advantage of these new markets by creating many new applications, products, and services such as telemedicine, mobile videoconferencing, and (real-time) mobile TV.

Now Japan, along with Korea, is poised to create three new markets that will profoundly affect future Internet-re-lated innovation: "Super 3G" mobile phones capable of re-ceiving 100-300 megabit-per-second downloads; ultra-fast 4G phones (100 to 1,000 Mbps downloads); and ubiqui-tous (combined ultra-fast broadband and wireless) networks. Shortly after 2010, these new mobile phones and networks of the future will present new extraordinary opportunities for innovation. And because they will first appear in Japan and Korea, innovators there will have first crack at creat-ing a vast array of new applications, products, and services for these truly "anytime, anywhere" devices and networks. Except for a small number of innovators in Silicon Valley and elsewhere who understand these markets, American residents will not have comparable opportunities for years to come.

When the Bush administration took office in 2001, such a situation was inconceivable. Eight years later, it was in-evitable. As the United States drifted lower in global broad-band rankings, a series of reports appeared urging measures to improve American competitiveness. At least three major studies called for rapid deployment of broadband: the Council on Competitiveness' "National Innovation Initiative," the Economic Strategy Institute's "America's Technological Future at Risk," and the National Academies' Committee's *Rising Above the Gathering Storm.* The Bush administration has ignored them.

But even if the government were to follow their recommendations, U.S. infrastructure deployment would not be appreciably faster. That is because the studies only hint at – most reject – new regulations to encourage competition and shy away from calling for any federal tax incentives and subsidies to spur deployment. Without competition, tax incentives, and subsidies, deployment of the fiber and wireless networks of the future in the United States will continue to be slow, uneven, and incomplete.

The innovation prognosis

The smooth innovation process in the United States was once referred to as the nation's "crown jewels," permitting it to lead the world. But while the process still works well, other nations have recognized the importance of innovation and the need to imitate the American innovation model – by procuring more talent, more R&D funding, more patents, better technology transfers, and so forth. Catching up won't be easy, because the Unites States has an enormous lead. But Japan and many other countries are gaining ground.

Japan stands second only to the United States in patent production. Its technology-transfer procedures are now in place and working. A younger generation of Japanese is more entrepreneurial. More venture capital is available, although not yet enough. An existing IT cluster will continue to expand, and it is possible that five new research centers may turn into innovation clusters. Japan's ultra-fast broadband and wireless communications has given rise – or will – to six huge new markets for innovation. In short, the Japanese government and private sector, using the country's customary top-down approach, are clearly determined to sharply boost innovation.

Daunting obstacles stand in the way, however. Innovation at any level depends heavily on individuals expressing unorthodox views. But that is not the Japanese custom, expressed in a popular saying: "the nail that sticks up gets hammered down." Although the government is trying to change this attitude, it will not be an easy task for a traditionally group-oriented society that values harmonious teamwork. The Japanese have more than their share of good ideas, and the younger generation is more individualistic than its parents. The question is whether the good ideas will be heard and acted on – or ignored.

The openness needed for innovation success may also prove difficult. Japanese companies are notoriously proprietary, as is most Japanese research. This approach can lead to impressive successes, as Microsoft and Apple have proven in the United States. But secrecy also has its drawbacks. Many patents developed by Japanese corporations lie dormant, and proprietary standards erected to protect Japanese products at home – the standards for mobile-phone handsets, for example – prevented Japan's manufacturers from becoming a global force. This is now changing. But how quickly will a transition to greater openness take place?

Risk-taking, too, is not something most Japanese embrace. Clearly the younger generation, which until recently knew only a bad economy, is less risk averse than its elders. And it was recently reported that Japanese housewives – from their kitchens – were betting billions of yen on currency futures. But as a general rule, the Japanese are conservative, especially when it comes to money, and with the partial exception of the Kyoto region, they are still reluctant to bankroll untested entrepreneurs.

An additional consideration: the degree of openness of Japanese society. The government seems intent on recruiting more IT specialists from overseas, despite considerable popular resistance to immigration generally. In sufficient numbers, foreign IT experts, particularly Indians and Chinese with their strong ideas, ambition and self-confidence, could go far to improve Japanese innovation and entrepreneurship, as they have in the United States. Yet there are questions here as well: even if foreign IT experts can be recruited, will they be welcomed and rewarded, and will they stay?

Despite these obstacles, there are three reasons to believe Japan will achieve greater innovation success. With its aging population and declining work force, the country must quickly increase productivity – the current goal is to boost it from 1.6% to 2.4% in five years[39] – and the key to that is innovation. The Japanese government understands this very well and has developed bold plans to improve the nation's innovative capacity and productivity. Furthermore, Japan's younger generation is remarkably unlike earlier generations – more individualistic, more confident, more open to the outside world. Not so different, in fact, from its peers in North America, Europe, and elsewhere in Asia. This suggests that, as in the past, it would be a mistake to sell Japan short.

Moreover, when it comes to innovation, the United States has its own problems. During the first five years of the Bush administration, the President and his top officials took their collective eye completely off the innovation ball. After that, U.S businessmen were only neutral to slightly positive about the innovation climate in the United States.[40] President Bush's competitiveness initiative provides barely a beginning in trying to fix the problems. The next President will have to do much better if the United States is to retain its lead in innovation.

Meanwhile, the dangers of losing that lead are real. As Stanford President John Hennesy recently summed up the situation: "Imagine that the next round of innovation is done in India or China [or, I would add, Japan or South Korea]. How many years is it before either Cisco relocates to India or China and grows most of its jobs there or the next Cisco is actually created there?"[41]

What should be done?

While the United States still leads in innovation, complacency is not an option. Some urgent recommendations:

1. Fix the patent office. The U.S. Patent and Trademark Office is being overwhelmed. It needs more resources; a tighter definition of patents – eliminating the "business methods" category, for example; and a thorough review of its operations in the new technology world. The United States would also benefit from a non-judicial method of re-solving patent disputes, quickly, fairly, and inexpensively. Too many lengthy, legal challenges are now being mounted simply to slow down competitors.

2. Monitor the technology-transfer process to ensure optimal functioning. Smooth transfer of a university's ba-sic research to private-sector applications is critical to the U.S. innovation effort. Since the inception of the Bayh-Dole Act in 1980, that process has worked well. Yet now there is evidence that university research agendas are increas-ingly being driven by commercial feasibility at the expense of *basic* work; that secrecy and patenting are limiting the scope of future research; and that the sale of a patent to one company is preventing the use of that knowledge in other fields. Those problems have apparently driven large cor-porations to seek basic research at universities overseas.[42] The optimal working of this transfer process is so central to U.S. innovation success that continuous, careful monitoring is required. The National Science Foundation and Depart-ment of Commerce are best positioned to do that. When problems arise, they should be quickly resolved, and given recent complaints, it is time to revisit the Bayh-Dole Act, now nearly 30 years old.

3. Encourage corporate R&D *in* the United States. At a minimum, this means increasing the tax incentives for corporate R&D conducted in the United States to make them comparable with those of other countries – and making the incentives permanent so that corporations can plan on them. But more should be done. The Commerce Department should carry out a study of what additional incentives (such as streamlining the visa process, mentioned earlier) would be needed to ensure the world's pre-eminent environment for innovation. The new, post-Bush administration should then follow through.

4. Encourage foreign innovator-entrepreneurs to remain in the United States. In recent years, reportedly over half of the Silicon Valley startups were launched by foreigners, mainly Chinese and Indian nationals. Clearly, then, foreign entrepreneurs are critical to U.S. innovation success. For obvious reasons, their governments are urging them to come home. While the choice is the individual's, these innovator-entrepreneurs should be encouraged to remain in the United States by giving them long-stay visas or, depending on circumstances, permanent residence.

5. Promote startups through tax incentives, and permit their use of stock options (without debiting). Startups – even those that fail, as most do – should be encouraged; they are the tangible result of the innovative process. As such, they should be fostered by all levels of government wherever possible. Among the useful incentives for fledgling startups: federal and state tax breaks, incubators where needed, and the use of stock options (without carrying them as an accounting debit). The key word here is "fledgling." These benefits should end when the enterprise reaches a certain size, say, $1 million in revenues, or a certain stage, say, sale to another company or launch of an IPO.

6. Fund innovation hubs. John Kao, in his book *Innovation Nation*, makes a compelling case for funding several (he urges 20) U.S. "innovation hubs" at $1 billion each.

The purpose is to create new Silicon Valleys for the industries of the future – wireless technology (mentioned earlier), nanotechnology, materials science, biotechnology, alternative energy sources, and many others. Several nascent innovation hubs already exist, such as those involving wireless technology in San Diego and biotechnology in Boston and Baltimore. Needed now are new public-private partnerships and additional public and private funding and other incentives to maximize their potential. Expansion of these hubs would encourage new cross-disciplinary research and attract not only researchers but also entrepreneurs and venture capitalists from around the world. Moreover, the hubs could never be outsourced. They would give U.S. innovation several shots in the arm plus the strong possibility of creating entire new industries and the skilled jobs that go with them.

7. Deploy ultra-fast fiber and wireless networks. Described earlier at length, these networks are essential to America's future innovation success. Silicon Valley, of course, has some of the fastest networks in the world. Spreading them across the country would provide countless additional opportunities for innovation.

Chapter 9.
The e-commerce dimension: online buying and selling

Electronic commerce – buying and selling online – invites a wide range of participants. For a manufacturer, the Internet offers the possibility of having scores of domestic bidders for a procurement contract and, as trust builds, of attracting them from around the world. For a wholesaler, it creates global opportunities for new customers. And for a retailer, the possibility of reaching potential customers around the country and overseas. In addition, one consumer can sell to another consumer directly or through online auctions – as far as the Internet reaches. All of this is e-commerce, and given its manifest importance, it is a dimension of Internet leadership.

Ira Magaziner, a law-school classmate of Bill and Hillary Clinton and an energetic Clinton administration aide, was among the first to grasp the potential of e-commerce in the mid-1990s. Working with a governmental task force, he came up with the basic principles that have guided the U.S. government's approach since 1997. Those principles called for a public-private partnership: the private sector should lead, but government must support a "predictable, minimalist, consistent and simple legal environment," and e-commerce should be encouraged globally through a consistent legal framework.[1] The minimalist legal framework was quickly put in place in the United States, essentially by revising existing commercial law to take into account the workings of the Internet – such as digital signatures, authentication, and electronic payments – and making commercial law applicable to online commerce.

With these pieces in place, Magaziner and other U.S. government officials led missions to tens of countries around the world, including Japan, to persuade them to adopt this approach as well. They were remarkably successful. By November 1998, 132 countries had agreed to adopt the U.S. approach to e-commerce and to forgo imposing tariffs on it.[2] The Japanese government signed on in May 1998, with both countries agreeing to uphold the stated principles and to work together.[3]

But the Japanese were slow to embrace e-commerce. Although a small rural company had begun selling noodles online in October 1994[4] and the government urged promotion of e-commerce in late 1998, little happened until Internet penetration in Japan reached the takeoff stage and the IT Strategy Council made expanded e-commerce a major goal in 2000. The Headquarters urged the Japanese, by 2003, to "far exceed" $635 billion[5] in business-to-business (B2B) e-commerce (a ten-fold increase from the 1998 level) and $27 billion in its retail sibling, business-to-consumer (B2C) e-commerce (a fifty-fold increase from 1998).

The Headquarters also prescribed changing laws and regulations that hindered e-commerce, and strengthening those that protected intellectual property rights and ensured consumer safeguards. Those ambitious goals, aimed at revitalizing the Japanese economy, galvanized the Diet and the bureaucracy. By spring 2001, the former had amended some 50 laws, and the government had eliminated most of the remaining obstacles to e-commerce transactions, a remarkable achievement in such a short time.

As all of that suggests, Japan, although the second-largest market in the world, was far behind the United States in e-commerce sales in 2000. Two figures tell the story: that year, total U.S. e-commerce sales (B2B and B2C combined) reached just over one trillion dollars ($1,056 billion)[6], while the Japanese total was only one-tenth of that amount ($112 billion). Several factors explained the disparity. The U.S. population and economy were more than twice as large as Japan's. At that point, U.S. businesses had invested more in IT than had the Japanese private sector. Dial-up connections were fairly cheap in the United States, and many more Americans had access to the Internet. Most of the legal and regulatory obstacles had been cleared away (although some confusion about sales tax existed). And despite the dot-com bust, Americans, and more importantly American businesses, remained far more trustful of online vendors than their Japanese counterparts.

Japan enjoyed a single advantage: millions of Japanese already had two years' experience with mobile-phone purchases – m-commerce – using i-mode and its competitors.

What was less obvious in the mostly dial-up world of that time was the relationship of advanced broadband and wireless infrastructure to e-commerce. Faster, more reliable networks – particularly fiber networks – permit business to make all of its operations, including e-commerce, more efficient. Such networks – broadband and wireless – also encourage consumers to spend more time online and make more purchases.

Bottom of the iceberg: business-to-business sales

Most of the e-commerce media stories are about online businesses: Amazon.com selling to consumers; consumers visiting the online mall at Yahoo; consumers selling to one another on eBay. But these stories miss the main point. Over 90% of the electronic commerce carried out in both the United States and Japan has little to do with consumers; it is *B2B*, businesses selling to other businesses.

In addition to increasing the number of potential suppliers, an electronic marketplace offers several advantages to business buyers and sellers. With more potential suppliers, business buyers can usually save money on their purchases. Buyers can also sharply reduce – by as much as 90% – the administrative cost of purchases, the time required to complete the transaction, and the inventory they must keep on hand. For sellers, B2B marketplaces offer potentially greater sales, lower costs of making them, and lower inventory needs. Moreover, in an electronic marketplace, buyers and additional suppliers may find each other.

The oldest B2B process used electronic data interchange (EDI) standards and was created by the U.S. trucking industry in the early 1970s to find cargoes for empty trucks on their way home from deliveries. Thirty-five years later, EDI services were still a major force in wholesaling. EDI automates purchasing – the usual order and bill of sale are sent electronically making them safe, secure, and verifiable – and makes the process fast and cheap. Wal-Mart, for example, now requires all of its suppliers to use EDI. Linked directly to the giant retailer's inventory databases, suppliers are automatically notified when Wal-Mart's stock runs low and authorized to send more. In the late 1990s, an estimated 95% of top *Fortune* 500 companies used EDI-based processes. And many still do, but EDI has serious flaws: the process usually requires an expensive private data network between trading partners; it takes time to set up; and it is not interactive. Nor does it permit discussion or negotiation. Many companies that used EDI services therefore began experimenting with *Internet* marketplaces, which are cheaper and more flexible.

These experiments mushroomed in the late 1990s when, during the dot-com boom, would-be Internet *business* marketplaces (estimates ranged from 700 to 1,500) emerged alongside existing data exchanges. Most of the nascent business sites failed in the bust, but some survived, often because they were sponsored by the major players in a given industry. For example, the World-Wide Retail Exchange, founded in 2000 by J.C. Penney, Gap, Marks & Spencer, and Tesco survived. Four years later its then-60 members received a variety of services that made them more efficient, and with more suppliers, they were able to buy goods more cheaply.

By that time, as reflected in statistics, B2B was ready to take off in the United States. In 2000, 94% of U.S. e-commerce was between businesses, which the Census Bureau, responsible for American e-commerce statistics, defines as simply electronic manufacturing sales and electronic merchant wholesale sales.. That year, total online B2B sales equaled $990 billion.[7]   Six years later, the percentage was down slightly from 2000; B2B then accounted for 92.5% of all U.S. e-commerce . But the value had soared: online B2B now totaled $2.7 *trillion*.[8]

In 2000, Japan's total B2B e-commerce accounted for $193 billion,[9] about one-fifth of the U.S. total. There were several reasons for this. Japan's smaller enterprises were several years behind those of the United States in IT adoption, whether PCs, local area networks, or Internet use. IDC, a global market intelligence firm, estimated that in 2000, Japan's total IT spending, as a share of GDP, was only half that of the United States.

Culture and custom also slowed Japanese domestic B2B e-commerce. It was impossible there to discharge thousands of suppliers, distributors, and middlemen, who might have been displaced by electronic marketplaces, because large-scale layoffs were unacceptable in a country where traditional lifetime employment made it nearly impossible to find other jobs. There were other obstacles as well: online security concerns, high telephone-line charges, and a shortage of engineers needed to design new B2B systems.

But on the plus side, Japan's *large* companies were already heavy users of EDI networks for business transactions. Two major trading companies, Marubeni and Mitsui, seeking to expand their traditional intermediary role into cyberspace, developed many e-marketplaces in the late 1990s.

Moreover, the trade and industry ministry (now METI) had made e-commerce a priority in 1995 and, over the ensuing five years, had spent $1 billion on over 200 projects, mostly for business applications and broadband infrastructure. The late 1990s saw increasing numbers of B2B exchanges, and the government soon took on an even-larger role.[10]

In 2001, e-commerce expansion became a major pillar of the e-Japan strategy. That strategy set a goal of $635 billion in B2B e-commerce transactions within three years, which meant a 60% increase in each of the following three years. The trade and industry ministry promoted a more IT-oriented economy. It adopted the U.S. minimalist approach to e-commerce, eliminating regulations that hampered e-commerce growth. And to make sure everyone understood the desired goals, the ministry, working with those affected, projected B2B e-commerce targets for each industry sector for each of the next five years.[11]

The ambitious e-Japan strategy goal, the ministry-private sector partnership, the industry-sector targets, and purely business interests produced striking results. By the end of 2003, Japan's B2B e-commerce had reached $703 billion, more than 15 percent above the e-strategy goal of $635 billion. In 2005, the trade and industry ministry, working with Japan's Electronic Commerce Promotion Council and the private research firm IDC Japan, claimed that Japan's B2B e-commerce exceeded that of the United States – although the American economy was well over twice as large.[12] (It should be noted that the ministry and the U.S. Census Bureau, which tracks e-commerce in the United States, use quite different definitions of B2B and B2C making direct comparisons impossible.)

In 2006, the trade and industry ministry claimed that Japan's B2B lead had increased. Including all online activity (Internet *and* private network data transactions), Japan's B2B volume had reached $2.1 trillion, compared with a U.S. total of $1.8 trillion.[13] Moreover, Japan, whose economy is less than half the size of the United States,' was doing more than twice as much B2B through the Internet.

B2C: Consumers buying online

In 2000, the United States led the world in business-to-consumer (B2C) e-commerce. With more computers and cheap Internet access, Americans were surfing the web (however slowly) in great numbers. Much of the country was in the grip of a dot-com mania: Scores of new Internet companies were being launched each week – flowers.com, Pets.com, and many more – and their stock prices were being watched closely, especially by a new group of online investors and Internet day traders. Many bought into predictions that online enterprises would soon virtually replace familiar bricks-and-mortar stores; 90% of the world's consumer-oriented websites were located in the United Sates.

Nearly all of the obstacles to online transactions, except Internet access speed, had been overcome. The government had long since eliminated the legal and regulatory constraints. Equally important, the private sector had invested in secure servers to ensure a safe payment process, and Americans (although frequently warned not to) readily used their credit cards for online purchases. Even those who chose to buy from local merchants began to do extensive research online before making their purchases. But most of all, America's transition to online shopping was encouraged by new and imaginative Internet businesses such as Amazon.com, eBay, and Yahoo!. By the end of 1999, business-to-consumer (B2C) sales hit $40 billion.

A year later, in 2000, total B2C sales reached $66 billion, a stunning 65% increase over the previous year. An *Economist* survey that year noted that three of four B2C online sales took place in the United States.[14] The American lead was so great, in fact, that some believed the United States might dominate global B2C e-commerce indefinitely. But 2000 was also the year of the dot-com bust, when scores of nascent online ventures failed. The vision of a quick American transition from mall shopping to online shopping went from blurry to black.

The bust killed all but the strongest online firms, and the surging B2C growth rates of the late 1990s nearly stalled. Consumer e-commerce gained only 6% from 2000 to 2001, less than one-tenth of the previous year's rise. But then, online retail sales and services picked up, and in 2006 B2C e-commerce reached $221 billion. More remarkably, from 2001 to 2006, online retail sales climbed at an average annual rate of over 25%, *despite* the dot-com bust, and the following year reached an estimated $127.7 billion, 3.2% of all U.S. retail sales.[15]

Why this continued success? Increasing use of broadband has been a major factor: as increasing numbers of Americans subscribed to broadband (now 55% of the population[16]), they spent more time online and made more purchases there. But America's online retailers have played an even larger part. They have advertised online and off. They have also made their websites easier to navigate and more secure by beefing up their IT systems. It became evident to many traditional retail stores that they needed an online presence to assure continued business success ("bricks and clicks"). As a result, many long-established Main Street retailers, from department stores and book sellers to office-supply and specialty shops, went online, leaving it up to the customer whether to end up buying there or over the counter.

The net effect was to expand, seemingly exponentially, the variety of goods available online, tempting a widening circle of buyers. Online service providers, from airlines and hotels to stock brokers and digital-photo printers, also burgeoned.

Three online enterprises continued to lead the way and, in fact, legitimized B2C e-commerce in the United States: Amazon, eBay, and Yahoo!. Each has its own approach and business model. Amazon, seeking to be a global general store, continually expands the variety of its online offerings, now ranging from books and music to tea and cameras, with little concern for profits (although it is now in the black). eBay, profitable from its beginning in 1995, pioneered auctions where consumers sell to one another in one huge global rummage sale. And Yahoo! took the familiar shopping-mall concept online, permitting its visitors to buy from a host of more or less familiar mall merchants through the Internet. What all three have in common is the concept of one-stop shopping and very sophisticated websites, order and payment processing, and fulfillment systems that make the online buying experience as efficient, pleasurable, and seductive as possible. Moreover, all have established overseas operations in major markets (when copycats didn't beat them to it).

In 2000, Japan was the second-largest B2C market in the world, at $7.5 billion, but that was just over a tenth of the U.S. total.[17] A handful of reasons accounted for most of that disparity: fewer PCs in Japanese households; the high cost of Internet access; limited use of credit cards; concerns about online privacy and security – and fears that the items ordered and paid for would not be delivered. In addition, legal and regulatory constraints remained.

Within that context, the IT Strategic Headquarters set its bold target of "well in excess" of $27 billion in B2C e-commerce by 2003. The Headquarters also urged prompt improvement of the e-commerce business environment. That was soon done: the Diet had passed a new IT Basic Law in late 2000, and the trade and industry ministry shepherded a revised commercial law through the Diet that removed constraints and adapted the existing commercial law to online transactions. METI also cleared away the regulatory underbrush and established an e-commerce promotion association, ECOM, with some 300 Japanese business participants. Finally, the ministry continued to monitor e-commerce results – B2B, B2C, and business-to-government – as it had since 1998.

Japanese business also got to work, coming up with imaginative solutions to consumers' fears – the deepest of which were that payment information provided online would be stolen and the items ordered would not be delivered. To work around the payment problem, Yamadaya, a noodle company that had an early online presence, offered several ways to pay: by credit card, debit card, bank transfer, or cash-on-delivery. In yet another twist solving both the payment and actual-delivery problems, the well-known Yamato Transport company, created its own online mall, and its drivers took cash when they delivered an online order. By 2002, a more convenient payment and delivery-insurance system emerged: buyers ordered items online, either at home or at one of the ubiquitous Japanese 7-11 or 7-11-like convenience stores, and the items were brought to the stores, to be paid for in cash.

Meanwhile, Japanese use of credit cards expanded rapidly, and online merchants made their systems more secure. (In 2000, Japan had only 15 secure servers per million people, compared to 170 in the United States.) Soon PayPal and PayPal-like systems emerged, permitting electronic credit- or debit-card payments. And Japan's consumer e-commerce continued to grow.

At the same time, the Japanese pioneered another promising form of B2C: mobile-phone purchases. Those began in 1999 with the advent of the "i-mode" mobile-phones with push-button Internet access. Mobile purchases began with ring tones, horoscopes, and entertainment news, but they soon expanded to buying tickets, articles in stores, and vending-machine items. By the end of 2000, online mobile sales accounted for about 7% ($491 million) of Japan's consumer *e-commerce*. Five years later, online mobile sales had rocketed to nearly 22% of total B2C transactions.[18]

In 2003, total online consumer sales exceeded the e-Japan strategy goal of $27 billion by nearly 50%.[19] And by the end of 2006, B2C electronic commerce hit $398 billion, up 27% from the previous year. But although Japan's market was growing faster than America's (27% to America's 21%), the nation's B2C total was still less than one-quarter that of the U.S. with $1.7 trillion.[20]

So despite the greater severity of the dot-com bust in the United States, it continues to lead the world in consumer e-commerce, with Japan still in (a distant) second place. The key factors remain as they were: America's greater and more trustful population, its greater numbers with broadband (however slow), its imaginative online retailers, and its seemingly insatiable consumption online as well as off. Japan, however, continues to lead the world in mobile-commerce, as it has since the introduction of i-mode in 1999. As more and more people use mobile phones for more and more tasks, mobile e-commerce may overtake the immobile version. In the meantime, Japan's ultra-fast broadband infrastructure provides new opportunities for imaginative online sales of products, applications, services, and content, especially video content. The emergence of linked ultra-fast broadband and mobile networks in 2010 will offer even more opportunities. We shall see whether Japan takes full advantage of them.

Summing up

Although most Americans believe the United States leads all other nations in e-commerce, that is not the case. When business and consumer e-commerce are combined, Japan comes out on top. True, the United States has a large lead in consumer e-commerce, but Japan has an even larger lead in business e-commerce – and, consequently, total e-commerce: in 2000, Japan's total was just one-tenth of America's; but, by 2005, Japan had taken the lead due to sharp increases in B2B commerce there. And in 2006, the latest year for which we have official statistics, according to the METI survey (and e-commerce definitions), Japan continued to lead the entire world in combined business and consumer e-commerce with $2.3 trillion to America's $2.0 trillion.[21]

What is to be done?

The short answer is, not much. Ira Magaziner got e-commerce right more than a decade ago: once laws and regulations are adjusted to the new reality of Internet commerce, the government should regulate or intervene minimally – and be sure to do no harm. That means the U.S. government shouldn't set e-commerce goals.

But it would be useful to:

Track the advance of e-commerce among developed countries and issue an annual report of global best practices. The Census Bureau has tracked U.S. e-commerce for years, using simplified definitions. It would be even more useful to standardize OECD e-commerce definitions so that reliable international comparisons can be made. Using those comparative statistics, the Commerce Department should prepare an annual report of international best practices for consideration by U.S. business.

Chapter 10.
The public dimension: e-government, e-education, universal access

The final Internet-leadership element is the public dimension. Consisting of three strands – e-government, e-education, and the imperative of universal Internet access – this vital element reflects the extent of government's direct participation. In all of the other leadership dimensions – broadband, wireless, human resources and R&D, innovation, and e-commerce – government may set the stage, encourage certain outcomes, or leave matters to others (or the market). In this, the public dimension, government itself is the central actor. What it does or doesn't do determines success.

America tackles e-government

As he set about reinventing government in September 1993, then Vice President Al Gore saw his information-technology agenda as part of his broader reinvention project. But he soon came to realize that information technology was the primary *means* of reinventing government. It was a way to encourage government departments to shift their focus from performing tasks to getting results, put their citizen "customers" first, and, paradoxically, use IT investments to reduce government spending.[1]

A number of important steps soon followed. Congress passed an IT management-reform act that created chief information officers in federal departments; President Clinton added a council of these chief information officers to advise on IT policy; and the White House announced a website that attracted worldwide attention. Congress passed an Internet privacy act that brought privacy protections in line with existing technology.

In the second Clinton term, the government provided more citizen services online, distributed federal benefits electronically, and, for businesses, published environmental, health, and safety regulations via the Internet.[2] Later, Clinton signed a paperwork-elimination act requiring that the 500 most-used government services be made available online. Congress mandated that the Defense Department create a single, online procurement website. And Gore introduced a comprehensive federal government portal, *FirstGov.gov* (now *USA.gov*). The results were impressive. At the end of 2000, the management consultancy Accenture ranked the United States third in its global survey of online government information and services, behind Canada and Singapore.[3]

Although he rejected most Clinton-Gore policies, incoming President Bush not only embraced those e-government initiatives, he sought to expand them. He was clear on what he wanted: e-government should be citizen-centered, results-oriented, and market-based. And he made it a priority – "expanded electronic government" was one of only five items[4] on the "President's Management Agenda" announced in July 2001. Bush sought to make it easier for citizens to access government services, reduce the federal reporting burden on businesses, lower the cost of government, and improve communication among all government levels. "Results," rather than "reinvention," was the motto, but it disguised considerable continuity.

President Bush signed a comprehensive e-Government Act in December 2002. The new law created an office of electronic government in the Office of Management and Budget and required all government departments and major agencies to report their e-government progress to the Congress annually. In addition, Bush himself asked for periodic progress reports on his management agenda, including e-government. That deeply impressed Karen Evans, his e-government chief, who said, "In my 23 years in government, I've seen many reform plans. But this time [with the President's management agenda], we have real accountability."[5]

According to Evans, the Bush administration sought to become "the world's leader in managing information technology to achieve the greatest gains in productivity, service, and results."[6] To do so, the administration carefully monitored over $68 billion in federal IT spending each year[7] with an eye to eliminating redundancy and improving the government's IT infrastructure. At the same time, they were providing the information and services citizens and business need. Each year the e-government office raised the bar and pushed harder.

By fall 2007, the administration could point to many successes. Federal IT systems were improving and nearly secured; IT workforce needs had been identified and were being filled; and half of the agencies were holding their IT cost overruns to less than 10% of project estimates.[8] In addition, in fiscal 2007, nearly 5 million referrals were made by the online government-benefits portal, more than 180,000 online federal-grant applications were received at *grants.gov*,[9] and over 90% of all 2006 tax returns were filed online.[10]

Meanwhile, the government streamlined its own personnel operations using IT: applicants for federal jobs posted their resumes online; some travel-voucher processing was being done there; and many federal employees received online training.[11] As a result, the United States had better and more efficient government, business and citizens had more information and an easier time dealing with government, and government departments communicated better with each other.

The United States held its own (3rd place – still behind Singapore and Canada) in Accenture's 2007 online government information and citizen services rankings. This success demonstrated clearly what the Bush administration could do when its ideology permitted the government to lead.

Toward the "paperless" office

By contrast, the Japanese trailed in e-government. Compared to the United States, Japan was slow to provide government employees with computers, slow to develop a central-government network, and slow to adopt the more efficient work style that widespread use of information technology permits. But the desire for administrative reform, the realization that Japan lagged behind other countries, and continuing budget pressures all convinced the IT Strategy Council that the Japanese government should do better.

The council made e-government one of the pillars of its e-Japan Strategy, persuaded that it was the key to completely reforming public administration. To set the reform in motion, it laid out exceptionally ambitious e-government goals. IT was to be used to make public administration much simpler, more efficient, and less burdensome for citizens and business. Administrative transactions within government and between government and citizens and industry should be handled online. Within three years, electronic documents, rather than paper, should be the norm; "paperless" offices should be the ultimate aim. But perhaps out of deference to its government sponsors, the council didn't specify any targets and deadlines for the e-government goals, and the bureaucrats, if only to avoid possible embarrassment, drafted implementation plans with few specifics.

Yet there was a seriousness of purpose. From the outset in 2001, the IT Strategic Headquarters encouraged each ministry to take a number of specific actions: put legal and regulatory information and administrative notifications online, work out procedures for online citizen services, develop a unified IT infrastructure within each ministry, and move toward online procurement.

These were general directives, however, and the headquarters left it to the ministries to decide how to accomplish these tasks. Each ministry, of course, had its own way of doing things; no one was made accountable for a ministry's e-government progress; and the IT strategic Headquarters was unwilling or unable to crack the whip. As a result, little was accomplished. Moreover, Japan's centralized administrative system forced the prefectural and local governments to wait for e-government guidance from Tokyo before taking action.

Although the planners persisted, the advance was slow. In 2003, a chief information officers' council drew up a plan for "next-generation electronic government," but implementation was again left to the individual ministries. In 2005, yet another e-government plan confessed there were "still e-government issues" and urged that the most important citizen and business services be put online within a year. The planners also exhorted their colleagues to *use* the improved central-government information network and the new network linked to local government offices. In 2006, the New IT Reform Strategy acknowledged some progress – "it is now possible to perform most procedures handled by the national government online" – but complained that use of these services (about 10%) was not increasing because they were inconvenient.

To increase the pressure, the strategic headquarters set up a government-wide IT management office and IT program offices in each ministry. It also turned to a committee of outside academic and business experts to carry out a "strict" evaluation of each ministry's information systems.[12] This gambit seems to have worked. After the outside experts examined the IT procurement process "in excruciating detail," for example, the government was able to reduce its procurement costs by 30%.[13] Many of these problems were reflected in Accenture's 2007 ranking of Japan's online citizen services as tenth best in the world.[14] The

Accenture analysts reported that the Japanese government still had no comprehensive citizen-service strategy and continued to struggle with persuading its citizens to use its online services.

Ironically, in tackling the five e-Japan strategy priorities, the Japanese government has been least successful with e-government, using IT to improve its own operations and online services. The reasons for this seem reasonably clear: lack of bold targets and deadlines at the outset; lack of central leadership and ministry balkiness; the difficulties of top-down network building and coordination; and (unsurprisingly) greater bureaucratic confidence in paper than in electrons. Unfortunate data leaks also fueled citizen mistrust of Japan's online services, and a recent scandal involving tens of millions of unfiled (paper) pension documents will make them even less trustful. In all, the Japanese government has made progress in e-government, but it still lags well behind the United States.

What should be done?

The United States has continued to advance e-government, because President George W. Bush made it part of his management agenda and oversight was given to the powerful Office of Management and Budget. But now it is time to raise the bar again.

Maintain e-government's priority status: make e-government a part of the incoming President's management agenda and set more challenging goals, reflecting private-sector practice.

Connecting the schools

Shortly after Clinton's 1996 re-election, the Federal Communications Commission (FCC) set about connecting all of the schools and libraries within four years. With the strong support of Senators Olympia Snow and Jay Rockefeller, Congress produced legislation that authorized the FCC to establish an "e-rate" fund. The FCC then ordered communications carriers to contribute about 1% of their revenues to the fund, which was nearly matched by the states and localities. Money from the e-rate fund continues to be distributed to school districts based on their ability to pay. Wealthier districts receive a 40% subsidy to underwrite school Internet connections and operating costs; poorer districts receive up to 90% subsidies.

Although the initial e-rate program had its critics, it was remarkably successful. By the end of the Clinton administration in 2000, fully 98% of all American schools were connected to the Internet – and nearly as many libraries.

By the time the Bush administration took office in 2001, however, the e-rate program was stretched to its limit. School districts and libraries had requested $5.2 billion to improve their Internet connections, but only $2.5 billion was available. The mismatch was eventually resolved by giving funding priority to districts where *schools* were not yet connected and, secondarily, to districts that wanted to provide Internet access in additional *classrooms*.[15]

At the same time, criticism of the e-rate program grew louder. Because so much money was at stake, rumors of fraud had circulated almost from the program's beginning.

The rumors were substantiated by a 2001 review of twenty-two schools (by the now-defunct Arthur Andersen accounting firm) that found several million dollars in "inappropriate payments and unjustified costs." In late 2002, the Justice Department successfully brought a number of criminal cases against fraudulent IT equipment and service providers.[16] On top of that, cash shortfalls in late summer 2003 led to an unannounced moratorium on all e-rate distributions – and to Congressional hearings. Eventually, safeguards were put in place and cash reserves bolstered so that distributions could be resumed late the following year (2004).[17]

Despite these problems, the Internet played an ever greater role in U.S. classrooms. By the end of 2005, nine in ten public schools used the Internet for instructional planning, student assessment data, and high-quality digital content, such as access to digital libraries and museums and other text, images, sound, and video. One-third of the schools turned to the Internet to provide distance education for their students; about half used it to provide professional development courses for teachers.[18]

Moreover, a 2006 survey of elementary and secondary school teachers found that two-thirds of them were using technology in the classroom at least twice a week and more than a third were using it every day. Even more striking, 54% agreed that information technology had changed the way they taught "a great deal." Still, the survey's authors concluded that American schools were about where American business had been twenty years earlier: "...on the cusp of radically transforming the learning environment."[19]

Two years behind

Japan began connecting its schools in 1998, two years behind the United States. Preoccupied with preparing their students for formal entrance exams to the next higher level of education, Japanese teachers initially showed little interest in information technology, and the education ministry didn't push them. So in the late 1990s, connecting the schools proceeded at a slow pace. In 2000, this situation led one parent, Masakuni Kumeda, a Cisco executive in Japan, to complain that his 10-year-old son was not learning about computers in school; Kumeda felt compelled to send him to a private, after-school computer course, called FutureKids, where computer and Internet skills were taught.[20]

At the end of 2000, only 54% of Japanese schools were connected to the Internet, just over half the U.S. total at that point. In fall 2000, however, the new e-Japan Strategy called for a "reinforcement" of IT-driven education in elementary schools, high schools, and colleges – and for outsiders to train teachers in the use of IT. But the first implementation plan, developed six months later, was overly ambitious, calling for all schools to be connected to the Internet within 12 months. Moreover, the plan called for all schools to have a school-wide, local-area network so that each classroom would have access to the Internet by the end of 2002. Japan did travel down this path, though not at that speed.

But by the end of 2005, all of the nation's *schools* had Internet access – as did nearly half of elementary-school, and nearly three-quarters of high-school *classrooms*. Moreover, nearly 90% of the former had broadband connections, and all of the latter had them. IT teacher training was generally available to everyone, and as in the United States, four out of five Japanese teachers felt prepared to teach using information technology.[21]

It is difficult to compare school use of the Internet (and information technology more broadly) in the United States and Japan. A 2005 comparison of technology at *one* suburban U.S. middle school and a comparable school in Japan found that the American school was better equipped, had better IT support, and the school's leadership was more committed to technology use in the classroom.[22] But a better indicator may be the Japanese government's own 2006 New IT Reform plan that suggests lingering dissatisfaction with Japan's e-education effort. Despite the impressive statistics about Internet access in Japanese schools and classrooms and related teacher training, the planners called for more IT use. As has been observed repeatedly, putting the hardware in place is the easy part; the more difficult task is changing the old ways of doing things.

To maintain Japan's international competitiveness, the planners wrote, the nation's children must become familiar with information technology at the elementary and high school levels. But, the planners continued, there were not yet enough computers for teachers, administrative functions have not been digitized, there are too few support personnel, and so forth. The plan then set targets for fixing most of these defects by 2010, while urging better standards for IT use, more distance education, and better digital educational content.[23]

Taken all in all, the United States and Japan now appear to be roughly equal in terms of schools and classrooms with Internet access, teacher IT training, and the possibility of IT and Internet-related instruction. Nonetheless, it appears that American schools generally have better integrated the Internet (and information technology) into their instruction and administration. Although American primary and secondary teachers are increasingly focused on "leaving no child behind," Japanese teachers remain preoccupied with the far more-difficult challenge of preparing students for unforgiving entrance exams that don't test computer skills. Thus American teachers have greater flexibility (and supervisory support) to introduce instruction in computer skills and Internet-related materials into the curriculum.

Still, although computer skills are being taught, neither the American nor the Japanese educational establishments (nor anyone else) has yet figured out the best way to integrate the Internet and its possibilities into the primary and secondary curriculum. That will require extensive reform of the entire curriculum – and considerably more time.

What remains to be done?

Review the entire K-12 curriculum with an eye to integrating IT and the Internet where possible. Virtually all schools and most classrooms are now connected to the Internet. Children are being taught IT literacy, that is, how to use, in an age-appropriate manner, a computer, certain software programs, and the Internet. Some schools are undertaking distance learning. And imaginative teachers are bringing the Internet's resources into the classroom in productive ways. But what is still lacking is a thorough review of the curriculum to determine how IT and the Internet might be used to augment and improve instruction across the curriculum and at all levels.

Five areas deserve special attention. First, IT is ideally suited to strengthening math instruction; easily downloadable exercises, drills, and games could be used to reinforce concepts and provide required practice. Second, an extensive series of laboratory demonstrations on the World Wide Web could be used in science instruction at all levels; such demonstrations could be introduced at school and reviewed by individual students as often as necessary in school or at home. Third, Internet drills can be used to improve English as a second language and foreign language instruction; again, explanations, exercises, drills, and games could be repeated until the student masters them.

Fourth, IT and the Internet could be used in special education, with explanations and drills tailored to different learning styles and difficulties for repeated use. And fifth, distance education should be vastly expanded as network speeds improve; this may be the best way to not only provide subjects, such as calculus and Chinese, not offered in a particular curriculum, but also to help equalize the quality of instruction across vastly divergent schools.

Closing the digital divide

If you believe, as most do, that the Internet really does change the way we live, and work, and play, universal Internet – these days "broadband " – access should be a very high priority. Over time, policy makers concluded that universal access to electricity and telephones was essential. Although they may differ on how to get there, most of those officials' successors now agree that universal broadband access is also indispensible. For that reason, progress toward universal broadband makes up the third strand of the public dimension of Internet leadership.

During the Clinton administration, universal Internet access was the oft-stated policy of the U.S. government. The aim of Gore's National Information Infrastructure initiative was to bring all Americans online, and the universal-access theme appeared in many speeches and policy statements during that era. At the time, universal access meant *dial-up* access. So the government devised strategies to make dial-up available to all.

Following passage of the Telecommunications Act of 1996, for example, Clinton's FCC sought to expand home Internet access and usage by making it more affordable. To drive down prices, the FCC required the regional telephone companies (the cable companies were not subject to regulation at the time) to open their residential telephone lines to outside Internet-service providers, the telephone companies' competitors. As intended, the ensuing competition drove down the cost of Internet access, and the number of Americans with home Internet surged. But realizing that this strategy would take time to reach everyone, the FCC, with Congressional approval, also created the e-rate program that brought Internet access to virtually all of America's schools and libraries by the end of 2000. As a result, children had access at school and, in theory at least, adults could go online at their local library. To chart progress toward the universal access goal, the government also issued a series of "Falling Through the Net" reports.

There was more. As his administration was winding down in April 2000, Clinton announced "A National Call to Action to Close the Digital Divide" that involved the federal, state, and local governments and relied on substantial private-sector support.[24] By the end of that year, 57% of Americans could access the Internet at home or work,[25] and 5.2 million of the nation's homes and small businesses already had broadband.[26]

When the Bush administration came to power in 2001, the nation was transitioning to broadband. And the broadband rollout, a Bush administration official soon made clear, would be led by the market, not the government. But because the government would have little control over this process, there were no pronouncements about universal broadband coverage. That was hardly a market objective. In fact, in 2003, the administration took a step in the opposite direction: it no longer compelled the telephone companies to open their local lines to outside DSL providers.

In 2004, however, pressured by presidential rival John Kerry, George Bush unexpectedly promised that all Americans would have affordable broadband by 2007. The broadband divide would be closed, according to the White House website, through broadband competition among the telephone and cable companies, along with the electric-power and wireless companies, all of which could provide broadband.

But the administration did little to promote universal broadband. Hoped-for broadband competition failed to materialize: the telephone vs. cable-company competition was slow to develop; the electric-power companies barely entered the market; and wireless competition continued to be mostly over the horizon. As a result, broadband in the United States remained relatively expensive, and the 2007 goal of universal access was not met.

Still, the number of U.S. broadband subscribers has increased sharply: in most demographic categories, subscribers nearly doubled between 2005 and 2008. In spring 2008, a Pew Internet Project survey found that 55% of the population had home broadband, 10% had dial-up service, and 3% had Internet service but didn't know which type it was. That left over 40% of American adults without broadband and 32% with no home Internet access at all. Also, when Pew asked both dial-up and non-Internet users whether home broadband was *available*, one-quarter said it wasn't and an additional 13% didn't know. Nor were mobile phones a help: only 2% of Americans subscribed to mobile-phone Internet access in mid-2007.[27]

Why don't Americans have broadband? Of the 10% with dial-up access (a group disproportionately female and living in rural areas), nearly two-thirds professed to be uninterested in faster access. But when asked what it would take to get them to switch to broadband, one-third said they would switch to broadband if the price fell, and one-sixth said they would subscribe when broadband became available.

But of the 32% without *any* Internet access, most were over 65 years old or earning less than $30,000 a year. Asked why they weren't online, one-third were not interested, 12% had no access, 9% found the Internet too difficult to use, and

7% thought it too expensive. But there was also good news: although access prices dropped only slightly (4%) from 2006 to 2007, broadband subscribers rose 17%, with the largest gains among those over 50 or living in rural areas. In fact, broadband lost ground (-11%) only among those earning less than $20,000 a year.[28]

Although some state governments, such as Kentucky, and several nonprofit organizations, such as the Benton Foundation, are working to close the broadband divide, the Bush administration continues to rely solely on market forces. Legislation has been introduced that would require "mapping" of where broadband is now available and where it isn't; but as of this writing, that bill has not received Congressional approval. Moreover, while northeast Asia and Western Europe were transitioning to much-faster *fiber* broadband, fiber was available to only 7% of American households at the end of 2007, and fewer than one in three of those subscribed.

In Japan, universal home Internet access was envisioned in the government's 1994 advanced communications society plan. During the latter 1990s, more and more Japanese dialed-up from their homes, although doing so was expensive. In 1998, to broaden Internet access and use, the government began its own program of connecting the nation's schools and libraries. The following year, Japan's telecommunications ministry began considering ways to encourage a competitive market for home Internet service providers that would lead to lower prices and greater access. That same year, after the launch of DoCoMo's "i-mode" service, millions of Japanese began to access the Internet via mobile phone.

As the century ended, nearly half (46% of the Japanese, compared to 54% of Americans) had home Internet access, connecting by dial-up or mobile phone. But only a few thousand had cable broadband access, and only a few thousand had a DSL connection.

Japan's 2001 e-Japan strategy focused on expanding broadband and bridging the digital divide. The goal was to make high-speed (DSL or cable) or ultra-high-speed (fiber) broadband available to 85% of Japan's 47 million households by 2005. When this target was met – and the Japanese schools were connected – by the end of 2002, the vast majority of Japanese homes had high-speed Internet service available to them, and more than 20% had access to fiber. The e-Japan strategy also urged government planning to narrow the digital divide, giving special attention to rural areas, the elderly, and the handicapped.

But broadband *usage* didn't keep pace with availability. So the government's 2003 strategy sought to increase consumer demand for the new, high-speed infrastructure by introducing IT literacy programs for adults and encouraging new uses of the Internet. Although this plan was less successful, sharp DSL competition that encouraged increasingly fast access speeds – and the lowest broadband prices in the world – brought millions online. In 2006, yet another government strategy explicitly called for making broadband available to *all* Japanese homes by 2010. To reach that goal, the ministry of communications then developed a roadmap that involved both the public and private sectors – as well as incentives.

Meanwhile, the Japanese continued to use their mobile phones to access the Internet at ever-increasing speeds.

Third-generation (3G) mobile phones were introduced in 2001 with access speeds of 200-300 *kilobits* per second (broadband by the old FCC definition). The nation's mobile infrastructure was soon upgraded, access speeds increased, and nearly everyone made the switch to 3G. On the drawing board for 2010 are 3.9G (often called 4G in the United States) mobile phones with download speeds of 100-300 *megabits* per second. Ultra-fast, combined fiber-mobile networks are on the board, too.

How well has Japan done in closing the broadband divide? The short answer is reasonably well. High-speed home broadband was available to 95% of the Japanese in 2007 – with 100% scheduled for 2010. High-speed, mobile-phone access is also available throughout the country. Fiber is also available to over 85% of Japan's households, and plans call for 95% of them to be within range of it by 2010. So the *availability* of high-speed Internet access, whether at home or roaming, will soon no longer be an issue.

But the Japanese face a broadband *usage* gap similar to that in the United States. At the end of 2007, nearly two-thirds subscribed to high-speed home broadband – and one-quarter had ultra-fast fiber access. In addition, nearly three-quarters of the population subscribed to mobile-phone service with high-speed Internet access.[29] Yet that left over one-third without broadband, which wasn't even available to 5% of the population at the end of 2007.

More surprising – and again similar to the United States – 31.5% of the Japanese *didn't use the Internet at all* in spring 2007.[30] According to a usage-trend survey by the communications ministry, Japan's non-Internet users tended to be older and poorer, but they didn't necessarily live in rural areas. The ministry's analysis indicated that people under 12 or over 50 were less likely to use the Internet, as were those earning less than $35,000 a year. But where one lived was far less important. According to a ministry survey in spring 2006, 80% used the Internet in larger cities, as did nearly 75% in "other cities," and nearly 70% in towns and villages.[31] Looking at trends in the later survey, the ministry found that from spring 2004 to spring 2007, the gap among age groups narrowed, while the income and urban-rural gap increased slightly. The ministry did not ask *why* people were not online.[32]

Which country has done a better job of closing the digital divide? The nod must go to Japan.[33] Home Internet usage is roughly equal in both countries, about two-thirds of the adult population, and home *broadband* usage – the correct standard for measuring today's digital divide – is also roughly the same. But Japan's broadband infrastructure is more developed (95% to America's estimated 80% or so), meaning that broadband access is *available* to substantially more households in Japan; it is just a matter of persuading people to use broadband – not bring it to them.

Japan has also vastly surpassed the United States in *mobile* Internet access, another aspect of the digital divide. Japan's 3G infrastructure is available to virtually all Japanese, while that in the United States is still confined to larger cities. That encouraged 70% of the Japanese population (88 million) to subscribe to mobile-phone Internet access, compared to 2% (5.5 million) in the United States.

In addition, Japan has an overwhelming lead in *fiber* infrastructure and usage – the digital divide standard of tomorrow. At the end of 2007, fiber was *available* to over 80% of Japanese households, but only 7% of those in America. Taking advantage of that infrastructure and relatively low cost, one-quarter of Japanese homes now subscribe to fiber, compared to only 2% of American. In addition, the Japanese government is committed to universal access and is taking active steps to achieve it, while the U.S. government is not.

What should the United States do to close the digital divide?

As the Pew surveys indicate, the task will not be easy. But here are some suggestions:

1. Make *ultra-fast* broadband available to all Americans. Until federal, state, and local governments commit themselves to the principle of universal, ultra-fast broadband, the United States will continue to have a patchwork broadband infrastructure.

The federal government eventually committed to making electric and telephone service available nationwide. It would be far better to pledge the government to providing universal ultra-fast broadband at the outset. But that can't simply be a campaign promise, as it was with President Bush; it must become a national priority. This will mean fiber broadband access for all but those living in the most remote areas – and ultra-fast wireless or satellite for them. How this should be done is discussed in Chapter 12.

2. Encourage all Americans to make use of these networks. As mentioned earlier, this would require public and private-sector educational campaigns aimed particularly at the elderly, the poor, and rural and central-city residents to overcome fears and describe benefits; cheap computers and even simpler access devices; simple, basic software; widely available IT training and technical support; and lower access prices. States and localities are best positioned to implement these programs – with federal incentives and help from the private sector. A restructured Universal Service Fund should play a large role in closing the divide in broadband, as it did in closing the telephone gap.

No-nonsense deployment and usage deadlines mentioned earlier would concentrate thinking and improve chances of success. Annual government progress reports of both availability and usage would remind us all how near we are to closing the digital divide.

Chapter 11.
Broadband lessons from South Korea, Canada, and France

Despite great handicaps, three countries – South Korea, Canada, and France – have become global broadband leaders.

South Korea's GDP per person is less than half that of the United States or Japan; moreover, it survived a financial crisis that brought the country to its knees just a decade ago. Canada is the world's second-largest country in terms of area; its rural and "remote" communities stretch from the Pacific well into the Atlantic, from North Dakota to the Arctic Circle. And France was so slow to enter the Internet age that it was described as technologically backward less than a decade ago.

Yet those societies now lead the United States (and most other developed countries) in broadband usage, speeds, and prices. Although the three used different approaches, government played a central role in advancing broadband in each.

South Korea wants to lead the world

South Korea has its own claim to global Internet leadership. From the outset, it has ranked among the world's leaders in broadband usage, ahead of Canada, France, Japan, and the United States by a substantial margin. Today over 80% of the South Korean population subscribes to broadband, and its success is by no means limited to that technology. South Korea was the first to offer third-generation mobile phones in 2000. It is among the world's leaders in IT manufacturing, IT literacy, e-education, e-government, and e-commerce. And it has its own plans for combining ultra-fast broadband and wireless networks – what it calls a Broadband Converged Network – by 2010.[1] How did this come about?

South Korea also had significant advantages. The country is relatively small and densely populated: half of its people live in apartments, and 40% live in the capital city of Seoul – ideal for the spread of broadband. The people are well educated and generally fascinated by new technology. The bureaucrats there, as in Japan, are unusually able and used to planning and leading large projects such as broadband expansion; and, just as important, the private sector is accustomed to following.

Having earlier developed plans to build the IT industry and expand IT use in administration, national security, and education,[2] Korean officials were quick to grasp the importance of Al Gore's 1993 National Information Infrastructure proposal. They were determined to further strengthen South Korea's IT industry, improve the nation's international competitiveness, and make Seoul a hub of the world's digital economy. They launched the Korean Information Infrastructure (KII) initiative in 1995 to create the high-speed Internet backbone that would be needed to connect subsidiary networks, the next stage of the nation's digital advance. The KII project also supported future Internet growth by funding IT research, several IT pilot projects, and the development of software applications. (All told, the government invested nearly $750 million in this strategy by the end of 2003.)

The following year, 1996, the government launched the first of a series of master plans to promote the use of IT and the Internet. It established an IT promotion committee headed by the president and advised by business and academic leaders. The committee's goal was to make South Korea a world Internet leader by 2010. Soon thereafter, the government announced a national framework for IT progress, with yearly targets to be met in critical areas. To energize the private sector, the government offered low-interest loans to encourage construction of high-speed networks and information-technology R&D, as well as subsidies for IT-industry-employee training.

These loans and subsidies came from a special fund to which both the government and the telecom companies contributed. By 2004, the fund had provided $5.7 billion in loans for industry proposals approved by the government, and the latter had invested an additional $8.2 billion from the national budget to promote IT. The private sector invested even more, approximately $23 billion on access networks alone by the end of 2005.[3]

South Korea's broadband breakthrough came early, in July 1998. A new cable company named Thrunet launched the first commercial broadband service using its own network. At that time, executives at Korea Telecom (KT), the government-owned national telephone company, were arguing among themselves. Some favored expanding the company's very slow ISDN digital service, others wanted to offer faster DSL broadband. They quickly came together and jumped in with their own DSL service when a second upstart, a new local telephone company with *its* own network called Hanaro Telecom, began offering DSL broadband in April 1999. KT quickly caught up with the front runners because of its existing nationwide network, its well-known brand, and its deep pockets. That set the stage for fierce broadband competition in urban areas and sharply falling prices (often to below cost). The government had made it easy for newcomers to enter the broadband market and compete vigorously.

As broadband access spread, the government took steps to encourage South Koreans to *use* the Internet. As part of another master plan, Cyber Korea 21, announced in the late 1990s, the government began a nationwide IT training program for 10 million South Koreans. People ranging from housewives to soldiers and to the disabled and elderly were taught how to use a PC, run some popular applications, and access the Internet at libraries and elsewhere. At about the same time, the government began offering basic PCs (and later used PCs) to the general public at bargain prices that could be paid in installments. That lowered prices in the commercial computer market as well. As a result, a great many Koreans could access the Internet with their own computers, sharply boosting demand for broadband.

Through an imaginative certification program for new apartment buildings, the government also spurred broadband demand, awarding three types of certificates to new apartment buildings depending on the capacity of their wiring for Internet use. The top certificate went to buildings wired with fiber and capable of handling 100 megabits per second or more. Buildings thus certified proved to be very popular, permitting their landlords to charge rental premiums – a powerful incentive for broadband use in a country where half of the population lives in apartment buildings that are replaced every 25 to 30 years.

Moreover, the government itself added to broadband demand by connecting its agencies, plus public research centers and major libraries, to the Internet. Also, beginning in 2000, elementary and high schools were offered discounted broadband access, and by December 2001, all were connected. Broadband usage surged, and by year-end, residential broadband subscriptions topped 7 million[4], and half of all Korean households had broadband – six years before the United States.

In 2002, the government launched yet another master plan, e-Korea Vision 2007, aimed squarely at achieving global Internet leadership. A main goal was to get 90% of the South Korean population online by 2006.[5] To reach that ambitious target, the government intervened directly in the broadband market by requiring the national carrier, KT, to open its residential networks to outside competitors at relatively low cost. That order was not intended to create competition in urban areas, where it already existed. The idea was to prevent broadband *overcapacity* in urban areas and to create competition in *rural* areas where little cable existed. Meanwhile, the earlier South Korean infrastructure plan was entering its final phase. Soon over 80% of all South Korean households had access to high-speed broadband.

The government then announced its next step: a long-range Broadband Converged Network plan. This plan calls for integrating existing broadband networks to provide high-speed (50-100 Mbps) network access to 20 million Koreans, two-fifths of the population, by 2010. That access may be delivered by fiber or by Very High-speed DSL (vDSL, capable of 50+ Mbps). The South Korean government has approached fiber far more cautiously than its Japanese counterpart. It has left the advance of that technology to the market, without offering any incentives or subsidies.

Initially, the private sector moved slowly with fiber. Although the urban DSL and vDSL markets were saturating, KT believed it was too expensive to lay fiber to living quarters or commercial buildings and developed instead a fiber-to-the-curb approach. But in early 2007, as demand grew, KT announced plans to invest $1.3 billion over the next three years to take fiber to the premises of *new* residential areas, and competitors soon made public their own plans. And by mid-2008, fiber Internet connections exceeded DSL and vDSL links, and South Korea lead the world in fiber usage with nearly 37% of its households connected to fiber, according to the FTTH Council's semi-annual rankings.[6]

South Korea has had remarkable success with mobile phones as well. Its companies were the first in the world to offer 3G mobile-phone service – in October 2000 (a year ahead of Japan). By 2007, they were approaching the high-water mark of one mobile phone per inhabitant, with teenagers driving the market. That saturation is essential to the success of the government's most recent "u-Korea" master plan, announced in 2006. Incorporating an earlier plan ("IT 839") that aimed at keeping the nation on the cutting edge of information technology, the more comprehensive u-Korea project envisions *unified* broadband, mobile, and sensor networks contributing to the world's first "u-society" by 2016.

Explanations of South Korea's remarkable broadband success usually center on five factors. First, compact geography, with 80% of the people living in urban areas. Second, the early, disruptive broadband competition among Thrunet, Hanaro Telecom, and KT that led to exceptionally low broadband prices and surging demand. Third, the role of government in providing infrastructure, encouraging the private sector to enter the broadband marketplace, creating broadband demand, and connecting the government and schools. Fourth, a world-class IT manufacturing industry, which kept equipment prices low. And fifth, a culture that is very receptive to new technology.

There are others factors as well. A killer app, Internet telephoning, drove the broadband advance. Ubiquitous *PC Bangs*, or computer cafes, introduced tens of thousands of young Koreans to ultra-fast broadband and team computer games. Families invested in broadband to further their children's education in a nation obsessed with education. Moreover, broadband (and IT) success satisfied, at least in part, the citizenry's intense determination that their country be recognized as a world leader.

What can the South Koreans teach us?

Among the nation's many contributions, three stand out:

- *A continuing government drive toward Internet leadership and cutting-edge IT status* is essential to making it happen. Without government determination, South Korea would not be a global Internet leader.
- *Government planning and incentives* are required to ensure that a nationwide broadband infrastructure is put in place. Reliance on market forces is not enough, but keen private-sector competition, encouraged by the government, is essential.
- *Government programs to increase broadband demand* should go hand in hand with deployment planning. Imaginative government programs, such as providing low-cost computers, IT literacy training, and expanded IT usage by government itself, can substantially increase demand – and Internet usage.

Canada connects its communities

Canada is determined to take broadband to the 4,200 communities strung across its huge landscape. A far easier task would be to reach the bulk of Canada's 32 million citizens. They live within a band – 3,000 miles long and 150 miles deep – atop the northern border of the continental United States – and half of them live in Canada's ten largest cities. Taking broadband to communities in exceptionally remote and isolated areas on the Arctic Circle and elsewhere presents a challenge of a very different order.

The Canadian parliament set the overall direction of the nation's Internet policy with its Telecommunications Act of 1993, passed three years before its American counterpart. The Canadian act mandated reliable, affordable communications services for "Canadians in all areas." To achieve that, the law stated, the government should "foster reliance" on market forces but should also consider the "social and economic needs of telecommunications users." Over the years, government officials have utilized market forces (and competition) to provide Internet access to urban Canadians. But from the outset, the officials understood that even a vigorously competitive market would not extend the Internet to the nation's rural areas. To do that, the government would have to develop targeted programs.[7]

The first of these, the Community Access Program (CAP), came two years later, in 1995. The CAP focused on connecting *all* 4,200 communities. In that dial-up era, the CAP sought to provide residents everywhere with affordable access to the Internet through schools, libraries, and community centers.

Canadian regulators encouraged competition among Internet-access providers in the profitable urban areas where telephone and cable service is nearly universal. In 1997, the Canadian Radio-television Telecommunications Commission (CRTC), an independent federal agency similar to America's FCC, required Canada's *telephone* companies to open their residential lines to outside competitors. A year later, the CRTC compelled the *cable* companies to open their residential lines as well. And in both cases, the CRTC set a relatively low interconnection price for outside competitors.

As a result, would-be competitors could choose to compete using either DSL or cable, without having to develop their own extensive networks. The induced competition caused the cost of Internet access to fall across urban Canada, and Internet demand rose.

Turning again to the rural communities in 1998, the federal government announced an even bolder vision and plan, "Connecting Canadians," which aimed at making Canada "the most connected nation in the world." To its increasingly successful Community Access Program, government officials added a "Smart Communities" element: competitively chosen demonstration projects in each of Canada's provinces, as well as one in the far north and one in a native American ("First Nation" in Canadian parlance) community.

These Smart Communities were meant to act as "learning laboratories," encouraging innovative use of Internet technologies at the grass roots.[8] Meanwhile, at the CRTC's urging, the telephone companies upgraded their infrastructure. By 1999, more than 97% of Canada's telephone lines were dial-up capable, and the telephone companies, with CRTC-approved plans, were working toward 100%. But despite those efforts, as 2000 ended, Canada still ranked tenth in the world in Internet *usership*, behind Korea, the United States, and Japan.[9] That would soon change as Canada turned to broadband.

In January 2001, as the Bush and Koizumi governments took office, Canadian Minister of Industry Brian Tobin announced the appointment of a 36-member National Broadband Task Force. Its mission was to advise the government on how best to make high-speed broadband services available to all Canadian communities by 2004. Tobin saw this as part of a challenge Canada had always faced: the challenge of connecting all citizens in the nation's vast territory. This time, it was essential that all Canadians share in the benefits of high-speed broadband – improved services, such as distance learning and "tele-health," along with regional and local economic development. All stakeholders had a seat at the task-force table. Nearly half of that body was composed of industry CEOs from the telephone and cable companies, and the equipment manufacturers; the rest represented rural and First-Nation communities, digital content producers, and educational, library, and health-center users.[10]

In its mid-2001 final report, the task force underscored the importance of taking broadband to all Canadian communities: "The task force is convinced that over the next 10 to 20 years...[b]roadband will transform the way we learn, the way we work, the way we use our leisure, the way we govern ourselves, the way we communicate, the way we express ourselves and the way we care for each other." Moreover, the technology had the potential to bridge the "systemic gap" in the quality of life enjoyed by Canadians living in or near urban areas and those in rural areas, a gap that exists "on every basic measure of human well-being."[11] But if the government did nothing further, if it relied solely on market forces, broadband would not reach three-quarters of Canada's communities – with one-quarter of the nation's population – by the 2004 deadline. Further government action was essential.

The task force then set out principles to guide the broadband deployment: the private sector should take the lead in developing and operating networks – and its risk should be maximized; public-private partnerships should be encouraged and communities should participate in the planning of the networks; governments at all levels should facilitate the deployment through policy decisions and "publicly assisted programs;" and the deployment should encourage the development of content and services as well as infrastructure.

More specifically, the task force urged that broadband be extended to public facilities, businesses, and homes, that the networks be open to all, that homes have symmetrical Internet access (equally fast uploads and downloads) of 1.5 megabits per second, and that the cost of service be comparable in urban and rural areas. The task force saw two models for extending broadband to the 3,000-plus communities the market wouldn't reach. One was a top-down "infrastructure support model," using incentives to supply broadband infrastructure and services. The other was a bottom-up "community aggregator model" aimed at stimulating demand for broadband. Often, the task force predicted, broadband expansion would require a mix of those two. And it wouldn't be cheap: the estimated cost of extending 1.5 Mbps broadband to all Canadian communities at that point was $867 million to $1.27 billion. (All dollar figures in this section are in *U.S.*, not Canadian dollars.)

The federal government then moved ahead. It launched a $66-million pilot program to help First-Nation, rural, and northern communities find ways to aggregate demand in order to attract broadband-service providers. This proved to be a slow process: communities had to apply for money to create business plans and then reapply for implementation funding.[12]

The government launched a second major effort. Convinced that satellite was the only way to bring broadband to some 400 localities (mostly First-Nation communities in the north), it announced a $110-million National Satellite Initiative in October 2003. The money was used to purchase broadband satellite capacity; but again the communities had to apply individually – and cover the cost of purchasing and setting up the necessary equipment to receive the satellite signal.[13]

The federal government also eventually invested $270 million in terrestrial broadband infrastructure. It funded the laying of fiber-optic cable along roads leading north (while permitting broadband service providers and towns to connect to the cable) and municipal infrastructure projects.[14] Ottawa also decreed that whenever government money helped fund a network's construction, it had to be open to all.

From 2002 to 2006, Canada's ten provinces also invested a total of nearly $490 million in broadband projects. Alberta spent $172 million on a 'SuperNet" that linked 422 communities outside the province's population centers; Quebec invested $134 million to link its schools and towns to the provincial government's network; and Saskatchewan laid out $104 million on three projects that brought broadband to well over 450 communities.[15] The private sector had invested even more. But despite all of these efforts, over 60% of Canada's communities did not have broadband by the original deadline, the end of 2004.[16]

In 2005, to chart a way forward, the federal government named a Telecommunications Policy Review Panel. Reporting in the following spring, the panel declared that the policy and regulatory framework put in place more than a decade earlier had served Canadians well. But it should be revised to reflect the profound advances in telecommunications technologies and markets. Reflecting a change in government philosophy, the panel urged phasing out the regulations requiring telephone and cable companies to open their lines to competitors. Instead, the panel called for retroactive regulation of the market and better incentives for private-sector investment in new networks.

The panel also raised the bar, urging the government to set a new target of "ubiquitous" (defined as 98%) broadband coverage by 2010. "Vigorous competition" should be the main driver of this undertaking, but "some" government action in high-cost rural and remote areas would still be needed. To fill this need, the panel recommended a new U-CAN program. U-CAN would offer limited subsidies to service providers that submitted the lowest-cost bids to extend the broadband infrastructure to rural areas – and complete the job of making broadband available to all Canadians.[17] As of fall 2008, however, the government had neither accepted nor rejected the report.

Meanwhile, the CRTC, without specifying a purpose, had earlier ordered the telephone and cable companies to establish special "deferral accounts," and to pay into them all of the profits they made in urban areas above "merited-service prices" (set by the CRTC). In 2006, it ordered the companies to begin spending down their "deferral accounts" on broadband services for rural and remote communities and the disabled. In time-honored Anglo-Saxon fashion, the companies immediately went to court to prevent this. But unless they succeed, an additional $650 million in private-sector money will be invested in taking broadband to the countryside. That sum, along with the federal and provincial government investments, would total $1.5 billion by the end of 2008.

At that point, nearly two-thirds of Canada's *communities* would have broadband with only two years to go to meet the new 2010 deadline.[18] But, viewed another way, 93% of Canada's *households* had access to broadband (with two-thirds subscribing) at the end of 2007. And Canada continued to rank number one among the world's most developed (G8) nations[19] in broadband usage.[20] Moreover, Canada's Prime Minister, Stephen Harper pledged, shortly before his October 2008 reelection, to invest $80 million for each of the next for each of the next five years to complete Canada's broadband network. But so far, the government has not taken the next step of encouraging the transition to fiber networks (although Bell Canada began fiber-to-the-premises trials in early 2006).

What does the Canadian experience teach us?

The importance of a number of key steps:

- *An inclusive vision.* Within months of Bill Gates's 1994 discovery of the Internet, the Canadian government launched a project to make Internet access universal by distributing it through schools, libraries, and community centers.

- *Timely (in this case, 2001) embrace of broadband,* along with the appointment of a national task force, comprised of all the stakeholders, to chart the way to universal access.

- *Regulatory creation of competitive, urban broadband markets* by requiring that residential lines of telephone *and* cable networks be opened to outside competitors.

- *Governmental recognition that other policies (and sub-sidies) would be needed* to extend broadband beyond urban and suburban areas.

- *Cooperative efforts of federal, provincial, and local governments* – which, in conjunction with the private sector, have made Canada a world broadband leader.

- *The importance of a Prime Minister's determination to take broadband to all Canadians* "to ensure a modern economy throughout rural and remote Canada," as the press release put it.[21]

France learns from others

Millions of French men and women enjoyed some Internet-like benefits long before the commercial Internet existed. That was possible, because in 1982, the French Post, Telephone, and Telecommunications ministry gave away some nine million "Minitels" to French telephone subscribers. These Minitels were small units, about the size of a football, that combined a screen and keyboard in one device, and connected to the telephone network with a modem. Using a Minitel, subscribers could learn the telephone number of anyone in France, purchase retail items online, order theater or train tickets, and even consult online databases or post a comment on a message board. Why were the Minitels given away? Because the ministry calculated that providing Minitels would be cheaper than producing and distributing millions of telephone books, the ministry could charge for Minitel use – and it helped French manufacturers.

Although the French turned increasingly to the Internet during the late 1990s, some were then troubled by continuing Minitel use. For example, French Prime Minister Lionel Jospin claimed in 1997 the Minitel was holding back France's entry into the information age.[22] Others believed Minitel use eased the French transition to the Internet. Yet at the end of the 1990s, French Internet use lagged well behind her European neighbors. Some unkind observers even called France technologically backward. But no one says that today: France is now one of Europe's broadband leaders, with low prices, high speeds, and sophisticated Internet services. And she now leads the United States, as well, with faster, cheaper broadband. How did this come about – and in such a short time?

In 2000, French telecommunications regulators made their first attempt to propel France into the information age. They encouraged French and even foreign companies to develop their own networks to provide Internet access. By doing so, they hoped to create a competitive market that would drive down prices and increase French Internet use. Initially, they were more than successful. Some 50 new companies entered the Internet service market backed by investors in France, elsewhere in Europe, and even the United States. But despite chaotic competition, the dominant national telephone company, France Telecom (FT), held its ground. And

soon the outside competitors, heavily dependent on stock offerings and bank loans, were decimated by the dot-com bust
of 2000.

The cable companies weren't strong competitors, either.
Although they had introduced broadband in 1997, they were
fragmented due to earlier regulation, still in debt from constructing their networks, and short on compelling service offerings. On top of that, France Telecom owned a 40% stake
in them. So, the French regulators' first attempt to create a
competitive market failed.

In spring 2002, the European Commission announced a
new "framework" to encourage and solidify competition in
telecommunications markets that had particular implications
for the emerging broadband markets across the European
Union. The EC's approach to creating these markets was
similar to the Japanese government's. Regulators should
subject the dominant player in the market, almost always
the national telephone company, to tougher regulation than
its competitors until a competitive market was established,
that is, when the dominant player and its competitors were
roughly balanced. As that market emerged (but only then),
regulators should remove the unequal prior regulations and
apply after-the-fact regulations to insure continuing competition. This course should be followed, the commission said,
by the regulatory authorities of the EU's member countries.

Inspired by the broadband success of Japan and Korea,
the French telecommunications regulators took action within weeks of the commission's announcement. To create a
competitive broadband market, they required the dominant
broadband provider, France Telecom, to open its residential

telephone lines to competitors and accept a very low lease fee. That would permit competitors to make a profit. The regulators also sought to extend DSL broadband service beyond the big cities to smaller towns and rural areas. Their intervention in the market succeeded, and as prices fell and new services appeared, many more people subscribed to broadband.

One French entrepreneur was eager to compete. Xavier Niel had made a fortune with Iliad, an online dating service, in the Minitel era. When Internet use increased, Niel, in 1999, created an Internet service provider called Free. The following year, Free began developing its own network, helped by a 15-million-Euro investment from the American financial firm Goldman Sachs. In 2001, Free's engineers developed the "Freebox," a small, TV-set-top box containing a modem to connect to Free's network and a device (DSLAM) that routed traffic in and out of the house. The Freebox was critical to the provider's success because it permitted Free to introduce new broadband services whenever it wished.

When the 2002 French regulatory shift came, Free was ready. Consciously modeling itself on upstart Yahoo!BB in Japan, Free began competing intensely with France Telecom for Parisian broadband subscribers. By spring 2003, Free was able to offer broadband service to a majority of the French population and, thanks to faster speeds and lower prices than France Telecom, it soon became the second-largest DSL service in the nation. That summer it offered France's first Internet telephone service; and that winter, Internet television service – thus becoming the world's first company to provide "triple-play" service (TV, telephone, and Internet access) over high-speed DSL. All that for 30 Euros a month, about $36 at the time.

That kind of bold entrepreneurship produced striking results. France's broadband market became "competitive" just two years after regulators ordered the opening of FT's residential lines. In spring 2004, France Telecom controlled only half of the broadband market, Free had nearly one-fifth, and other competitors shared the rest. Moreover, Internet telephone use was approaching 40% of all fixed-line calls.

In 2005, the European Commission sought to extend France's success (and that of Scandinavia and the Netherlands) to the rest of the EU members. It issued an "e-Europe" directive aimed at making Europe "the most dynamic and competitive knowledge-based economy in the world," in part by making broadband widely available. The commission directed EU governments to develop broadband expansion strategies, create competitive broadband markets where they didn't exist, and encourage deployment of the technology to rural areas. The commission and national governments also put money behind the project, investing $21 billion up to 2006.

Around this time, some observers thought France might be headed for a "DSL cul de sac." DSL broadband then accounted for 85% of the French broadband market, and neither France Telecom nor any other major company had announced plans to build a fiber network. Yet there were smaller fiber networks in operation. Many rural areas and regions without broadband, after appealing in vain to FT for DSL service, began constructing their own fiber networks from 2004 to 2006, most with French government administrative and financial assistance.

In summer 2006, facing increased competition, FT made a dramatic shift, announced it would become a major player in fiber, and began testing a fiber-to-the-home network in six Paris districts and six nearby cities.[23] Two years later, FT had begun fiber deployment in Paris and other major French cities and was scheduled to pass 1 million living units by the end of 2008; during the following three years, from 2009 to 2012, FT now plans a massive FTTH rollout across the entire country.[24]

For its part, Free had built out its own FTTH network – using the Paris sewer system that leads into each building – to nearly a third of Paris by the end of 2007 and planned to deploy fiber to all of Paris and an additional six cities by 2010.[25] Other companies announced FTTH plans as well. And just as quickly, the French regulators suggested sharing the new fiber networks, given the huge investments needed, and promised action to prevent a possible monopoly.[26] Just now, they are seeking to compel service providers who install fiber to a building to share it with other operators to avoid redundancy; the regulators are expected to decide this question by the end of 2008.[27]

By spring 2008, the regulators' broadband success was even more obvious: France had surpassed its European neighbors – as well as the United States – in broadband usage, with 16.2 million residential and business subscribers.[28] Meanwhile, in December 2007, Free was offering its 3 million French subscribers more than 80 TV channels, unlimited Internet phone calls within France and to some 70 foreign countries, and high-speed (28 Mbps) Internet service for the same 30 Euros a month, then worth about $43.

What should we take away from the French achievements?

- *Regulators should consider carefully how intense competition is likely to be* between those providers using a single technology, such as DSL, and between those using differing broadband technologies, such as DSL and cable – *and how long it might take for that competition to emerge.* Declaring open competition is seldom sufficient to overcome the advantage of existing large-scale providers.
- *Learn from others.* French regulators, along with their Japanese and other European counterparts, created a competitive broadband market in a very similar way (as the European Commission urged): by handicapping France Telecom, the dominant player.
- *Encourage bold competitors*, like Free, that are able to compete intensely while remaining profitable.
- *Support local and regional entities* if they can provide a viable business case for broadband infrastructure deployment.
- *Identify existing infrastructure* (such as sewers) which might speed broadband infrastructure deployment.
- *Use intense competition in the high-speed (DSL and cable) broadband market to drive the transition to ultra-fast (fiber) broadband.* This, of course, is what happened in Japan as well.

The indispensible leader

What is the central lesson from all three of these countries, one that is shared by all of the world's broadband leaders? It is that government must play a central role in broadband expansion and not simply leave it to the private sector and market forces. Although the South Korean, Canadian, and French private sectors invested heavily in broadband, did all of the deployment, and now own and manage the networks, the governments intervened where necessary to *spread* broadband. Among the leadership roles the governments played were: describing a vision of the benefits broadband might bring; developing a national broadband strategy; funding or subsidizing backbone and network infrastructure; creating truly competitive broadband markets; increasing demand for broadband by providing cheap computers and boosting IT literacy; extending broadband to rural and underserved areas by aggregating demand and in other ways; and speeding the transition to ultra-fast fiber networks.

Moreover, governments have balanced the interests of the broadband network owners and developers with those who are dependent on them: applications, services, and content providers; businesses large and small; critical public institutions such as schools, libraries, and hospitals – and consumers such as you and me and our rural neighbors. Unfortunately, the market can't do these things or can do them only indirectly – and not as well and much more slowly.

That is why Japan – and South Korea, Canada, France, and ten or so other countries – now lead the United States in broadband. Their governments showed the way.

Chapter 12.
Returning to the Information Superhighway

When former Prime Minister Mori announced in 2000 that Japan would be the world's Internet leader by 2005, he was aiming to end U.S. dominance within those five years. After all, in 2000, the United States was the world's acknowledged Internet leader. That leadership was evident across all but one dimension of Internet leadership: wireless, where Japan (and Korea) were showing the way.

Clearly, the United States no longer leads. But has Japan supplanted it, achieving Mori's goal? To answer this question, let's look again briefly at each of those seven Internet leadership dimensions:

In *broadband*, Japan now has an enormous lead over the United States. In the deployment of infrastructure, Japan is now several years ahead. High-speed broadband reaches 95% of Japan's households and ultra-fast fiber passes more than 85%. In the United States, DSL or cable broadband reaches perhaps three-quarters of the homes, and fiber less than 10%. In usage, according to the Organization for Economic Cooperation and Development (OECD) , the countries are roughly equal in that just over 16 out of every 100 inhabitants subscribe to broadband, but Japan's version is much faster and cheaper. Taking speed and cost, as well as usage, into account, as a leading index does, Japan, again, has an enormous lead, ranking second in the world compared to the United States' 15th. Moreover, Japan's fiber network is the most reliable anywhere.

Japan has an even greater lead in *wireless*. The government is now preparing to upgrade its reliable, nationwide, 3G mobile-phone infrastructure that makes calling virtually anywhere in the country possible. In the United States, 3G infrastructure is spotty, and available only in larger cities, and roughly half of the country's land area has no wireless service at all. As for mobile-phone usage, 83% of the Japanese had them in December 2007, and nearly nine-tenths of those (87%) had wireless Internet subscriptions.[1] An estimated 84% of Americans had mobile phones, but only 2% of those subscribed to Internet service.[2] While Japanese mobile-phone bills are generally higher, Internet subscriptions are cheaper and downloads are far faster. Both countries are using WiFi in homes, offices, and other "hot spots," and making limited use of WiMax.

The United States leads in the third dimension: *the number of Internet experts and the amount of information-technology R&D funding*. Japan educates more native-born experts – defined as electrical engineers and computer scientists with master's or doctoral degrees. But the United States trains as many non-Americans as it does Americans, giving it a substantial lead in overall numbers. Moreover, the United States grants professional work visas to a larger number of foreign IT experts in a year than Japan did in five, resulting in a far larger number of resident Internet experts than Japan. On the other hand, although Japan's economy is only one-third as large as America's, the Japanese government, from 2001 through 2005, invested almost as much in information-technology R&D.

The United States continues to lead in *innovation*, although Japan has clearly analyzed U.S. success and is seeking to imitate it. For example, the number of patents filed by Japanese – with less than half the American population – almost equaled those filed by Americans in 2006. In recent years, the Japanese government has also allowed university (and corporate) researchers to profit from their research and has encouraged the transfer of university research to the private sector. (But those steps came twenty years later than they did in the United States.) In venture capital, the Japanese government is seeking to pattern a network on America's. As a result, Japan's environment for innovation is steadily improving, and, although the United States remains dominant, one study now ranks Japan second in telecommunications innovation, including broadband.[3]

Japan led in *e-commerce* at the end of 2006. America continues to top the world in retail e-commerce (B2C), thanks to Amazon, e-Bay, Yahoo!, and others, but Japan's greater business-to-business (B2B) e-commerce sales more than offset that advantage.

The United States and Japan are roughly equal in *the public dimension* of Internet leadership: e-government, e-education, and universal broadband access. America remains a world leader in e-government, because President George W. Bush made it a part of his management agenda from the outset of his administration. By contrast, the Japanese government, despite many plans and revisions, is still struggling. The United States may also have a slight advantage in e-education. Although schools in both countries are now almost completely equipped and connected to the Internet, American teachers seem to be making (somewhat) greater use of the IT resources at their disposal.

But Japan has an enormous lead in the third (and most important) element of the public dimension: universal broadband Internet service. Having made universal broadband access a national priority, fully 95% of the households in Japan now have broadband access, roughly 20% more than in the United States. And as mentioned above, third-generation mobile-phone infrastructure with basic broadband speeds covers virtually the entire country, while in the United States it is confined to major cities. That important difference stems from the fact that the U.S. government hasn't made universal broadband access a priority in the past eight years, and universal wireless access never was.

America overtaken

All in all, it is fair to say that Japan has overtaken the United States as Internet leader. While America remains ahead in important dimensions of Internet leadership – the number of Internet experts and IT research spending, innovation, e-government, and e-education – Japan, along with several other countries, is gaining in each of these areas. But more important, Japan has deployed the world's leading fiber and wireless infrastructures. And a "ubiquitous," ultra-fast, fiber-wireless broadband network is in the offing. These are the communications networks of the 21st century, and without them, the United States can't contend for global Internet leadership. Moreover, without effective national broadband and wireless strategies, the United States will continue to lose ground.

If Japan has overtaken the United States, is it now the *world's* Internet leader, as former Prime Minister Mori predicted? One could argue that it is, but there is another contender for that title: South Korea. Whether Japan or South Korea is the world's Internet leader today depends on the importance you assign to each of the leadership dimensions. For example, South Korea leads the world in broadband *usage*, while Japan has the most extensive fiber *infrastructure*; and so on. But if world leadership is uncertain at present, it will be determined shortly. Both Japan and South Korea plan ubiquitous networks – seamlessly connected, ultra-fast fiber and wireless. The undisputed global Internet leader will surely be the nation that first reaches that goal – and can exploit the extraordinary possibilities those networks open up.

Japan still has some unfinished tasks. Its most obvious challenge is to increase demand for its expanding fiber network, whose spread has been slowed by lack of sufficient demand. Because a completed fiber network is essential for wireless as well as landline services, the government should do more now to spur demand for fiber access. As in South Korea, ways to boost demand might include providing inexpensive PCs to those who can't afford them; offering additional adult IT literacy training, especially to rural residents and the elderly; encouraging the creation of popular new applications and content that appeal to those without fiber access; and perhaps even extending modest Internet-service subsidies. But the best way to increase demand is by offering the kinds of services foreseen in the e-Japan Strategy II, services such as extending telemedicine to rural areas, tracking food items, easing transportation bottlenecks, expanding distance learning, developing home-sensor networks, and so on.

Japan's second challenge is to promote greater technological innovation. Its world-leading fiber infrastructure and usership give it first crack at developing new fiber-oriented applications, services, and content. Similarly, Japan's existing 3G mobile-phone networks and Internet usership – and progress toward 3.9G and 4G networks – provide innovative possibilities that other countries simply don't have. Development of ubiquitous fiber-wireless networks will offer yet another set of innovative possibilities. But if Japan is to take advantage of those (no-doubt-fleeting) opportunities, it should take these steps: further encourage domestic researchers and potential entrepreneurs, as well as home-grown venture capital firms; consider inviting in more foreign entrepreneurs and venture capitalists; and set standards that will yield a leg up in the global market, rather than protect its home market.

A third major challenge for Japan is e-government. Here, the government has failed to carry out its own strategies. There are several reasons for this lack of progress. But the prime minister and the IT strategic headquarters should make better e-government a priority and set the kinds of goals and deadlines that it has imposed so successfully in other dimensions of Internet leadership. The benefits would be substantial.

The answer to yet another basic question needs clarification: why did the United States fall behind Japan and other nations so quickly? The explanation begins with President George Bush's (and Vice President Dick Cheney's) lack of interest in Internet leadership and science and technology more broadly (except as it applied to military operations). In addition, they failed to grasp the essential role of technology – and Internet leadership, in particular – in driving sustainable economic growth. Their view that sustainable growth will result from reduced taxes and increased defense spending has been proven disastrously wrong.

Ideology has also played a critical role. Based on its distrust of government (except in the military realm), the administration saw no role for it in ensuring America's continued Internet leadership. The President and his advisers insisted that market forces, without any government leadership or even guidelines, would advance the nation's broadband (and wireless) infrastructure – and that deregulation should precede a truly competitive market. On top of that, information-technology R&D funding remained flat for most of the Bush administration's eight years, and DARPA, the government's leading developer of promising but risky technologies, turned almost exclusively to military projects. Until 2006, little thought was given to expanding the number of America's highly skilled IT professionals through education or immigration. And by failing to encourage a world-class IT infrastructure, it handicapped America's innovative entrepreneurs as well as her Internet and mobile-phone users.

Finally, and perhaps most tellingly, the administration failed to take notice of the progress other nations were making. Confident of U.S. superiority, it did not learn from other nations and ignored repeated warnings, issued by respected organizations and individuals, of America's relative decline. Amazingly in 2008, U.S. officials still argued that the country was leading the world in broadband and that international rankings showing the United States in 15th place were methodologically flawed. Obliviousness to overseas Internet progress followed by denial of America's lost Internet leadership came to characterize the Bush administration. The truth is that the United States is no longer an Internet leader but a middle-tier broadband nation, as confirmed by the OECD and other objective observers.

The benefits lost due to the administration's neglect have been profound. First, of course, is forgone economic growth, estimated in the hundreds of billions of dollars. Lost productivity has been evaluated in the range of 0.5% of growth per year. Tens of thousands of jobs weren't created in deploying new networks. Innovative new discoveries weren't made because the broadband and wireless advance has been so slow. And America's IT industry is not as strong as it might have been.

Equally important, Internet leadership – and the cutting-edge broadband and wireless networks that go with it – are essential to solving the nation's pressing problems. Take health care, for instance: the use of IT and nationwide fiber, wireless, and sensor networks could be used to monitor sick and elderly citizens at home, even in rural areas. Those networks could be used to extend sophisticated diagnoses and surgical guidance throughout the country. They could make medical records available to those who need them wherever they are located.

Or take another pressing problem: education. Nationwide fiber connections and wireless local-area networks within schools could make critical resources – textbooks, maps, source materials, videos, statistics – available to every building, classroom, and teacher. This network could also make possible model presentations by top teachers on subjects at all levels, along with a wide variety of distance-learning courses for schools where demand does not justify "live" teachers. Such networks could also provide the kinds of repetitive practice necessary to master certain aspects of mathematics, foreign languages, and other subjects.

And consider energy conservation. Nationwide fiber networks and reliable videoconferencing applications would permit most people to telecommute and teleconference across the country, saving an enormous amount of time and fuel, reducing road and air congestion, and improving productivity. Moreover, advanced fiber broadband and wireless networks could vastly improve homeland security.

Those lost benefits raise a critical question: is America destined to remain in the middle of the Internet leadership pack? The answer is "no" – *if* the country is willing to face unpleasant facts and make a fresh start. It must first admit that it *is* in the middle of that pack and recognize that it will take several years to get back into contention for the leadership. It will have to learn from the successes of other nations and adapt their experience to American conditions. Most important, it will have to enlist and sustain enlightened political leadership and determination.

Returning to the Information Superhighway

Specific recommendations were made in several earlier chapters. Let me reiterate the most important steps the United States should take now:

1. **Think strategically: declare affordable, nation-wide, ultra-fast fiber and wireless networks a national priority.** Ultra-fast means data transmission speeds of 100 megabits per second or more. Why ultra-fast? The historical pattern of U.S. broadband access speeds shows a fivefold increase every five years; if this pattern continues, the United States will require access speeds of nearly 40 Mbps in 2010, 200 Mbps in 2015, and 1,000 Mbps by 2020. Only the ultra-fast fiber and wireless communications networks of the 21st century can handle those huge data flows of the future. Built for other purposes, the DSL and cable networks that are now the norm in the United States are, in fact, transitional. Although they may eventually be able to reach speeds of 100 megabits per second or more, future demand will soon outpace them. Thus the Connect Kentucky and Connected America plans that call for extending today's basic broadband networks are too little, too late. The political will and money needed to implement those programs should be spent on making the existing fiber network universal.

Within a decade, the United States will also need nationwide, ultra-fast *wireless* networks with download (and upload) speeds over 100 megabits per second. That will require substantial upgrading of the existing wireless networks; extending those networks to cover virtually the entire nation; and developing WiMax networks for the most remote areas. The eventual goal, of course, should be to connect the ultra-fast fiber and wireless networks.

2. Provide those ultra-fast fiber and wireless networks to the vast majority of American households by 2012 – and to nearly all by 2016. As the past eight years have shown, the market can't implement goals such as these. As things now stand, Verizon, the only company now offering fiber to the home, will provide that access to only about 10% of America's (mostly affluent) households by 2010. And at that point, Verizon and other mobile-phone companies will still be *experimenting* with ultra-fast wireless networks.

Only government leadership can ensure Americans access to those networks of the future within a reasonable timeframe. In declaring the networks a national priority, the new President should set the targets of providing fiber to 80% of American households and wireless to 70% in his first term, and fiber to (virtually) 100% and wireless to 90% four years later. In doing so, he will have to persuade the nation that they are essential: to solving the nation's pressing problems; to ensuring sustainable economic growth, increased productivity, and the creation of tens of thousands of new, well-paying jobs; to opening up new vistas for U.S. innovation and entrepreneurship and new markets for U.S. applications, services, and content providers; and to creating better, more productive, and interesting lives for all Americans. In short, the nation's new chief executive must present a compelling vision of the brighter American future those networks would bring.

3. Spur demand for those new networks by setting usage targets: 60% household usage of available ultra-fast networks by 2012 and 75% by 2016. If you build them, people will come – eventually. But Japan's experience has shown that, unless demand is actively promoted, it can take six years to reach a 25% household-usage rate. Moreover, that measured take-up will slow the expansion of the fiber network itself. South Korea's experience, on the other hand, shows that concerted effort on the demand side can encourage four-fifths of the population to adopt broadband, and that, of course, fosters the expansion of fiber networks. Thus promotion of demand should go hand in hand with the network expansion. Government at all levels and the private sector should join in educational campaigns that highlight the ways the new networks can benefit individuals and communities.

4. Name a Supernetworks Task Force to develop strategies to deploy those networks, fund their construction, and promote their use. The new President should appoint a task force that includes all of the major stakeholders: high-level federal, state, and local government officials; the CEOs of the major companies offering broadband and wireless Internet services and the head of their union; the CEOs of the major Internet equipment makers and applications, services, and content providers; and top representatives of the health, education, library, and consumer groups, along

with recognized networking experts.   Those high-rank-
ing men and women are needed to bring the country's best
thinking to bear and hammer out the compromises needed to
develop strategies that will meet the deadlines.

The task force should also recommend ways to finance
the project. Funding will require a mix of sources, including
the private sector through direct investment in profitable areas; public-private partnerships in potentially profitable areas; and tax incentives, long-term guarantees, and subsidies
in unprofitable areas, along with a reconceived Universal
Service Fund. Rural areas, smaller cities, and towns should
be encouraged to construct their own networks, adhering to
federal standards. One way to promote that would be for the
federal government to offer incentives for laying fiber along
the entire interstate highway system, creating a network to
which any company, regional entity, or municipality could
connect. Networks built with any government incentives or
funding should be open to all.

Working together, governments at all levels and the private sector can also do much to promote demand, as we have
seen in the Connect Kentucky model. Among the methods
are educational campaigns describing the benefits of ultra-
fast networks; demand aggregation; recycled, inexpensive,
or subsidized computers; new applications, services, and
content aimed at groups that are not using broadband or even
the Internet; IT literacy training; and so forth. Failure to
promote demand will slow the expansion of the networks.

**5. Call on the National Research Council to develop
ways to use the expanding Supernetworks to solve the
nation's urgent problems.** Because each of them – energy,

healthcare, education, national security – poses its own challenges, each will require the attention of an expert group composed of issue and IT specialists. The healthcare group, for example, might ponder the IT and networking resources needed to provide standardized digital health records; remote vital-signs monitoring of the ill and elderly; quick transfer of data-intensive records (such as x-rays and MRIs) across the country to facilitate diagnosis and second opinions; videoconferencing links to permit offsite medical consultations and guidance of surgical operations; and many other matters. That would involve reviewing best practices at home and abroad, suggesting new approaches, developing new standards, pointing out areas for innovation, and suggesting new research. The idea, of course, is to bring the best possible technology and standards to bear in producing the highest quality and least costly outcomes.

6. Begin research now on fourth-generation (4G) mobile networks, sensor networks, and ubiquitous networks – linked fiber, wireless, and sensor networks – and planning for the transition to a new Internet address system (IPv6) that will be required. In other countries, such as Japan, research labs linked to telecom companies and equipment makers carry out this research. But in the United States those research facilities are now very modest, spending an estimated $250-$350 million per year (compared to $13.5 *billion* spent in the European Union). After documenting the crisis in U.S. telecommunications research, the National Research Council recently called for a DARPA-like Advanced Telecommunications Research Activity to stimulate and coordinate telecom research.[4] This demonstrates that the research needed to create these new networks will have to be underwritten by a public-private partnership or the government. Either way, the research should follow the ARPA model of funding one or more technological approaches to reach a given end result.

The transition to the new Internet address system will present a different challenge, mainly because the old (IPv4) address system originated in the United States and is so well established. Still, the U.S. government itself is making the transition to the new system, and with Y2K-like planning, the private sector can as well. A reasonable date for completion of the needed research and the transition to the new address system would be 2012.

7. Shore up the technological base: expand the pool of IT specialists, increase and rebalance IT research funding, and closely monitor the innovation environment. The U.S. technological enterprise and innovation environment remain the envy of the world. But other nations have grasped the importance of innovation and, using the U.S. model, are closing the gap. And in the United States, some obvious things need fixing.

Fewer and fewer Americans are studying computer science and engineering at the undergraduate and graduate levels, too few foreign students are studying these subjects in the United States, and visa requirements force too many foreign IT specialists to leave. The reasons for all of this are outlined in Chapter 7 and can be fixed with determination and some money.

Since 2001, the U.S. government has invested just slightly more than its Japanese counterpart in IT research, although the Japanese economy is less than half as large. In fact, the Japanese aim to spend as much on all government-funded research as they do on their military establishment. While the United States is unlikely to do that, it should fund substantially more R&D– and set its own goal of 1% of GDP annually. It should also develop an overall IT research strategy and rebalance the federal government's research portfolio to increase the funding of basic research, blue-sky projects, and ARPA-model research aimed at promoting promising (but risky) civilian technologies.

The U.S. innovation environment is one of the nation's greatest treasures, and it should be treated as such. That means keeping a close eye on it – and the efforts of other nations to emulate it. Some problems are already well documented and need fixing: an overloaded patent office; overly commercial university research agendas; uncertainty about federal tax breaks for corporate R&D; unnecessary tax and accounting burdens for startups. The list goes on, but correcting those items would be a good start.

8. Monitor e-commerce best practices. Although e-commerce is best left to the private sector, U.S. businesses would benefit from knowing more about what their overseas counterparts are doing. For example, businesses may be operating at a disadvantage by using dedicated networks that favor a specific group of suppliers, rather than using the Internet to expand the number of potential bidders. The Commerce Department is well placed to survey and publicize overseas practices.

9. Continue to make e-government a Presidential priority, better integrate IT and the Internet into the

K-12 curriculum, and commit to closing the digital divide. The United States continues to be a world leader in e-government, because George W. Bush made it part of his Presidential Management Agenda. But that doesn't mean the government has done as much as it should have. The next President should set the bar higher.

Virtually all American schools now have Internet connections, and most classrooms do. School children are now learning computer and Internet skills appropriate to their age. But the computer and the Internet have yet to be integrated into the K-12 curriculum. Much more could be accomplished and more efficiently – math and language drills, Internet geography lessons, science experiments, for example – but IT is unlikely to be the panacea many would like. Studying IT and Internet integration seems a job for the Harvard School of Education working with MIT.

Closing the digital divide, just as closing the electricity and telephone divides of earlier times, is a matter of commitment, determination, and some money. It needs to be done.

10. Learn from others. During the past eight years, the U.S. government and much of the private sector have acted as if they have nothing to gain by studying what other nations have done. At the outset, that attitude stemmed from a widespread conviction that the United States was still the global Internet leader. But after more than a dozen warnings from prestigious study groups, associations, and specialists, it is past time for Americans to recognize that their country has fallen behind. It should now learn from the successes and mistakes of others. If there is an advantage to falling behind, that is it.

All is not lost for the United States. Although eight years of uncertainty, sluggish competition, and government inattention have been costly, they have taught us several important lessons. We have learned, for example, that fiber networks are the essential networks of the 21st century; there is little point in continuing to invest in DSL over copper lines or cable Internet access over coaxial cable. Even at their fastest, up to 100 megabits per second or so for the former and 500 Mbps plus for the latter, those networks are simply too slow for tomorrow's needs. We have also learned that ultra-fast wireless networks are feasible and essential, because most people, most of the time, will want to use a handheld device to access the Internet. That means it is counter-productive to leave parts of our largest cities, much of the countryside, and literally half of the nation's geography without cutting-edge wireless service and Internet access.

We have learned, too, that nationwide, *ubiquitous* fiber and wireless networks represent the benchmark for 21st century networks in advanced nations. Those that don't develop them will be at a significant competitive disadvantage, will prove less adept at solving their problems, and will handicap their citizens.

Perhaps most important, we have learned that inflexible, ideological approaches to these issues don't work. They only ensure that those who own today's obsolescent networks will dictate what is best for themselves, not the nation. It is time, then, to return to government leadership, public-private partnerships, and the flexible, imaginative approaches that created the Internet in the first place. If the new administration is able to take those lessons to heart, the United States could leave the middle tier of Internet leadership and rejoin the top rank in four years' time. In eight years, it could regain its rightful place, once again contending for global Internet leadership.

ENDNOTES

Chapter 1. A look ahead – to 2015

[1] Robert W. Crandall and Charles L. Jackson, "The $500 Billion Opportunity: The Potential Economic Benefit of Widespread Diffusion of Broadband Internet Access," July 2001. p. iv. http://www.att.com/public_affairs/broadband_policy/ BrookingsStudy.pdf.

Chapter 2. America takes the lead

[1] Quoted in Katie Hafner and Matthew Lyon, *Where Wizards Stay Up Late: the Origins of the Internet* (New York: Simon & Shuster, 1996), p. 38.

[2] Ibid., pp. 40-42.

[3] From a Robert Taylor interview for a videotape, "History of the Future," commissioned by Bolt Beranek and Newman to celebrate the 25th anniversary of ARPAnet, as described in *A Brief History of the Future*, pp. 87-88.

[4] John Naughton, *A Brief History of the Future* (New York: The Overlook Press, 2000), p. 133.

[5] Hafner, *Where Wizard Stay Up Late*, pp. 143-151.

[6] From *EFFector 4.01*, December 1992, available online at the Electronic Freedom Foundation site: http://www.eff.org/effector/ effect04.01.

[7] Hafner, *Where Wizards Stay Up Late*, pp. 243-245.

[8] M. Mitchell Waldrop, *Dream Machine* (New York: Viking, 2001), p. 459.

[9] Juan D. Rogers, "Internetworking and the Politics of Science: NSFNET in Internet History." *The Information Society*, 14:213-228, 1998, pp. 218-219.

Chapter 3. Gore galvanizes the government

[1]   Waldrop, *Dream Machine*, p. 459.
[2]   Although the term "information superhighway" is associated with Gore, Nam June Paik, a South-Korea-born American video artist, claims to have coined the term in 1974.
[3]   Senate Subcommittee on Science, Technology, and Space hearings transcript, August 11, 1988, p. 3.
[4]   Ibid. p. 19.
[5]   Ibid. p. 36.
[6]   Waldrop, *Dream Machine*, p. 462.
[7]   All of this is detailed at much greater length in Jim Clark and Owen Edwards' *Netscape Time: The Making of a Billion-Dollar Start-up That Took on Microsoft* (New York: St. Martin's Press, 1999).
[8]   Bill Clinton and Al Gore, *Putting People First* (New York: Times Books, 1992).
[9]   Clinton, *Putting People First*, pp. 143-145.
[10] "Technology – Position Paper of the Clinton Campaign." http://www.ibiblio.org/nii/tech-posit.html
[11] Ibid., p. 1.
[12] David Maraniss and Ellen Nakashima, *The Prince of Tennessee* (New York: Simon & Shuster, 2000), p. 283.
[13] *EFFector 4.01*, December 1992.   http://www.eff.org/effector/effect04.01.
[14] This version of an oft-repeated administration position was taken from a mission statement for the Information Infrastructure Task Force, formed shortly after the NII announcement. http://www.ibiblio.org/nii/NII-Task-Force.html
[15] Interview with the author, August 22, 2002.
[16] Interview with the author, October 18, 2005.
[17] Some argue that Gore's 1991 High-Performance Computing Act gave the NSF authority to open the network to all, but the Boucher bill made an NSF decision to open the networks legally unassailable.
[18] National Information Infrastructure "Agenda for Action," September 1993, p. 12. http://ibiblio.org.nii/.
[19] Ibid., p. 1.
[20] From "Remarks on the Internet and Information Technologies" by Albert Gore, Jr. in D. Michael Hester and Paul J. Ford, *Computers*

and Ethics in the Cyberage (Upper Saddle River, NJ: Prentice Hall, 2001), pp. 424-430.

21   Additional information at: http://www.ibiblio.org/nii/NII-Task-Force.html.

22   NII 2000 Steering Committee, National Research Council, *The Unpredictable Certainty: Information Infrastructure through 2000* (Washington: The National Academies Press, 1996), pp. 3-26.

23   Speech by Vice President Al Gore to the National Press Club, Washington, December 21, 1993.

24   Reed E. Hundt, *You Say You Want a Revolution: A Story of Information Age Politics* (New Haven: Yale University Press, 2000). p. 155.

25   Interview with the author, August 22, 2002, Washington.

26   "From "Red Tape to Results: Creating a Government That Works Better and Costs Less," September 7, 1993.

27   Executive Order 13011 of July 16, 1996.

28   Hundt, *You Say You Want a Revolution*, p. 184.

29   Ira C. Magaziner, "Creating a Framework for Global Electronic Commerce," Progress & Freedom Foundation's "Future Insight," Release 6.1 – July 1999. http://www.pff.org/issues-pubs/futureinsights/fi6.1globaleconomiccommerce.html

30   PITAC Report to the President. "Information Technology Research: Investing in Our Future." February 24, 1999. http://www.nitrd.gov/pitac/report.

31   Democratic Candidates' Debate at Dartmouth College, October 27, 1999.

32   President's Council of Economic Advisers, *Economic Report of the President, 2001* (Washington: Government Printing Office, 2001), p. 25.

33   From a GOP candidates' debate in Manchester, NH, January 26, 2000.

Chapter 4. Japan takes on the world

1   Author interview with Dr. Tadao Saito, February 25, 2003, Tokyo.

2   From their importation in the 8th century until today, Chinese characters, now somewhat different from those used on the mainland, have formed the core of the Japanese written language.

3   Haruhisa Ishida, "Networking in Japan," Asian Technology Information Project Report, July 16, 1992, and the February 25, 2003 interview with Dr. Saito.

4   France's 1978 Simon Nora-Alain Minc Report and Britain's 1979 Carter report, according to Ezra Vogel, in *Comeback: Case by Case: Building the Resurgence of American business* (New York: Simon & Shuster, 1985).

5   Murai is always careful to call this an experimental network, because it was still illegal for outsiders to send packet data over NTT telephone lines. That changed with the partial NTT privatization in April 1985.

6   In Carl Malamud, *Exploring the Internet: A Technical Travelogue*, 1993.

7   Ishida, "Networking in Japan," op cit..

8   Haruo Yamaguchi, *Telecommunications: NTT's Vision of the Future*, translated by Norman Havens (Tokyo: NTT Publishing Co., Ltd., 1991). The book was originally published as *21 seiki terekomu shakai no kozu*. (Tokyo: Diamond, Inc., 1990).

9   Ibid., pp. 118-130.

10 Ishida, "Networking in Japan," op cit.

11 This "war" is described in considerable detail in Chalmers Johnson, "MITI, MPT, and the Telecom Wars: How Japan Makes Policy for High Technology" in Chalmers Johnson, Laura D'Andrea Tyson, and John Zysman, editors, *Politics and Productivity: The Real Story of Why Japan Works* (New York: Ballinger Publishing Company, 1989).

12 Author interview with Koichiro Hayashi, September 30, 2002, Tokyo.

13 Martin Fransman, *Japan's Computer and Communications Industry* (New York: Oxford University Press, 1995), pp. 175-176.

14 Asian Technology Information Program Report ATIP98.057, dated July 15, 1998. Many of the earlier comparisons come from another ATIP report, ATIP96.014, dated February 7, 1996.

15 Officially, DoCoMo means "do communications over the mobile network."

16 Much of this information is taken from Jeffrey Funk's *The Mobile Internet: How Japan Dialed Up and the West Disconnected* (Hamilton , Bermuda: ISI Publications, 2001), pp. 19-45.

17 Stephanie Strom, "Cold Pizza Hits the Spot in Japanese Politics," *The New York Times* online, July 23, 1998. Good-humoredly, Obuchi later personally delivered hot pizza to journalists covering him.

18 *Mireniamu Purojekuto* (Millennium Projects) online. http://pol. cside4.jp/cabinet/9.htm (in Japanese).

19 Author interview with Shigeki Suzuki, February 5, 2002.

20 Jim Hoagland, "Koizumi's Korean Surprise Counters Gloom at Home" in *The International Herald Tribune*, September 20, 2002.

21 John Nathan, *Sony: The Private Life* (New York: Houghton Mifflin Company, 1999), p. 321.

22 "IT Basic Strategy", p. 2. http://www.kantei.go.jp/foreign/it/network/0122full_e.html

23 David Ibison, "Japan points to weakness in use of information technology," *Financial Times*, May 22, 2001.

24 From the "New IT Reform Strategy," op cit., p. 4. http://www.kantei.go.jp/foreign/policy/it/ITStrategy2006.pdf.

Chapter 5. The landline broadband dimension: getting to fiber

1 These are my *current* definitions of "basic," "high-speed," and "ultra-fast" broadband in the United States. These definitions change over time as the broadband infrastructure improves. It is also worth noting in this connection that, until recently, the FCC defined "high-speed" Internet service as anything over 200 *kilobits* per second.

2 Sources for high-speed and fiber broadband availability come from the Fiber to the Home Council (http://www.ftthcouncil.org/?t=253) and Japan's Ministry for Internal Affairs and Communications. By March 2008, fiber was available to 86.5% of Japanese households.

3 Business use of broadband is not considered here, because well over 90% of larger businesses in both countries had broadband connections at then end of 2000.

4 Unfortunately, the U.S. FCC, the authoritative source of these statistics, combined these two categories at that time.

5 The Japanese defined "high-speed" and "ultra-fast" broadband by the type of connection: "high-speed" meant a DSL or cable connection; "ultra-fast" meant a fiber connection.

6 These are called "central offices" in the United States.

7   Author interview with Sachio Senmoto, March 1, 2002, Tokyo.

8   Ken Belson, *The New York Times*, June 28, 2003.

9   Source: Japanese Ministry of Internal Affairs and Communications.

10 And a December 2002 "Report on Building Out Broadband" by the President's Council of Advisors on Science and Technology went unnoticed.

11 "The Great Digital Broadband Migration", a speech to the Progress & Freedom Foundation, December 8, 2000, Washington, DC.

12 Speech by Nancy J. Victory, Assistant Secretary for Communications and Information, U. S. Department of Commerce, October 25, 2001.   http://www.ntia.doc.gov/speeches/2001/broadband_102501. htm

13 FCC's Cable Modem Order, March 2002.

14 The policy was foreshadowed in Catherine Yang, "Here Comes Broadband John," *Business Week* online, April 19, 2004. http://www.businessweek.com/magazine/content/04_16/b3879111. htm.   The policy was actually announced in mid-June 2004 in San Jose, California: Aaron Ricadela, "Kerry Pledges $30B For Tech R&D, Broadband," *InformationWeek* online.   http:// www.informationweek.com/news/management/showArticle. jhtml?articleID=22102231

15 "ITU's New Broadband Statistics for 1 January 2005." http://www. itu.int/osg/spu/newslog/ITUs+New+Broadband+Statistics+For+1+ January+2005.aspx

16 Saul Hansell, "The Supreme Court: The Service Providers; Cable Wins Internet-Access Ruling," *The New York Times*, June 28, 2005 online.

17 Amy Schatz, "FCC Unanimously Approves Deregulation of DSL Service," *The Wall Street Journal*, August 5, 2005.

18 Information from the Connect Kentucky website: http://www. connectkentucky.org

19 Ann Carrns, "Faster and Stronger," *The Wall Street Journal*, July 28, 2008.

20 Low-interest loans were of little value because Japanese interest rates were near 0% at that point.

21 Those companies offered broadband over powerline (BPL) service, using the extensive fiber networks they used to monitor their provision of electric power.

22 Source: Japan's Ministry of Internal Affairs and Communications.

23 "NTT Lowers Fiber Subscriber Target from 30mn to 20mn," *NikkeiNet Interactive*, November 10, 2007. http://www.nni.nikkei. co.jp/AC/TNKS/Search/Nni20071109D09JFA13.htm.

24 High-definition TV reception over the Internet requires 17 megabits per second or so, *if* the speed does not fluctuate. If it does, as is almost always the case, something on the order of 25 megabits or so is needed to insure a reliable 17 megabits, hence the range given. But it should be noted that new compression techniques are reducing the speeds required.

25 SBC Communications, the regional telephone company for the central part of the country, purchased AT&T, a long distance and mobile-phone company, and adopted the latter's name in November 2005. In December 2006, AT&T acquired yet another regional telephone company, Bell South and became sole owner of the Cingular Wireless.

26 Stephenson's viewpoint was expressed in Paul Sloan, "AT&T's New Operator," "Fortune 500" Special Issue, *Fortune*, May 5, 2008, p. 144.

27 Author conversation with Verizon chief economist Dennis Weller, January 31, 2008.

28 E-mail from AT&T spokeswoman Destiny Belknap Varghese, May 6, 2008.

29 These networks are used to monitor the flow of electricity and can, with modification, be used for residential service as happened in Japan.

30 John Horrigan, "Home Broadband 2008: Adoption Stalls for low-income Americans even as many broadband users opt for premium services that give them more speed," Pew Internet Project, July 2, 2008. See PDF of Questionnaire, page 19, Question 20. http://www.pewinternet.org/pdfs/PIP_Broadband.2008.Topline.pdf. FCC statistics, although official, are less reliable than the survey, because the FCC reports broadband access by zip code; if even one household in a zip code has access, all households in the zip code are included. Extrapolating from this data, one study estimated that broadband was available to 86% of U.S. households in December 2005. See Jed Kolko, "A New Measure of Residential Broadband Availability," a paper delivered at the 2007 Research Conference on Communication, Information, and Internet Policy, September 28-30, 2007. Paper at: http://web.si.umich.edu/tprc/papers/2007/716/measuring%20BB%20availability%20v6%20081707.pdf.

31   OECD Broadband Statistics, December 2007. Table 1d. Broad-
      band subscribers per 100 inhabitants. http://www.oecd.org/
      dataoecd/21/35/39574709.xls.

32   Daniel K. Correa, "Assessing Broadband in America: OECD and
      ITIF Broadband Rankings," The Information Technology and In-
      novation Foundation, April 2007, p. 4. http://www.itif.org/index.
      php?id=57 Updated by the author in May 2008 to take into account
      June 2007 OECD statistics. http://www.itif.org/index.php?id=143

33   FCC, "High-Speed Services for Internet Access: Status as of June
      30, 2007," Washington, March 2008, Table 5. http://www.fcc.gov/
      wcb/iatd/comp.html

34   China Internet Network Information Centre, "Statistical Report on
      the Internet Development in China," January 2008. http://tinyurl.
      com/288v77.

35   And a Senate Resolution introduced by Senator Jay Rockefeller on
      May 7, 2007 puts the date at 2027 or later. The resolution urges
      100 Mbps-service for all Americans by 2010; then Senator Barack
      Obama was a co-sponsor of the resolution. http://www.benton.org/
      node/5912

36   "A Blueprint for Big Broadband," an EDUCAUSE White Paper,
      January 2008, pp. 72-73. Windhausen assumes Verizon will pass
      18 million of America's 115 million households, leaving 97 mil-
      lion without fiber. Assuming an average of $1,000 to pass each of
      the remaining households, you reach the $100 billion total. Wind-
      hausen notes that Verizon has told investment analysts it currently
      (early 2008) costs $817 to pass a home, but Verizon is, for the most
      part, stringing fiber from telephone poles in relatively densely pop-
      ulated suburbs. The EDUCAUSE White Paper can be found at:
      http://net.educause.edu/ir/library/pdf/epo0801.pdf.

Chapter 6. The wireless dimension: anytime, anywhere

1   FCC, "High-Speed Services for Internet Access: Status as of June
      30, 2007," March 2008, Table 3. http://www.fcc.gov/wcb/iatd/
      comp.html

2   In addition, many Japanese used Personal Handy Phones, a simpler
      technology that permitted slower Internet access, at that time.

3   OECD Communications Outlook – 2003. http://www.oecd.org/
      LongAbstract/0,3425,en_2649_34225_2514080_1_1_1_1,00.html

4   FCC, "Sixth Commercial Mobile Services Report," Adopted June 20, 2001. http://wireless.fcc.gov/index.htm?job=cmrs_reports

5   The Ohboshi description is taken from John Beck, *DoCoMo: Japan's Wireless Tsunami* (New York: AMACOM, 2003), pp.73-85.

6   Ibid., p. 98.

7   "i-mode", according to Keiji Tachikawa who succeeded Ohboshi as president of NTT DoCoMo, means information, interactive, Internet, and "ai" (pronounced "eye" in Japanese, meaning love). As noted in John Ratliff, "DoCoMo as National Champion", End Note 11. http://citeseerx.ist.psu.edu/viewdoc/summary?doi=10.1.1.22.9078.

8   J-phone's name was changed to its parent company's name, Vodaphone, in 2003 to promote the global brand. With the purchase of Vodaphone's Japanese operations by Softbank, it became Softbank Mobile.

9   Michiyo Nakamoto, "A pioneering but risky mobile call," *Financial Times*, October 1, 2001.

10 Michiyo Nakamoto, "Entering a new world of high speed data access," *Financial Times*, November 21, 2001.

11 Ministry of Internal Administration and Communications White Paper 2004, Figures 1-1-5 and 1-1-7.

12 Telecommunications Carriers Association. www.tca.or.jp.

13 Although laptop WiFi connections, which were discussed in the previous chapter, are capable of running at 11 Mbps, they cannot run faster than the underlying broadband service which supports them. At the end of 2005, the average DSL and cable-modem broadband services in America, whose signal WiFi connections use, ran at 1.5Mbps, 25% slower than Japan's *mobile* download speeds.

14 Hundt, *You Say You Want a Revolution*, p. 14.

15 The terms cell(ular) phone and mobile phone are virtually interchangeable. Nearly all mobile phones are cellular phones based on the original Bell Lab concept. These phones receive wireless radio signals in a "cell" defined by the transmitting power of the cell's radio tower. As the phone passes to an adjacent cell, the call is "handed off" to the adjacent cell's tower. But for efficiency's sake, the wireless call is transmitted by wireline whenever the call's destination is more than a few cells away. A mobile call, then, almost always goes from a cell tower to wireline back to a distant cell tower (if the call is being made to another mobile phone). Other mobile

phones use newer wireless technologies, such as WiFi and WiMax, or satellites to communicate.

[16] Hundt, *You Say You Want a* Revolution, p. 92.

[17] FCC, "Eighth Annual Report and Analysis of Competitive Market Conditions with respect to Commercial Mobile Services," released June 26, 2003. www.fcc.gov.

[18] FCC's "Eighth Annual Report and Analysis of Competitive Market Conditions with respect to Commercial Mobile Services," released June 26, 2003. http://wireless.fcc.gov/index.htm?job=cmrs_reports

[19] Quoted in Dan Steinbock, *Wireless Horizon: Strategy and Competition in the Worldwide Mobile Marketplace* (New York: AMACOM, 2003), p. 109.

[20] E-mail from Jeffrey Nelson, Verizon Corporate Communications, March 7, 2006.

[21] Matt Richtel, "Technology Group Plans Wireless Network," *The New York Times*, May 7, 2008.

[22] E-mail from Ritch Blasi, Cingular media relations, March 7, 2006.

[23] Sacha Segan, "G'Bye WiFi, Hello 3G," *PC Magazine*, March 21, 2006, pp. 26-27.

[24] The FCC issued the Twelfth Report on the Commercial Mobile Radio Services Industry, covering 2006, on February 4, 2008, thirteen months later. Japan's MIC, by contrast, issued its early report on *2007* on February 27, 2008.

[25] FCC, "Twelfth Annual Report and Analysis of Competitive Market Conditions with respect to Commercial Mobile Services," released February 4, 2008, paragraph 223, p. 99. http://hraunfoss.fcc.gov/edocs_public/attachmatch/FCC-08-28A1.pdf.

[26] By June 2007, these percentages had increased to 72% and 87%, respectively. Source for both: "ICT Policy in Japan," a presentation by Kiyoshi Mori, Vice-Minister for Policy Coordination, Ministry of Internal Affairs and Communications, January 13, 2008, p. 1.

[27] Neither the FCC nor CITA publish figures for 3G or 3.5G subscribers. Thus 3G subscriber number is taken from FCC, "High-Speed Services for Internet Access: Status as of June 30, 2007," March 2008, Table 1, "Mobile Wireless." The source for the number of subscribers who surfed the web during November 2006-January 2007 is based on estimates of the private research firm M:Metrics, as quoted in the "Twelfth Report," op. cit., para. 211, p. 94.

[28] "Twelfth Report," op. cit., para. 227, p. 101. .

29 "Twelfth Report," op. cit., p. 9.
30 Verizon, for example, spent only one-third as much on infrastructure in a recent year as DoCoMo did, although the United States is twenty times larger.
31 Matt Hamblen, "Verizon Wireless plans LTE trial next year," *ComputerWorld*, November 29, 2007. http://www.computerworld.com/action/article.do?command=viewArticleBasic&articleId=9050018&intsrc=hm_list
32 "Twelfth Report," op cit., Table 11, p. 68.
33 The latest as of this writing was a plan by Sprint Nextel, Google, Intel, Comcast, Time Warner, and Clearwire: Matt Richtel, "Technology Group Plans Wireless Network," *The New York Times*, May 7, 2008.

Chapter 7. The human dimension: computer scientists and IT research

1 John Kao, *Innovation Nation* (New York: Free Press, 2007), p. 30.
2 New York: HarperBusiness, 2005.
3 Committee on Prospering in the Global Economy of the 21st Century, *Rising Above the Gathering Storm: Energizing and Employing America for a Better Future* (Washington: National Academies Press, 2007), p. 3.
4 A recent news report stated that 40% of 8th grade math teachers were not certified to teach math.
5 John Kao, *Innovation Nation*, p. 34. The test from which these results were taken is the Program for International Student Assessment (PISA).
6 "Drop in Bachelor's Degrees Granted," *CRA Bulletin*, March 8, 2007. http://cra.org/wp/index.php?p=105.
7 National Science Foundation, "Science and Engineering Indicators 2008," Appendix tables 2-30 and 2-32.
8 Julia Oliver, "First-Time, Full-time Graduate Student Enrollment in Science and Engineering Increases in 2006, Especially Among Foreign Students," NSF *InfoBrief* (NSF 08-302), December 2007. nsf.gov.
9 NSF, Science and Engineering Indicators 2008," Appendix table 2-38.

10   Martin Fackler, "High-Tech Japan Running Out of Engineers," *The New York Times*, May 17, 2008.

11   These two paragraphs rely heavily on a June 18, 2005 *Nikkei online* article on the software engineer shortage and the Keidanren program, and Martin Fackler, "High-Tech Japanese, Running Out of Engineers," *The New York Times*, May 17, 2008.

12   "Hitachi Systems to Boost Chinese Computer Engineering Staff by 50%,"*Nikkei online*, May 27, 2006.

13   "Japan to train 1,000 Vietnamese doctoral students," VietNamNet Bridge, March 26, 2008.
      http://english.vietnamnet.vn/education/2008/03/775293/

14   Martin Fackler, "High-Tech Japanese, Running Out of Engineers," op cit.

15   The report was titled: "Information Science and Technology: Investing in Our Future."

16   Speech by John H. Marburger III, director of the White House Office of Science and Technology Policy, to the 2006 AAAS Policy Forum, April 20, 2006, Washington, DC.

17   The Computer System Policy Project headed by Intel CEO Craig Barrett. Their report was made public on January 7, 2004: Jonathan Kim, "U.S. Could Lose Technology Dominance, Executives Say," *The Washington Post*, January 8, 2004.

18   Quoted in William C. Symonds, "A Breakthrough for MIT – and Science," *Business Week*, October 4, 2004.

19   National Innovation Initiative Summit and Report, p. 11. Available online at:
      http://www.compete.org/images/uploads/File/PDF%20Files/NII_ Innovate_America.pdf.

20   *Rising Above the Gathering Storm*: quote, p. 3; recommendations, p. 7.

21   This is based on the fact that 58% of all government-funded R&D is defense-related research and the reasonable assumption that the figure is even higher for federal IT-research programs.

22   *OECD in Figures 2007*, Science and technology, Research and development (I) and (II) 2005.

23   Japan's fiscal years begin in April and end in March.

24   NSF Tokyo Regional Office, "S&T-related Budget for JFY 2005 – Quick Summary," Report Memorandum #0501, January 6, 2005.

25   Ibid.

26   NSF Tokyo Regional Office, "2007 Survey on Research and Development in Japan: Increase in Expenditures for Six Consecutive

Years," Report Memorandum #08-02, February 8, 2008, p. 6. The dollar figures are calculated at $1=JPY 115 throughout this book, unless otherwise indicated.

Chapter 8. The innovation dimension: patents, tech transfer, venture capital

[1] Thomas L. Friedman, "The Secret of Our Sauce," *The New York Times*, March 7, 2004.

[2] *Rising Above the Gathering Storm,* Executive Summary, p. 3.

[3] John Kao's excellent book *Innovation Nation* has influenced my thinking about innovation. His definition of the term, abbreviated here, appears on page 19, and his description of the various stages of innovation on pp. 20-21.

[4] William R. Brody, "Thinking Out Loud," *The JHU Gazette*, February 6, 2006.
http://www.jhu.edu/gazette/2006/06feb06/06brody.html.

[5] European Commission, Director-General for Enterprise and Industry, *European Innovation Scoreboard 2007: Comparative Analysis of Innovation Performance,*. www.InnoMetrics.eu.org.

[6] The others are: Institutions, Infrastructure, Macro economy, Health and primary education, Higher education and training, Market efficiency, Technological readiness, and Business Sophistication.

[7] OECD, *Compendium of Patent Statistics 2008*, September 12, 2008, p. 6.
http://www.oecd.org/dataoecd/5/19/37569377.pdf.

[8] "Innovation," *Economist* Weekly Indicators, May 17, 2007.
http://www.economist.com/markets/indicators/PrinterFriendly.cfm?story_id=9193893.

[9] OECD, *Compendium of Patent Statistics 2008*, OECD, 12 September 2008, p. 14-15.
http://www.oecd.org/dataoecd/5/19/37569377.pdf.

[10] The General Electric website, for example, has forms for employees to submit promising ideas for which they hope to be compensated.

[11] The study was conducted by James Bessen and Michael J. Meurer with data from 1976 to 1999, reported in *The New York Times*, July 15, 2007.

[12] For example, the *National Innovation Initiative* urged by the Council on Competitiveness and the National Academy of Sciences publication *A Patent System for the 21st Century*.

[13]   *Rising Above the Gathering Storm,* Executive Summary, Recommendation D-1, p. 11.

[14]   Steven W. Popper and Caroline S. Wagner, "New Foundations for Growth: The U.S. Innovation System Today and Tomorrow: An Executive Summary," RAND, January 2001, page 1. www.RAND. org.

[15]   According to a May 29, 2006 METI press release, "Report of Fundamental Survey of University-based Startups in FY 2005," there were 1,112 university-based startups at the end of March 2005. By the end of March 2006, the number had climbed to 1,503.

[16]   Presentation by Gerald Hane, Managing Partner, Q-Paradigm, at the Woodrow Wilson Center, March 17, 2004, Washington.

[17]   METI, online at www.meti.go.jp/policy/innovation_policy/index. html.

[18]   METI, "Today's New Topics, September 3, 2007. www.meti.go.jp/ english/newtopics/data/n070903e.html.

[19]   A March 2002 survey of 323 universities by Tsukuba University included in a presentation by .Noboru Maeda at the "Japan-U.S. Entrepreneurial Forum," Tokyo, February 2, 2003, slide 17.

[20]   Author interview, March 1, 2002, Tokyo.

[21]   Hane presentation, *op. cit.* But one international study indicates that the Japanese have been less successful in helping startups to extend their financial and business networks. See Tetsuya Kirihata and Kathryn Ibata-Arens, Chapter 14, "Comparative Management of University Ventures in the UK, US and Japan, Strategic Cooperation Between R&D Type Ventures and Supporting Experts, Research Project Report, Nara (Japan) Institute of Advanced Science and Technology (NAIST), Ministry of International Trade and Economy, Management of Technology, March 2007 (in Japanese).

[22]   Niels Bosma, Kent Jones, Erkko Autio, and Jonathan Levie, *Global Entrepreneurship Monitor* 2007, Table 1, "Prevalence Rates of Entrepreneurial Activity and Business Owner-Managers Across Countries 2007," p. 16. http://www.gemconsortium.org/download/ 1226104453311/GEM_2007_Executive_Report.pdf.

[23]   Tim Kelley, "Venture Professor" *Forbes.com*, February 13, 2006. http://www.forbes.com/global/2006/0213/056A.html.

[24]   Richard Waters, "Silicon Valley adjusts its expectations" *Financial Times*, February 20, 2003.

[25] Center for Venture Research, University of New Hampshire, "The Angel Investor Market in 2007: Mixed Signs of Growth." www.unh.edu/cvr.

[26] PriceWaterhouseCoopers/National Venture Capital Association, "Money Tree Report Q1 2008." IT was defined at the total investments in computers and peripherals, IT services, networking and equipment, and software. PWCMoneytree.com.

[27] Randall S. Jones and Tadashi Yokoyama, "Upgrading Japan's Innovation System to Sustain Economic Growth," OECD Economics Department Working Paper No. 527, November 29, 2006, Figure 2, p. 9. http://www.olis.oecd.org/olis/2006doc.nsf/LinkTo/NT000073EA/$FILE/JT03218797.PDF.
Japan's 2000-2003 GDP calculated at Y115=$1.

[28] Paul D. Reynolds, William D. Bygrave, Erkko Autio, and others, *Global Entrepreneurship Monitor*, 2003 Executive Report, pp. 60-61. http://www,gemconsortium.org/download/1222969314181/ReplacementFINALExecutiveReport.pdf.

[29] Jones and Yokoyama, "Upgrading Japan's Innovation System to Sustain Economic Growth," op cit.

[30] PriceWaterhouseCoopers/National Venture Capital Association, "MoneyTree Report" for 4Q 2007. PWCmoneytree.com.

[31] Venture Enterprise Center Foundation, "Fiscal 2006 Survey of Venture Capital Investment Trends (Heisei 19 nendo bencha kyapitaru nado tooshi dookoo chosa)," Chart 2-12, p. 12. $1=JPY115. http://www.vec.or.jp/vc/survey-19j.pdf.

[32] Council on Competitiveness, "Clusters of Innovation: Regional Foundations of U.S. Competitiveness," 2001, p. 1. http://www.compete.org/

[33] The other three actions were: The U.S. must take science seriously, make science research funding a priority, and remove politics from research funding decisions.

[34] Hamilton Project presentation: "Promoting Opportunity and Growth through Science, Technology, and Innovation" at the Johns Hopkins' Nitze School of Advanced International Studies, December 5, 2006, Washington.

[35] PriceWaterhouseCoopers/National Venture Capital Association, "MoneyTree Report" for 1Q 2008. PWCmoneytree.com.

[36] Quoted in G. Pascal Zachary, "When it Comes to Innovation, Geography is Destiny," *The New York Times*, February 11, 2007.

37   Robert Huggins Associates (Cardiff, Wales), "World Knowledge Competitiveness Index," as reported in Scheherazade Daneshkhu and Maure Dickie, "Silicon Valley tops high-tech league," *Financial Times*, December 12, 2005.

38   Council on Competitiveness, "2005 National Innovation Survey." http://www.compete.org/

39   NSF Tokyo Regional Office, "S&T Items in the Japanese Government's Basic Policies on Economic and Fiscal Reform 2007," Report Memorandum #07-06, July 3, 2007, p.1.

40   Council on Competitiveness, "2005 National Innovation Survey." http://www.compete.org/

41   Quoted in Michael D. Lemonick, "Are We Losing Our Edge?," *Time*, February 5, 2006.

42   Janet Rae-Dupree, "When Academia Puts Profit Ahead of Wonder," *The New York Times*, September 7, 2008.

Chapter 9. The e-commerce dimension: buying and selling online

1   "A Framework for Global Electronic Commerce" announced by President Bill Clinton at the White House, July 1, 1997.

2   "Memorandum on Electronic Commerce," November 30, 1998, weekly compilation of Presidential documents, Volume 34, Number 49, pp. 2387-2429.

3   U.S.-Japan "Joint Statement on Electronic Commerce," May 22, 1998, weekly compilation of Presidential documents , Volume 34, Number 21, pp. 883-956.

4   Arthur Mitchell, "How the Internet Will Change Japan," published online, January 2001. http://www.coudert.com/practice/ebook/toc.htm.

5   The exchange rate for all figures in this chapter only is: $1=JPY110.2; in other chapters it is: $1= JPY115.

6   Sources: For the U.S.: Economics and Statistics Administration, U.S. Census Bureau, *E-commerce 2000*, March 18, 2002; for Japan: IT Strategic Headquarters, "E-Japan Priority Policy Program," March 29, 2001. These figures, however, are only *roughly* comparable because the two sources define e-commerce differently. See Footnote 9.

7   *E-commerce 2000*, March 18, 2002.   http://www.census.gov/eos/
     www/ebusiness614.htm

8   *E-commerce 2006*, May 16, 2008.

9   METI, "Summary of 'Market Research on Electronic Commerce
     2001,'" a survey conducted by METI, Electronic Commerce Pro-
     motion Council of Japan and NTT DATA Institute of Management
     Consulting, Inc., February 18, 2001. NOTE: the U.S. and Japanese
     governments define B2B and B2C differently. The U.S. Census Bu-
     reau uses a "simplified" definition, lumping all electronic manufac-
     turing and wholesale sales into "business-to-business" e-commerce
     and all retail and services transactions into "business-to-consumer"
     e-commerce. The Japanese Ministry of Economics, Trade, and In-
     dustry (METI) does not simplify. It assigns certain manufacturing
     and "wholesale" sales to B2C, as well as B2B e-commerce, and cer-
     tain services to B2B and others to B2C. As a result, their respective
     e-commerce totals provide only very rough comparisons.

10   This analysis is based, in part, on Jason Dedrick and Kenneth L.
     Kraemer, "Japan E-Commerce Report," Center for Research on In-
     formation Technology and Organizations, University of California/
     Irvine, December 2000.

11   The targets are contained in METI, "Summary of 'Market Research
     on Electronic Commerce 2001,'" by METI, Electronic Commerce
     Promotion Council of Japan (an industry group) and NTT DATA
     Institute of Management Consulting, Inc., dated February 18, 2001
     (though the correct date is almost certainly February 18, 2002, since
     the report includes complete data for 2001), p. 7.

12   METI, using its own definition of B2B (see Footnote 9), stated
     that the 2005 Japanese B2B total was $2 trillion compared to a
     U.S. total of $1.7 trillion: METI, "Announcement of the Results
     of the 2005 e-Commerce Market Survey" press release, June 26,
     2006. See Footnote 9 for U.S. and Japanese B2B definitional
     differences.

13   METI-ECOM, "*Heisei 18-nendo Denshisho Torihiki ni kansuru
     Shijo Chosa*" (2006 E-Commerce Market Survey), May 11, 2007,
     p.1. Publication of U.S. e-commerce statistics by the Census Bureau
     runs about one year behind the comparable METI-ECOM surveys.

14   John Peet, "Shopping Around the Web," an *Economist* Survey of
     e-commerce, February 24, 2000, p.49.

15   "*E-commerce 2006*," May 16, 2008, pp. 2-4.

16   John B. Horrigan, "Home Broadband Adoption 2008," July 2008. www.pewinternet.org.

17   METI-ECOM-NTT DATA Institute of Management Consulting, Inc., "Summary of Market Research on Electronic Commerce 2001," February 18, 2001. But these figures are only roughly comparable due to differing definitions of B2C e-commerce in the two nations' statistics. See Footnote 9.

18   Ministry of Internal Affairs and Communications, *2006 White Paper* (in Japanese). http://www.johotsusintokei.soumu.go.jp/whitepaper/ja/h13/html/D1123000.htm

19   METI, "Briefing for Journalists 2004" on METI-ECOM-NTT Data's "Survey on Actual Condition[s] and Market Size of Electronic Commerce for 2003," June 11, 2004, p. 24.

20   METI-ECOM 2006 e-Commerce Survey (in Japanese), May 11, 2007, p. 3.

21   Ibid., p. 3.

Chapter 10. The public dimension: e-government, e-education, universal access

1   Outlined in Al Gore, *Common Sense Government: Works Better & Costs Less*, Third Report of the National Performance Review. Washington: September 7, 1995

2   *Access America.*   http://govinfo.library.unt.edu/accessamerica/reports/access.html

3   Accenture, "*e-Government Leadership: Rhetoric vs. Reality – Closing the Gap*," an Accenture comparison of e-government progress, April 2001.   http://www.accenture.com/Global/Services/By_Industry/Government_and_Public_Service/PS_Global/R_and_I/CRMGaps.htm

4   The others were: strategic management of human capital, competitive sourcing, improved financial performance, and budget and performance integration.

5   Author interview with Karen Evans (Administrator of e-Government and Information Technology, Office of Management and Budget), September 10, 2004.

6   Office of Management and Budget, "Expanding E-Government: Making a Difference for the American People Using Information Technology," December 2006. www.egov.gov.

7    $68.2 billion was spent in fiscal 2007, $68.1 billion was approved in fiscal 2008, and $70.7 billion was requested for fiscal 2009. Source: "Report on Information Technology (IT) Spending for the Federal Government for Fiscal Years 2007, 2008, and 2009." Available through the FY 2009 Budget link at www.e-gov.gov.

8   Executive Office of the President, "Expanding E-Government: Achieving Results for the American People," May 2008, p. 9. www.e-gov.gov.

9   Executive Office of the President, "Report to the Congress on the Benefits of the President's e-Government Initiatives, Fiscal Year 2008," February 2008. www.e-gov.gov.

10   Internal Revenue Service, "Table 4. Number of Returns Filed Electronically, by Type of Return and State, Fiscal Year 2007." www.irs.gov.

11   Executive Office of the President, "Report to Congress on the Benefits of the President's e-Government Initiatives, Fiscal Year 2008" www.e-gov.gov.

12   International Council for Information Technology in Government Administration, "ICA Country Report: Japan's e-Government (2006)," August 31, 2006. www.ica-it.org.

13   Accenture's 2007 e-government survey, *Leadership in Customer Service: Delivering on the Promise*, p. 34. http://www.accenture.com/Global/Services/By_Industry/Government_and_Public_Service/PS_Global/R_and_I/DeliveringonthePromise.htm.

14   The Accenture ranking weights "service maturity" (the government's online presence) at 10%; "customer service maturity" (the extent to which government agencies manage customer interactions and deliver services) at 50%; and "citizen voice" (the results of an opinion poll) at 40%.

15   Rebecca S. Weiner, "Education: Government Internet Subsidy Stretched to Its Limits," *The New York Times*, May 15, 2001.

16   John Schwartz, "Schools' Internet Subsidies Are Called Fraud-Riddled," *The New York Times*, January 10, 2003.

17   Cara Branigan, "eRate flows again; '04 apps still pending," *eSchoolNews*, November 9, 2004. eschoolnews.com.

18   National Center for Education Statistics, Institute of Education Sciences, U.S. Department of Education, "Internet Access in U.S. Public Schools and Classrooms: 1994-2005," November 2006, p. 10. http://nces.ed.gov/pubsearch/pubsinfo.asp?pubid=2007020.

19 From CDW-G, "Teacher's Talk Tech 2006." http://newsroom.cdwg. com/news-releases/news-release-06-26-06.html.

20 Alexandra Schmertz, "There's a lesson for educators," *Financial Times*, September 19, 2000.

21 Ministry of Education, "Japan's Education at a Glance 2006." mext. go.jp/english/statist/07070310/005.pdf.

22 Eri Ono, "Technology Integration at a Japanese Middle School," in Griff Richards (ed.), *Proceedings of World Conference on E-Learning in Corporate, Government, Healthcare, and Higher Education (ELEARN) 2005* (Chesapeake, VA: AACE), pp. 982-985. Made available by courtesy of the author.

23 IT Strategic Headquarters, "New IT Reform Strategy," January 2006, and "IT Policy Priority Program, 2006." http://www.kantei. go.jp/foreign/policy/it/index_e.html.

24 White House Press Release, "A National Call to Action to Close the Digital Divide," April 4, 2000. http://clinton4.nara.gov/textonly/ WH/New/html/20000404.html.

25 John Horrigan and Lee Rainie, "Getting Serous Online," Pew Internet Project, March 4, 2002. http://www.pewinternet.org/PPF/r/55/ report_display.asp

26 FCC, "High-Speed Services for Internet Access as of December 31, 2000," August 2001, Table 3.
www.fcc.gov /Bureaus/Common_Carrier/Reports/FCC-State_Link/ IAD/hspd0801.pdf.

27 Source of the mobile-phone statistic only: FCC, "High-Speed Services for Internet Access, Status as of June 30,2007," March 2008, Table 3. http://hraunfoss.fcc.gov/edocs_public/attachmatch/ DOC-280906A1.pdf.

28 The remainder of these statistics are taken from John B. Horrigan, "Home Broadband Adoption 2008," July 2, 2008. pp. i-iii. http:// www.pewinternet.org/PPF/r/257/report_display.asp.

29 Ministry of Internal Affairs and Communications, "Number of Broadband Service Contracts, Etc. (as of the end of December 2007)," March 18,2008. http://www.soumu.go.jp/joho_tsusin/eng/ statistics.html.

30 The latest usage statistics are for Japan's FY 2006, which ended March 31, 2007. *MIC Communications News*, "Results of Telecommunications Usage Trend Survey 2007," August 29, 2008. http:// www.soumu.go.jp/joho_tsusin/eng/Statistics/pdf/080403_1.pdf.

31 Source for the geographic data only: MIC News Release, "Results of Telecommunications Usage Trend Survey for [Fiscal] 2005," May 19, 2006, p. 3.

32 Source for the remaining usage data: Ministry of Internal Affairs and Communications, *DO Site* [Digital Opportunity Site], "Differences in the use of the Internet." http://www.dosite.go.jp/e/do/j-state_net.html.

33 While Japan has done better than the United States, remember that South Korea and the Scandinavian countries have done far better than either Japan or the United States in closing the digital divide.

Chapter 11. Broadband lessons from South Korea, Canada, France

1 National Information Society Agency, Republic of Korea, *2007 Informatization White Paper*, September 2007, p. 47. www.nia.or.kr (then Publications, Public, 07.10.09).

2 "Measures to nurture the IT Industry (1987-1985 [sic])," focused on manufacturing, and "National Basic Information System" (1987-1996), aimed at using IT for administration, defense, public security, finance, and education. Source: Dr. Tim Kelly, Head, Strategy & Policy Unit, International Telecommunication Union, "Ubiquitous Network Societies: Case Study of the Republic of Korea," delivered at New Initiatives Workshop on Ubiquitous Network Societies, Geneva, April 6-8, 2005. http://www.itu.itl/osg/spu/ni/ubiquitous/Papers/UNSKoreacasestudy.pdf.

3 From Inho Chung, "Broadband, the Information Society, and National Systems," in Martin Fransman (ed.), *Global Broadband Battles* (Stanford Business Books, 2006), Table 3.4, p. 102.

4 National Internet Development Agency of Korea, Ministry of Information and Communication, "Internet at a Glance," *2006 Korea Internet White Paper*, p. 6.

5 In fact, only 80% of Koreans were online at the end of 2007, but that was an achievement no other nation could match. National Internet Development Agency, Ministry of Information and Communication, "Survey on the Computer and Internet Usage," February 2008, p. vii. http://isis.nida.or.kr/eng/.

6   Fiber to the Home Council, "With Robust Growth in Fiber to the Home subscribers, Asia-Pacific Continues to Lead in FTTH Penetration," July 23, 2008. http://www.ftthcouncilap.org/

7   International Telecommunications Union study, "Promoting Broadband: The Case of Canada," Document PB/05, April 9, 2003, Geneva, p. 14.

8   Ibid., Annex 2: Connecting Canadians, pp. 43-45.

9   Ibid., pp. 8 and 11.

10 Industry Canada News Release, "Minister Tobin Announces Members of the National Broadband Task Force," January 11, 2001. www.ic.gc.ca.

11 National Broadband Task Force, "Executive Summary of the 'Report of the National Broadband Task Force,'" pp. 3-4. http://broadband.gc.ca/pub/program/NBTF/summary.html.

12 Industry Canada "Broadband" website: http://broadband.gc.ca/pub/program/about.html

13 Infrastructure Canada News Release, October 5, 2003. http://infrastructure.gc.ca.

14 Canadian Radio-television and Telecommunications Commission, "Telecommunications Monitoring Report, July 2007," Appendix 5, Table A.5.2. Summary of programs for broadband deployment initiatives and investments, p. 9. http://www.crtc.gc.ca/eng/publications/reports/PolicyMonitoring/2007/tmr2007.htm#a5

15 Ibid., Appendix 5, Table A.5.1. Summary of provincial governments' broadband deployment initiatives and investments.

16 Ibid., Appendix 5, Figure A.5.1, Communities with and without broadband access. The percentage of communities without broadband was projected to drop to 38% by the end of 2008..

17 Telecommunications Policy Review Panel Report, March 2006. www.telecomreview.ca.

18 CRTC, Telecommunications Monitoring Report, July 2007, op cit., Appendix 5, pp. 9-10.

19 The G8 nations are Canada, the United States, the United Kingdom, France, Germany, Italy, Japan, and Russia.

20 CRTC, Telecommunications Monitoring Report, July 2007, op. cit., pp. ii and 77.

21 "Ensuring a modern economy throughout rural and remote Canada," October 11, 2008. http://www.conservative.ca/EN/1091/107195

22 Dermot McGrath, "Minitel: The Old New Thing," *Wired*, April 2001. http://www.wired.com/print/science/discoveries/news/ 2001/04/42943.

23 Light Reading Europe, "FT Launches FTTH Trial," January 17, 2006. http://www.lightreading.com/document.asp?doc_ id=86954&print=true.

24 Dieter Elixmann, et al., "The Economics of Next-Generation Access - Final Report," WIK Consult Report, September 10, 2008, p. 124. http://internetthought.blogspot.com/2008/09/wik-report-for-ecta- on-economic-of-next.html.

25 Om Malik, "Xavier Niel, France's Broadband Maverick," in his blog "GigaOM," December 21, 2007. http://gigaom.com/2007/12/21/ xavier-niel-free-fr/.

26 La Lettre de l'Autorite de Regulation des Communications Electro- niques et des Postes, "ARCEP [formerly ART] 2006 Annual Re- port," March/April 2007. http://www.arcep.fr.

27 Dieter Elixmann, et al., op. cit., pp. 136-137.

28 ARCEP, "L'Observatoire de l'Internet haut debit – 1er trimestre 2008 – Resultats provisoires publies le 30 mai 2008," May 30, 2008. http://www.arcep.fr/index.php?id=9654&type=98&L=1&L=1.

Chapter 12. Returning to the Information Superhighway

1 Ministry of Internal Affairs and Communications, Press Release- Telecom, "Status of Numbers of Subscribers to Telecommunica- tions Services (As of the end of December 2007)," February 27, 2008, Attachment: Table 3. Mobile Phones and PHS.

2 Source for mobile phone usage: CTIA, the wireless industry as- sociation. Statistics available at http://www.ctia.org/advocacy/ research/index.cfm/AID/10323. Internet subscriptions: FCC, "High-Speed Services for Internet Access: Status as of December 2007," March 2008, Table 3, p. 8.

3 "Venture Capitalists Around the Globe Identify Pockets of Technol- ogy Innovation According to a Study by Deloitte and the National Venture Capital Association," June 3, 2008. http://www.deloitte.com/dtt/press_release/ 0,1014,sid%253D2283%2526cid%253D209317,00.html.

4   The R&D estimates were made by Jake MacLeod, Bechtel Communications chief technology officer, as quoted in "A Blueprint for Big Broadband," an EDUCAUSE White Paper, January 2008, p. 33. The National Research Council recommendations are summarized on the same page.
http://net.educause.edu/ir/library/pdf/epo0801.pdf.

Acknowledgements

This book project was launched with an Abe Fellowship awarded by Japan's Center for Global Partnership, an arm of the Japan Foundation. The generous grant that accompanied the fellowship underwrote four months of research in Japan and a year's effort. I am deeply grateful to the Center for their confidence in me.

Another Abe Fellow (and Keio University associate professor), Motohiro Tsuchiya, introduced me to the International University of Japan's Center for Global Communications (GLOCOM), its respected director, Professor Shumpei Kumon, and its very able staff. GLOCOM proved to be a congenial professional home in Tokyo. Kumon-*sensei*, several staff members, and others affiliated with the Center devoted many hours to educating me about the Internet experience in Japan. Without their help, this book would not exist.

In Washington, I am grateful to Professor Dianne Martin, former chair of the Computer Science Department in The George Washington University's School of Engineering and Applied Science, for permitting me to spend a year at the Cyber Security Policy and Research Institute (formerly the Cyber Policy Institute) as a Research Fellow, and to the staff of the University's library.

Early research for this book led to an article, "Down to the Wire," in the May-June 2005 issue of *Foreign Affairs*. I am indebted to my editor there, Stephanie Giry, for sharpening the argument and smoothing my prose. I was also pleasantly surprised by the remarkable effectiveness of the *Foreign Affairs* public affairs staff that resulted in many interviews and presentations.

Several individuals deserve special thanks for exceptional helpfulness during the writing of this book: Izumi Aizu, Robert Atkinson, James Baller, Robert Cannon, Takashi Ebihara, Stuart Miller, Michael Nelson, Adam Peake, Yasuhiko Taniwaki, and Motohiro Tsuchiya. My debt to them is enormous. Permit me also to thank the scores of interviewees in Japan and the United States who spoke with me at length and often answered follow-up questions. They are too numerous to list, but I remain grateful for the time they spent with me.

Reviewers in Canada, Germany, Japan, and the United States helped to reduce the book's errors of fact and judgment. I would especially like to thank the following for reading portions of the manuscript: James Baller, Joan Burrelli, Robert Canon, Dieter Elixmann, John Horrigan, Kathryn Ibata-Arens, Toshiya Jitsuzumi, Keisuke Kamimura, Tadamasu Kimura, Jim MacKenzie, Michael Nelson, Julia Oliver, Eun-A Park, Lawrence Rausch, Yasuhiko Taniwaki, Motohiro Tsuchiya, Donald Westmore, and Stephen Wolff. Stuart Miller read the entire manuscript. Each of them offered useful insights, comments, and corrections. For the mistakes that remain, I alone am responsible.

Special thanks to my editor, Roger Williams, for adding polish to my prose, LeeAnn Jackson for the index, and the ever helpful staff of the Arlington (Virginia) Central Library, where I spent many hours writing this book.

Finally, loving thanks to my wife, Natasha Simes, who provided just the right measure of encouragement, and my children and friends who refrained from asking whether the book was finished yet. At long last, it is.

Arlington, Virginia
November 2008

INDEX